ABSOLUTE VALUE

ABSOLUTE VALUE

WHAT REALLY INFLUENCES CUSTOMERS IN THE AGE OF (NEARLY) PERFECT INFORMATION

Itamar Simonson *and* Emanuel Rosen

HARPER
BUSINESS

An Imprint of HarperCollins*Publishers*
www.harpercollins.com

HarperCollins books may be purchased for educational, business,
or sales promotional use. For information, please e-mail the Special Markets
Department at SPsales@harpercollins.com.

FIRST EDITION

Designed by Jo Anne Metsch

Library of Congress Cataloging-in-Publication Data has been applied for.

ISBN: 978-0-06-221567-3

14 15 16 17 18   OV/RRD   10 9 8 7 6 5 4 3 2 1

To Yael and Daria,
for your absolute support

CONTENTS

Introduction   ix

I. THE SHIFT FROM RELATIVE TO ABSOLUTE

1 From Relative to Absolute   3
2 The Decline of "Irrationality"   18
3 New Patterns in Consumer Decision Making   33
4 Why We're Bullish About Absolute Values   44

II. HOW MARKETING CHANGES FOREVER

5 When Brands Mean Less   59
6 Satisfaction, Loyalty, and the Future of Past Experience   77
7 Absolute Diffusion: From Pinehurst to Pinterest   89
8 Pointless Positioning and Persuasion   101

III. A NEW FRAMEWORK

9 The Influence Mix   115
10 Communication: Match Your Customers' Influence Mix   133
11 Market Research: From Predicting to Tracking   147
12 Segment Evolution: From Susceptible to Savvy   163
13 The Future of the Absolute   173
14 Absolute Business: A Final Word   184

Acknowledgments   193
Notes   195
Index   221

INTRODUCTION

HERE ARE FIVE widely held beliefs about marketing and decision making that we collected from recent publications. This book explains why these (and other) statements are becoming less true today, and why they are likely to be even less true in the future:

> *"A company's brand is more important today than it has ever been."*
> *"Nurturing loyalty should be the marketer's primary, day-to-day concern."*
> *"All customers are irrational."*
> *"An overload of options may actually paralyze people."*
> *"Positioning is the most important part of the marketing game."*[1]

Why do we think that these mantras will become less relevant? Our answer is rooted in a fundamental shift in consumer decision making: Consumers used to make decisions relative to other things—a brand name, their previous experience with a company, an inflated list price, a brand's advertising message compared to competing brands' messages, or the other products a marketer chose to display on a catalog page or on the shelf. Conventional wisdom still holds that people's choices can be greatly influenced by the context or the framing of an offer.

But for the first time this is starting to change and we're moving toward an age of nearly perfect information. Review sites, shopping apps on smartphones, an extended network of acquaintances available through social media, and unprecedented access to experts and other sources, all mean that many consumers today operate in a radically different, socially intensive information environment. In a world where consumers enjoy complete access to informed experts and various information services, where they can instantly read the opinions of previous users, it's much easier for consumers to predict their likely experience with a product or a service—it's easier to know the absolute value of things.

When we talk about "absolute value" we refer to the experienced quality of a product. For example, the experience at a restaurant, the pleasure (or boredom) one might experience reading a book, the closeness of the shave, the actual comfort of headphones, or the usage value you get from using your camera. So "absolute value" doesn't only refer to the technical specifications and reliability of a camera, but to what it is like to own and actually use it. In short: The new information environment around us allows consumers to predict much more accurately the experienced quality (or absolute value) of products and services they consider getting.

The implications for consumers and businesses are enormous. First, reliance on absolute values means that, on average, consumers tend to make better decisions and become less susceptible to context or framing manipulations. For businesses it means that marketing is changing forever. When consumers can more easily assess absolute values, this means that the influence of "relative forces" (such as branding, loyalty, and positioning) that used to drive predictions of the experienced quality of things is, for numerous products and services, rapidly declining.

The fundamental shift from relative to absolute requires managers, marketers, and business strategists to reexamine *everything*, and it gives rise to the need for a new way of thinking about marketing (and for a new language to talk about it). This is why we offer an entirely new framework (which we call the Influence Mix) for making more effective marketing decisions based on the mix of influence sources that your customers rely on. The reality is that the shift from relative to absolute is taking place in some product categories and for some consumers much faster than for others. This framework will let marketers better understand where things are changing and where they are not, and apply the marketing strategies and programs that are appropriate in each case.

Our agent, Jim Levine, always likes to say that a good business book should address three questions: 1) What? 2) So what? and 3) Now what? We can summarize everything we said so far by answering these questions: What? There's a fundamental shift in consumer decision making. Instead of relying on relative evaluations, for the first time in history consumers have the tools to assess the absolute value of things. So what? This means that consumers are likely to make better decisions (on average) and that marketing is changing forever because people will rely less on proxies for quality such as brand names, loyalty, or positioning. Now what? All this gives rise to the need for a new framework and approach to marketing, which we call the Influence Mix.

To help you navigate through our book, we divided it into three sections which (more or less) correspond to the three questions above. In Part I—*A Shift from Relative to Absolute*—we establish the foundation. In Chapter 1 we show how a company can benefit from the shift: Since brand names play a reduced role as proxies for quality, ASUS was able to reach the fifth place in worldwide PC shipments without heavily investing in building its brand. Of course, we'll go deeper into the theory (and will present some experimental evidence) regarding the shift away from relative evaluations in today's shopping environment. In Chapter 2, we explain why some of the key demonstrations of "irrational" consumer decisions are becoming less relevant. We all have been flooded with books and articles about how "irrational" we are, but the new information environment actually allows us to make better choices overall that are based on absolute values—the building blocks of effective decisions. We've also heard a lot in recent years about choice overload—the notion that we are overwhelmed by too many choices—but in Chapter 3 we question the robustness of this notion. Using a variety of information search aides, most consumers can handle the available information selectively and efficiently; we also describe some new patterns in decision making that emerge in the age of abundant, low-cost information. In Chapter 4 we address a question that some readers may have on their minds: With the constant trickle of stories in the media about fake reviews and other attempts to game the system, why are we still bullish about absolute values?

In Part II—*How Marketing Changes Forever*—we describe previously unrecognized implications of the current environment for business, marketing practice, and consumer decision making. In Chapter 5 we explain why brands are losing their role as proxies for quality. We explore, for example, how Yelp affected the revenues of big chain restaurants, and the opportunities it opens to other businesses. In Chapter 6 we explore the topic of loyalty and satisfaction. When consumers rely on absolute values and less on their past experience, loyalty declines. What are the implications to business? You can never rest on your laurels (think Nokia or BlackBerry), but it also opens some opportunities. In Chapter 7 we discuss how some theories of diffusion are changing when uncertainty about innovations is resolved much faster than in the past. We'll discuss, for example, how Pinterest defied the traditional thinking about technology adoption in Silicon Valley. Then, in Chapter 8 we argue that when it's easier to assess absolute values, positioning and persuasion techniques are likely to become less effective. (In the old days, Volvo could position itself as the safest car. It's much harder to do when customers use different information sources.)

In Part III—*A New Framework*—we introduce the Influence Mix, which should help managers determine where their products fall with respect to the evolving customer decision making. As we explain in Chapter 9, there are categories, segments, and situations where consumers still heavily depend on relative evaluations (while absolute values drive the choice of a new camera, brand names and habits continue to be key drivers in choices of beer). Once a company determines the mix of sources that influence its customers, that mix should drive their strategy. This applies to its communication strategy (which we discuss in Chapter 10) and its market research program (the subject of Chapter 11), and it can also differ by segment (which we cover in Chapter 12). Throughout this section we emphasize that the Influence Mix is dynamic. A segment that is currently influenced by traditional information sources can move to new sources rather quickly. This is particularly true as new sorting and search tools (which are even easier to use than existing ones) will keep emerging, which is the topic of Chapter 13. Then, in Chapter 14 we make some final comments about the shape of things to come and illustrate how particular managerial practices such as pricing or organizational structure might be revised to fit the new reality.

When we introduce the idea of absolute value to people, we get all kinds of questions, so let us briefly address the two most frequent ones (and we'll expand on these and other questions later on). The first question that often comes up: Is there even such a thing as absolute value? Our answer is that when we talk about absolute value, we don't necessarily mean to say that people will find *the* absolute best option (assuming that an absolute best option exists), and some ambiguity about the absolute best is likely to remain, in part because our own preferences are often vague and unstable. We're talking about a "good enough" answer or about getting closer to (but usually not reaching) the absolute value of things. The second question we often hear: Doesn't value depend on the individual? Isn't it subjective? Our answer: Yes, an absolute value may very well differ from one person to another (though it may be similar for consumers who have similar tastes). Our point is that today you can more easily determine the absolute value of something to *you*, because you can get information from so many experts and users, some of whom may share your tastes. And even when an absolute factual answer cannot be determined, consumers usually prefer it over the answer they'll get from a marketer.

Perhaps the simplest way to understand what we mean by "absolute" is to think about it as the opposite of "relative." In the old days, consumers were much more susceptible to being influenced by relative things. When considering what laptop to get, Jeff made his decision relative to things like the brand name or his past experience with that brand, whereas today, with not much effort, Jeff can obtain good diagnostic information regarding his likely experience with that laptop, and thus get closer to the absolute value of that product.

We both used to believe in the currently accepted mantras regarding branding, positioning, loyalty, information overload, and consumers' "irrationality." Relative thinking is deeply embedded in the business world and, like everyone else, we've heard for decades that it's all (or mostly) about how companies frame or position things. For each of us, this book represents a major journey away from our original beliefs.

As a researcher, Itamar started with a deep conviction that consumers typically do not have real preferences, are easily malleable, tend to act irrationally, and can't really evaluate real quality. He, in fact, made his own contributions to reinforcing these beliefs, for example by discovering the compromise effect (consumers' tendency to select the middle option from any option set placed in front of them). The rise of the Internet didn't change these core beliefs. If anything, it seemed that the Internet added to the information overload and made consumers even more irrational and confused than in the old days. Yet a few years ago, Itamar started having second thoughts. He published some papers that raised questions about the effect of the current information environment on the validity of his own (and others') prior research about consumer irrationality and inability to determine product quality.

Emanuel's journey was different. Coming from the world of advertising, he was initially an avid believer in the power of promotion, branding, and positioning. In his mind, marketing started with brand awareness so you needed to hammer the brand name into people's minds. As he made the shift to technology marketing, he started to appreciate the power of word of mouth and interpersonal influence and he wrote extensively about the topic. Although he was one of the first authors to write about the expected rise of interpersonal influence in marketing, his discussion was still within the framework of established marketing concepts and diffusion of innovation theory (which was rooted in a world of much greater uncertainty).

In 2008 we got together to write a book about the future of marketing. It didn't take us long to agree that as humans we're not well equipped to predict the future. But we also recognized that even though we can't really tell what will happen, we see enough evidence in the present to discuss some possible directions. Itamar brought insights from decision making theory and consumer psychology. Emanuel brought his practical experience and his knowledge on interpersonal influence. We felt that together, perhaps we can truly understand what is really changing in the new environment and go beyond the rhetoric of recent buzzwords such as "the newly empowered consumer." Over the past five years we've witnessed tools and platforms evolving to further enable access to absolute values: Review sites got better at sorting and summarizing information. Shopping apps on smartphones brought the trends we discuss to brick-and-mortar stores. New tools, apps, and websites kept coming and helped us realize the extent to which things are changing. That when consumers can get closer to absolute values, *everything* needs to be reevaluated.

We're sure we'll get some things wrong, and hopefully some things right. Our objective is not to pinpoint what will happen, but to think—and provoke thinking—about the future of marketing and consumer decision making.

Stanford/Menlo Park

May 2013

1

The Shift from Relative to Absolute

1

FROM RELATIVE TO ABSOLUTE

WHEN JONNEY JHIH started talking about selling laptops under the ASUS brand, it didn't raise too much concern among established players in the PC industry. Shih is the chairman of ASUSTek (known simply as ASUS), a Taiwanese company that was a contract manufacturer of notebook computers and game consoles. While ASUS was well respected among industry insiders, few consumers were aware of its existence. Conventional wisdom holds that you need to build a trusted brand in order to get people to open their wallets, and establishing a brand is notoriously expensive. Friends and colleagues warned Shih that he wouldn't get far without brand awareness, name recognition, and heavy advertising.[1]

When we talked to him in 2013, it was clear that they were wrong. In 2012, ASUS reached the fifth place in worldwide PC shipments, at the expense of more established players, with prominent growth as the overall industry shipments declined. In the first quarter of 2013, ASUS reached the number-three position in worldwide tablet shipments, according to IDC.[2]

How could a company be so successful with almost no initial brand awareness?

We argue that Jonney Shih, and the $15 billion company that

he heads, benefit from a fundamental shift in the way consumers make decisions. Consumers used to make decisions relative to other things—a brand name, a list price, or their own past experience with a company. But today, more and more decisions are based on the absolute value of things. What do we mean by that? As we explained in the introduction, when we talk about absolute value, we are not talking about some universal truth about a product, but about the actual experienced quality of the product for a certain consumer. In other words, we're referring to a consumer's ability to get closer to knowing her likely experience with a product.[3]

While relative evaluations are based on comparisons with whatever happens to be most prominent, or placed in front of you (the "local context"), absolute evaluations go beyond the local context, to use the most relevant information available about each product and feature, and they usually produce better answers. We want to say that absolute evaluations get people closer to the truth, but "truth" is too strong a word here. They get people closer to knowing what to expect.

Here's one way that ASUS benefits from the shift away from relative evaluations. In the old days, consumers often used their own past experience with a brand as a key quality proxy. When Jane was thinking of buying a new laptop, the most accessible piece of information in her mind might have been this: "In the past, I used a Dell laptop that worked fine." This was an easy reference point to use, and it led Jane to conclude that the new Dell models on the market must be good, too. Some of this way of thinking will continue, of course, but today Jane can easily find out much better information about any model made by Dell, HP, ASUS, or any other company. Even if you've never heard about ASUS before, you can do this exercise right now: Go to a review site such as CNET or gdgt .com and read reviews by experts and regular users. After reading a few reports, you'll have a pretty good idea regarding your likely experience with a laptop from ASUS. As we are writing this, one laptop from ASUS has a rating of 88 (out of 100) on gdgt.com (the highest score for a Windows-based laptop). It gets a similar score on Decide.com, a tool that aggregates expert and user reviews.[4]

When quality can be quickly assessed, people are less hesitant to try something new, which means that newcomers like ASUS can enjoy lower barriers to entry. Shih and his team got a pretty dramatic demonstration of this when ASUS introduced its Eee PC in 2007. To say that competitors didn't take the new product seriously is an understatement. "They laughed at us," Shih says. But shortly after its announcement, the Eee PC started getting the attention of geek bloggers around the world. It had several things going for it. It was light. It had built-in wireless (unique at the time for its price point). Its operating system was a limited version of Linux, which meant that you didn't have big memory-hungry Microsoft software. Most important, it was dirt cheap—$399. When the device shipped, users started discussing it online, and you could go to any review site and read the pros and cons from other users. By the end of 2008, this new device from a company virtually unknown in the United States sold almost 5 million units. All competitors jumped on the bandwagon with their own device, creating a new category known as netbooks.

ASUS is not known for its marketing. When Jonney Shih makes product announcements, you cannot avoid comparing him to Steve Jobs and his legendary demos. Shih is passionate, and his presentations can get quite dramatic, but with his business attire, parted hair, and the technical details he cites, it's clear where he's coming from—ASUS has a strong engineering orientation, and marketing usually takes a backseat. He has learned a lot, though, by watching Apple. An engineer by training, Shih used to be focused almost exclusively on specs and performance, but by studying Apple's success over the years, he now understands the advantage of putting the consumer experience at the center. So in the past few years he shifted the company's focus from its spec orientation to "design thinking," which better fits today's environment. The Eee PC was an early product of this shift in orientation.

There were several other interesting things that happened with the Eee PC, and they can give us a taste for what happens in the current information environment. We'll talk later about the fact that there was no traditional market research done when the product was developed. Or that the adoption of the Eee PC didn't follow classic diffusion theory. In one area where ASUS did things according to the textbook, it got its biggest surprise. We'll come back to Jonney Shih toward the end of this chapter, but before we do, we want to go deeper into the shift from "relative" to "absolute" and discuss some research that demonstrates this shift.

EXPERIMENTAL EVIDENCE

You may have heard this story: Back in the 1990s Williams-Sonoma was selling a bread-baking machine. Sales were not great. Then the company added a second bread machine that was much more expensive, and something very interesting happened. Few customers bought the expensive model, but much to the company's surprise, sales of the first machine nearly doubled. This is a classic example for how relative evaluations work. You may have also heard the advice consultants and scholars frequently associate with this story: If you want to boost the sales of a product, launch a more expensive one. Steering consumers to midrange products by introducing a high-end option sounds like a solid strategy, but how useful is it in today's shopping environment?

We decided to examine this question. The above advice builds on Itamar's dissertation and on research he published in the early 1990s with the late Amos Tversky, the leading psychologist of judgment and decision making. In a study that Itamar and Amos published in 1992, participants in one group had to choose between two Minolta cameras, one priced at $169 and the second priced at $239. Another group of participants was presented with the same two cameras and a third, more expensive one (priced at $469). The results of the original experiment were intriguing. The $239 camera was more popular in the second group than in the first one. In other words, just by adding the $469 camera, some people were influenced to choose the $239 camera instead of the cheapest one.[5] Just as in the Williams-Sonoma example, this study demonstrates that people's choice can be greatly affected by the set of options placed in front of them. Specifically, the camera experiment shows that people tend to choose the middle or compromise item among a set of options.

But are people susceptible to this compromise effect when they shop online?

In 2012 Itamar and a PhD student named Taly Reich ran a new study. In it two groups of participants were under very similar conditions to the 1992 experiment. One group saw two Canon PowerShot cameras, and the second group saw three Canon PowerShot cameras. What happened? The results were very similar to what was shown twenty years earlier: Adding a third (more expensive) camera drastically increased the relative percentage of people who chose the mid-priced camera. This wasn't too surprising. After all, the human brain has not changed in the past twenty years, so we expected this experiment to show the same results when conducted under similar conditions.

But we were more interested in two other groups of participants, who were put in more realistic shopping conditions. People in these groups first saw what consumers usually see when they shop for a camera on Amazon.com: lots of options, a variety of prices, reviews written by consumers, and so on. After they looked at all the Canon PowerShot cameras available on Amazon, participants in these groups were asked to assume that they have narrowed their choice down. Now participants in one of the groups saw two cameras while participants in a second group saw three cameras, as in the original study.

What was the outcome? The compromise effect was gone. It completely disappeared. It vanished.

This new experiment demonstrates the shift from relative evaluations to absolute evaluations. What happens here is easy to explain:

Participants in the restricted conditions compared a camera to whatever was in front of them. When there were just two cameras, they compared them to each other, and when a very expensive camera was put in front of them, it dramatically shifted their preferences. But this wasn't how things worked for the two "Amazon groups." They were not restricted by the "local context." This is much more similar to what happens in today's reality. In many cases today, our decisions are no longer driven only by what happens to be in front of us or is top-of-mind. Instead, we can easily and quickly evaluate things based on a global context—other sources, information, and options that are not under anyone's control. Judgments are still relative, but the reference points can be based on the best of what's available out there.[6] As a result, a tendency to prefer compromise options has diminished (though it is unlikely to go away).[7]

Why did consumers used to rely on relative evaluations so much? Relative evaluations derive from limitations that we all share as humans: First, we tend to be "cognitive misers." What do we mean by that? It's not necessarily that we're lazy, but our mind tends to do whatever is easiest. When making a decision, we use only a small amount of information and it tends to be the information that is easiest to access. It may be, for example, the most easily accessible prior knowledge, or whatever we happen to see at the moment.[8] This comes at the expense of harder things like searching our brain for potentially relevant information or looking for other options somewhere else. Second, we have a hard time looking at something and assessing its quality, so we do the next best thing and rely on evaluations relative to generic, top-of-mind (though often not very useful) reference points or quality proxies. Such proxies may include brand name, prior satisfaction with other products by that brand, the image of the store where it is sold, or the reputation of the country where the product was manufactured. That's just the way we are: absolute-value challenged, cognitive misers who are addicted to comparisons. We can't look at a dishwasher and determine its value or how well it will clean the dishes. But place two dishwashers in front of us, and we will instantly start comparing their features and prices.

When we examine the practice of marketing through the twentieth century, we can say that it was largely geared to communicate values relative to reference points. As consumers, we depended heavily on relative evaluations: We chose one item on the shelf because it looked better or cost less than the one next to it. We evaluated products relative to our prior experience with a particular brand. We evaluated the price of a car relative to its sticker price. In short, we evaluated things relative to whatever was most accessible to us. But what would happen if one morning we woke up and were freed from our addiction to relative evaluations because we suddenly were able to assess absolute values?

PLANET ABSOLUTE

Let's imagine a planet—we'll call it Planet Absolute—that is almost identical to Planet Earth. There's only one difference: Before you buy something on Planet Absolute, you press a magic button and know everything you want to know about it—you know exactly how good or bad that product or service is going to be, and how you will like it after using it. Economists would call this "perfect information."

How would people make decisions on Planet Absolute?

They wouldn't rely on a brand to determine the quality of a product. They would just press the button. They would not be too impressed by the fact that a product is made in Germany or any other country with a reputation for high quality. They would just press the button. They wouldn't even care as much about the fact that they loved the last model of a product. When evaluating a new model, they would just press that button. When a consumer would shop for a car on Planet Absolute, she would not need a bunch of indirect proxies to assess her likely experience with a specific model. While she would still be affected by image and status, she would not need a brand name to assess the car's quality.

A state of perfect information is of course theoretical and we obviously will never reach the hypothetical Planet Absolute, but in more and more areas of life, we're starting to get closer to absolute values, which make us less dependent on relative evaluations. The human brain is not changing, but a fundamental shift in our information environment is under way, with far-reaching, evolving implications for consumer decision making. As we pointed out earlier, when we talk about absolute values, we're talking about a "good enough" answer. We don't mean to say that people will find *the* absolute best option in every category. In all likelihood, this won't happen unless they waste too much time. Furthermore, some ambiguity about the absolute best will remain in many cases, in part because our own preferences are often vague and unstable. However, there is no doubt that, with little effort, people can obtain today high-quality, diagnostic information regarding their likely experience with a product or a service.

It's also worth emphasizing that we're not talking about the obvious observation that consumers can easily find a great deal of information these days. The main difference we are talking about refers to the assessment of quality. In the past, consumers had a hard time assessing quality before purchase. This gave rise to much of what we know as marketing—various quality cues such as brands, prices, country of origin, much of advertising, and so on. But this is changing.

WHAT DRIVES THE SHIFT FROM RELATIVE TO ABSOLUTE?

A technological revolution, still in its infancy, is driving this shift, as new tools help us assess the quality of products and services we're considering. Aggregation tools, advanced search engines, reviews from other users, social media, unprecedented access to experts, and other emerging technologies—these things make it possible for consumers to make better decisions without having to rely on relative evaluations.

Examples are all around us: A woman compares prices of video games at a big retail store. Using "relative" tactics, the retailer can influence her choice by placing a game they want to push next to a very expensive one, making the former look like a bargain. But then the woman scans the bar code of the game, using her smartphone, and finds out that it's available at the store next door for less than half the price (and even cheaper online). Another example: A young man is considering buying a new TV. In the past, he would evaluate his options relative to his prior experience with a particular brand, say Sony. Today he's more likely to read reviews on Amazon.com or BestBuy.com, or go to some product rating site.

Some of the tools that we talk about won't be new to many readers, but this doesn't make their impact less dramatic. Sometimes taking stock of what has transpired in front of our eyes can be startling, and it's worth stopping for a moment to look at what has happened in the past decade. Review sites (from Amazon and CNET to Yelp and Zagat) tell us about the reliability and usefulness of products, and help us predict the experience we can expect at restaurants or hotels. Through social media, it's become so easy to get recommendations from friends and acquaintances. Post a quick question on Facebook or Twitter ("Can anyone make a camera recommendation?") and you are likely to get customized advice from a knowledgeable friend. Use Facebook's Graph Search to find out what your friends (or their friends) say about a particular restaurant or movie.[9] Assessing value and price has become much easier, too: Mobile apps such as Decide.com, ShopSavvy, or Bakodo inform us about the resale values of products.

Unprecedented access to experts is another fundamental shift that often goes unnoticed. Think about it: At its peak in the 1990s, *PC Magazine*'s circulation was 1.2 million copies. This may sound like a lot, but today expert reviews are available to anyone who uses the Internet—more than 200 million people in North America alone.[10] These days you can also find very quickly and quite accurately how popular (or unpopular) things are. The publisher of our book may publicize it as a "national bestseller," but claims about the book's popularity won't be that effective, because you can see our book's ranking on Amazon at any time. Similarly, a maker of a new gadget can tell you that "everyone's talking" about his latest invention, but a quick search on Twitter or a myriad of other tools will tell you if this is indeed true.

And this is just the beginning. In the coming years, we can expect to have access to even more data that will be better organized and interpreted. We explore some of these future trends later on in the book. We're not going to try to predict future technologies (humans are limited in this respect), but we'll discuss where things may be going. The cumulative effect of even just the existing technologies, and their dramatic effects on how consumers make decisions, pose a major challenge to established ideas about marketing and related business functions. Simply put, it makes influencing through relative tactics and indirect cues (such as brand and price) much harder.

Aggregation tools and review sites are not without problems, so we're sure some readers have some (valid) questions on their minds: Can't these technologies be manipulated by unscrupulous marketers? Isn't the wealth of information creating tremendous clutter that makes decision making even more difficult? Since people are different from each other, how can an evaluation by one person help another one? What about matters of taste? And will people actually take the time to use these tools? We'll address these and related questions throughout the book, but here is a brief preview of our answers:

First, can't these technologies be manipulated? No doubt some companies try (and will always try) to game the system, for example by planting positive reviews. Yet despite alarming articles that pop up periodically in the press about fake reviews, paid bloggers, fake "Likes," or other manipulations, we think that manipulators will usually have limited impact, and their effectiveness will decline as rating systems find better ways to deal with them. Reviews are not perfect, but the one solution that consumers are *not* turning to is trusting marketers as the main source for information regarding quality. Consumers are much more likely to migrate to sources they *do* trust, such as experts, or recommendations from friends and acquaintances (which are much more accessible today). We discuss this in great detail in Chapter 4.

The second question: Isn't the wealth of information creating tremendous clutter that makes decision making even more difficult? We've heard a lot in recent years about the concept of "too much choice" and information overload, the notion that too many options and too much information may overwhelm consumers to a point where they don't buy at all or make poor decisions. Many observers use these concepts to support their belief that brands and loyalty are more important than ever. We don't think so. First, the idea that consumers should or will consider all or most of the available information indiscriminately is an unrealistic "strawman," as we'll explain in more detail later. The web provides very effective tools for sorting and using the most relevant information. Also, based on a recent review, it appears that the choice overload problem is not nearly as serious as one might expect based on some highlighted findings. The review article, which combined the results of fifty experiments dealing with the phenomenon, concluded that "the overall effect size in the meta-analysis was virtually zero."[11] And with the steady improvement in information and option-sorting tools, the overload problem will become even less significant. While we agree that under certain conditions people can be overwhelmed by too many disorganized options, in most real-world buying situations, options are already well sorted (more on choice overload in Chapter 3).

Since people are different from each other, how can an evaluation by one person help another one find the absolute value of a product? First, the absolute value of a product consists of some components that are universal. For example, everyone prefers reliable products over unreliable products. So evaluations from other consumers and experts can be very helpful on that front alone. But it goes beyond that: There are indeed components of absolute value on which people differ based on their tastes, interests, and abilities. For example, some shoppers for a camera may define quality based on whether a camera is easy to use and fully automatic, whereas other shoppers prefer cameras with sophisticated manual override features. Some people may evaluate a cruise on whether or not it is family-oriented, while other people may evaluate it on whether the cruise is oriented for older people who are sensitive to noisy kids. The good news is that consumers can select those reviews (or expert opinions) according to what's important to them. They can usually rather easily determine if the source of the information fits their type; for example, when assessing absolute values of cameras or cruises, one can usually determine if the source of the information is knowledgeable about the topic and how similar they are to the reader. Which leads us to matters of pure taste. When it comes to such decisions, it's true that it's harder to talk about absolute values. Who's to say if *Midnight in Paris* is a good film or if Giorgio Armani is the right perfume for you? But clearly, this doesn't prevent people from relying on reviews and other tools to find out how those similar to them rate a movie, a book, or a restaurant. Just look at the number of reviews of food, perfume, and fashion (to name just a few categories where personal taste plays an important role). There are tools that allow you to find large groups of people who share your taste, but the key point is that even when an absolute factual answer cannot be determined, consumers clearly prefer it over the answers provided by marketers.

Finally, will people actually take the time to use these tools? People already use—and trust—these tools in a big way, which turns them into an important factor in decision making regardless of any limitations. Consider just three facts:

- Consumer confidence in reviews around the world is increasing. In 2012, 70 percent of consumers surveyed online by Nielsen indicated that they trust online reviews—an increase of 15 percent in four years.[12]

- Thirty percent of U.S. consumers start their online purchase research with Amazon.com, which, with its wealth of reviews, has become a clearinghouse for product information.[13]
- Research done for Google in 2011 found that the average shopper consults 10.4 sources of information prior to purchase—almost twice as many as in the previous year.[14] Although more studies are needed and the actual number of sources consumers consult varies greatly from one purchase and product category to the other, the trend is clear.

Back to Jonney Shih and the launch of the Eee PC. As we said, there was one thing that Shih and his team tried to do according to the textbook. This was to clearly position the Eee PC and define its target market. But this is where they had their biggest surprise. ASUS tried to position the Eee PC as a low-end device geared at people who haven't owned a PC before—children and the elderly. But most people who actually bought the Eee PC already had a computer. Many of them were businesspeople and other users on the go who wanted to have a second (lighter) laptop. That's another (not uncommon) phenomenon in this new information environment: You offer a product or a service and certain "target" segments adopt it and position it as they wish. It's hard to position things in people's minds when they have access to all the information they need.

There was also no traditional market research done in developing the Eee PC. We actually doubt that it would have predicted the success of this device. One reason is that if ASUS were to have conducted research, they would have picked a sample from their target market (first-time PC users) and not from the people who ended up buying it. The broader reason is that market research tries to predict people's preferences, but increasingly, decisions are influenced by the opinions of other consumers and experts. As we discuss in a later chapter, some market research, for example, missed the success of the iPhone: In 2007, a study among ten thousand people around the globe concluded that there is no real need for a convergent product such as the iPhone in affluent countries like the United States.

The adoption of the Eee PC didn't follow classic diffusion theory. A lot of business thinking is still based on the belief that a product is first adopted by a few innovators who are willing to take risks, then by early adopters, then by the early majority, and so on. This gradual model (which made perfect sense in an environment characterized by high levels of uncertainty) is becoming less relevant when anyone can find useful information shortly after a new product launches. Not long after the Eee PC shipped you could easily find information about it on blogs, review sites, and in mass media.

All of ASUS's success stories don't mean that its future is secure. The same forces that enabled its rise may allow the company to fall just as fast. Some marketing experts love to talk about brand loyalty, yet this is another thing that is changing in this new era. When quality was hard to predict, it made sense to stick with a familiar brand. But when you can quickly assess the quality of things, loyalty doesn't help consumers as much. Brand equity is simply not as valuable as it used to be. Don't get us wrong. Being Apple is still better than being ASUS. Brand equity is still valuable in terms of name recognition, continuity, and in some cases, emotional attachment and prestige. (As we are writing this, Shih is benefiting in this sense from some highly visible partnerships with Google.) But brands play a reduced role when it comes to assessments of the quality of a product.[15]

ASUS is not an anomaly. Throughout this book we'll meet companies that benefit from the shift to absolute evaluations in a variety of industries: HTC in mobile, Pinterest or Instagram in apps, Acer (Shih's former employer) in laptops, Hyundai in automotive, Shark in vacuum cleaners, Ninja in kitchen products, LG and Samsung in . . . everything.

We realize that some of the points we made in this chapter call for much explanation. From telling people about this book, we have learned that some of our points (such as the decline of brand or loyalty as quality signals) tend to generate resistance (and even hostility) from some marketers. In the next few chapters we'll go into great length to explain and support these claims. And some other things have to be said here: First, revolutions are messy and rarely happen overnight. The shift we're discussing here is far from being an instantaneous, smooth ride to perfect information. Second, the trends we describe in this book will not happen evenly across the board. As we explain in Part III, we don't expect these trends to apply in the same way to cars and toothpastes, to well-connected and to less connected consumers, and to decisions made with or without time pressure. There are categories, segments, and situations where consumers still heavily depend on relative evaluations. Finally, it's worth mentioning that people are not becoming smarter or more logical. No worry; we'll all continue to be susceptible to some irrelevant influences and make some error judgments.

For now, even if you're not convinced about all the implications we described, let's recap the main point of this chapter, which is the shift in consumer decision making from reliance on relative values to absolute values. In the past, we made decisions relative to other things that happened to be most accessible. Today, in many cases, our decisions are no longer restricted to what happens to be in front of us. In today's socially intensive information environment, we can easily evaluate things based on the best information out there, and thus get closer to the absolute value of things. We have a much better idea about our likely experience with products and services. So, counter to what we frequently hear, consumers will, on average, make better choices and act more rationally, which takes us to the next chapter. . . .

2

THE DECLINE OF "IRRATIONALITY"

A FUNNY THING has happened to the concept of "irrationality": Over the past four decades, thousands of experiments have suggested that by changing things like the context or framing of an offer, marketers can easily sway people to act in "irrational" ways. In the past few years, this idea has started percolating into the mainstream. Ironically, just as the concept is gaining popularity, it's becoming less representative of reality.

It's easier to be *rational* when you rely on absolute values.

No, we're not suggesting that people will start behaving fully rationally (the way economists assume they would) anytime soon, that any basic cognitive abilities are changing, or that they will be totally immune to manipulation. (And this, of course, includes the authors of this book. We have our share of embarrassing stories where we bought lemons or useless products but made every effort to use them to "get our money's worth"). But a shift is indeed taking place as a by-product of the new reality.

Putting it all in historical perspective, we can say this: In the beginning, economists and other scholars believed that people are generally rational utility-maximizers, know exactly the value of each product feature, and that those susceptible to decision errors will learn from their mistakes. Over the past forty years, many decision researchers have portrayed people as inherently "irrational" and error-prone (and to set the record straight, Itamar is among those responsible for the portrayal of consumers as susceptible to various seemingly irrational influences).[1] They showed in numerous (often intriguing) lab experiments that with the right framing or context, an experimenter can cause people to reverse their preferences. In this book we try to go a step further: We of course recognize that people's minds have limitations that won't change, but we examine what happens to these limitations in a new environment that is less hospitable and conducive to such "irrationality" effects.

We need to clarify the term "irrationality" in our context. We put the word in quotation marks because, as Daniel Kahneman points out in his book *Thinking, Fast and Slow*, the word connotes impulsivity, emotionality, and a stubborn resistance to reasonable argument. Without quotation marks, it's too strong a word in our context. In fact, Kahneman writes: "I often cringe when my work with Amos [Tversky] is credited with demonstrating that human choices are irrational, when in fact our research only showed that Humans are not well described by the rational-agent model."[2]

So what do scholars mean when they say someone is "irrational"? Probably the least ambiguous definition is related to behavior that is inconsistent with the economic concept of value maximization. For example, a consumer who selects an option that is clearly inferior or switches from choosing A over B to choosing B over A due to seemingly irrelevant factors is said to exhibit "irrationality." Are people who believe in UFOs irrational? Not in this context. A decision is regarded as irrational if it clearly shows that the person's decisions are inconsistent, incoherent, or unambiguously represent an inferior choice for that person given his or her beliefs, values, and preferences. While we may be critical or even ridicule the belief in UFOs, there's nothing "irrational" about it as the term is used in this field.

Numerous studies have demonstrated that consumers' decisions can be influenced in different ways. These influences fall into three broad categories—framing effects, choice context effects, and task effects. "Irrationality" studies are rather intriguing and new studies keep coming, but how representative are they of today's reality? What happens to these theories of choice manipulation and influence in the "noisy," information-rich, and socially intensive environment that is developing? We argue that the new environment significantly changes how things work. First, the relevance of these influence tactics has diminished in a world where people can easily assess quality. On average, better decisions are being made based on the information that's available. Second, the noise that all this information creates has a surprising effect. In the next few pages we'll discuss each of the categories—framing, context, and task— and explain why they are less relevant in the new information environment.

FRAMING EFFECTS

On the same day in March 2012, *USA Today* announced that the Federal Reserve annual stress test failed four of nineteen big banks, while the *New York Times'* headline read: "15 of 19 Big Banks Pass Fed's Latest Stress Test."[3] So in this case an editor at *USA Today* chose to frame the news more negatively than a counterpart at the *New York Times*. It turns out that framing can significantly affect our perceptions, memories, and the choices we make. An intriguing study illustrates how framing can affect even the perception of taste. In an experiment conducted at the University of Iowa by Irwin Levin and Gary Gaeth, participants rated beef that was presented to them as "90 percent lean" as better tasting than beef that was presented as containing "10 percent fat." It was the same beef and the same information. Clearly, the taste of beef should not depend on how it's labeled. But when the researchers tweaked the message to sound more positive, those people who saw it as "lean" tended to like it better.[4]

Framing still works just fine in the lab, and many marketers continue to believe that they can affect people's perceptions by framing something positively. But what happens to this effect in today's reality? In 2012, we saw an example of how framing works today (or doesn't): There's a food product used in the United States that's produced from the bits and ends left over in the butchering process. The fat is removed by heating and spinning, and then this leaner mix is treated with ammonium hydroxide to kill bacteria. The makers of the product found a nice-sounding name for it— "lean, finely textured beef"—and, for a while, framing seemed to be working like in a textbook.

Except that in 2002 a microbiologist at the U.S. Department of Agriculture by the name of Gerald Zirnstein offered a less flattering framing for the product. In an email message to colleagues, he referred to it as "pink slime" and added: "I do not consider the stuff to be ground beef, and I consider allowing it in ground beef to be a form of fraudulent labeling."[5] As long as Zirnstein's framing was not made public, the makers of the product were doing fine, but in 2009, the *New York Times* published the term in an article. Sometime later, celebrity chef Jamie Oliver discussed the topic on his TV show and a blogger named Bettina Siegel, whose blog "The Lunch Tray" focuses on kids' food, picked the term and started an online petition asking Secretary of Agriculture Tom Vilsack to stop using "pink slime" in school lunches. After just nine days, more than two hundred thousand people signed the petition and the USDA announced that it would offer school districts a choice of beef without the product. With additional coverage on ABC News, public perception of the product shifted, and the largest U.S. supermarket chains announced that they would no longer sell products containing "lean, finely textured beef." The bottom line is this: Framing works in the lab where people are not exposed to any alternative frames. When consumers rely on information from multiple sources, framing effects are likely to be weaker and, in some cases, dissipate completely. Of course, marketers, such as political consultants, will continue to look for just the right terms that might help promote their causes and hurt competitors, and in some cases they will be successful. But frames offered by marketers face tougher competition and are sometime neutralized by alternative frames.[6]

CHOICE CONTEXT EFFECTS

Remember the camera experiment from the previous chapter? As you recall, adding an expensive camera to the choice set caused some consumers to choose the moderately priced camera instead of the cheapest one. This is a perfect example for a context (or choice set) effect (the context of the offer affected people's decisions). Let's look at another one: Suppose you're shopping for a shredder and you see two options. One shredder costs $20 and can shred up to 7 sheets of paper at a time. The second shredder costs $50 and can shred up to 11 sheets of paper at a time. Which one would you choose? If you care about cost you would probably choose the first one; if you care about the number of sheets, you would choose the one with higher capacity.

Now, suppose that you're shopping under different conditions and you actually see *three* shredders: one at $20 that shreds 7 sheets at a time, the second at $50 that shreds 11 sheets, *and* a third shredder that costs $95 and can shred up to 12 sheets of paper at a time. Which shredder would you choose now? When Taly Reich and Itamar ran this study recently, adding the $95 shredder that shreds 12 sheets increased the number of consumers who chose the $50 shredder instead of the cheapest one. While this may look at first glance like another case of the compromise effect, what's going on here is different. This is known as asymmetric dominance, an effect that was first shown in 1982 by Joel Huber and his coauthors from Duke University. Essentially, those who chose between just two options saw a cheaper shredder that shreds fewer sheets against a more expensive shredder that shreds a higher number of sheets. But adding the $95 shredder that shreds 12 pages made the $50 shredder look like a winner: This shredder shreds almost as many pages for almost half the price! Companies can (and do) use this effect (sometimes referred to as the decoy effect) in selling hard drives, MP3 players, and other products.

But what happens to this effect when people shop online with full access to information? As with the camera experiment, Taly and Itamar also tested this effect in "Amazon" conditions. As opposed to the two groups that saw the shredders in isolated conditions, there were two groups of participants that were put in more real-life conditions. They first saw what consumers usually see when they shop for a shredder: a variety of options and prices, plus some reviews written by consumers. Once they looked at all the options, they were asked to assume that they have narrowed their choice down. Now, participants in one of the groups saw the two shredders (costing $20 and $50), while participants in a second group saw three shredders (costing $20, $50, and $95).

What was the outcome? The asymmetric dominance effect was gone. Not a shred of the effect was left.

Here's a story we came across that can help us further discuss the diminishing relevance of context effects in today's world: Not long ago, an Israeli real estate agent met an acquaintance who was selling his apartment in Jerusalem. When the agent inquired about the asking price, the man said he's listed the apartment for 2.1 million shekels, which surprised the experienced agent, who pointed out that similar apartments in the area usually sell for about 1.85 to 2 million shekels. With a mischievous wink, the man shared the little trick he had devised. In addition to listing his own apartment, he placed ads for three fictitious apartments in the same neighborhood for much higher prices ranging from 2.2 to 2.35 million. His idea was that potential buyers would see these ads and therefore feel that his asking price was a bargain. This is a context effect similar to examples we discussed earlier. Putting aside the serious ethical and legal questions that are beyond the scope of our book, let's ask a simple question: How likely is this trick going to work in two different markets? In one market, buyers have no information whatsoever about past transactions. In the other market, buyers know every single detail about all past transactions. Clearly, the man's trick is less likely to work in the second environment.[7]

While we're still far away from "knowing every single detail about past transactions," a buyer in the United States today can use several tools that will give her a very good idea of what's a reasonable price for a property. A quick search on Zillow.com will give her an estimate for the value of a particular house that is based on past transactions around that property. She can then view the details of many of the houses sold in the area to develop a sense of what's a reasonable price. Zillow is far from being perfect, but it limits sellers' ability to play such tricks.[8]

TASK EFFECTS

The way consumers' preferences are expressed and formed can also significantly affect people's choices. It turns out that if you ask people to select a product one way, they will choose product A, and if you ask them in a different way, they will choose product B. In a study that Stephen Nowlis and Itamar ran, subjects were asked to select between two toasters. When people were asked to simply pick one of the two toasters, they picked the less expensive brand (Kmart store brand). When people were asked to *rate* the two toasters, they preferred the better-known brand name (Black & Decker). This concept has many practical implications to marketers. For example, many retailers present their private-label brands next to the corresponding national brands. Conversely, products with a main advantage that is more qualitative (a well-known brand, for example) and harder to compare than price are likely to sell better if they are presented in a way that makes it difficult for buyers to compare (for example at an end-of-aisle display, also known as an end cap).[9]

This type of effect is also likely to be weaker as shopping environments are changing. A marketer of an expensive product who pays extra for an end cap display can hope to avoid direct comparison. But things can be very different when consumers are armed with smartphones and apps such as ShopSavvy that let them scan the bar code of a product and display prices in other retail stores. An app like GoodGuide displays alternative products based on attributes the consumer cares about. When assessing the quality of offers is supported by these types of technologies, swaying people's choices using "irrationality" tactics is far from being trivial.

Up to this point, we've seen how framing, context, and task effects are becoming less effective and less relevant. Part of the reason is that people are able to better assess the quality of things, but there's another, less obvious reason. . . .

THE SURPRISING POWER OF NOISE

Influence and manipulation work best when there's full control over what people are exposed to, and "noise" is kept to a minimum. What exactly do we mean by noise? Noise refers to any information that is not under control, often consisting of diverse pieces of data from different sources, about different aspects and options.

The following experiment hints at the difference between how people decide in isolation, and how they decide in a dynamic noisy environment. In 2006, Raymond Fisman, Sheena Iyengar, Emir Kamenica, and Itamar published a paper about speed dating. A few days before the actual speed dating event, participants were asked what factors were most important to them in a mate. Not surprisingly (and consistent with prior research) women were much less likely to say that physical attractiveness would be important. That was their theory when all they saw was a well-structured survey on a computer screen. But something completely different happened once these women participated in the actual event: They appeared to have forgotten their stated criteria. Attractiveness was almost as important for women as it was for men. Part of this may be explained by the fact that when speed dating, women couldn't accurately predict the "earning potential" of men (which has often been found to be a key driver for women). Yet a more relevant factor in our context has to do with the noise associated with speed dating—up to twenty dates, each lasting four minutes, all happening in the same (literally) noisy room. Instead of a clean survey, you're exposed to hundreds of diverse pieces of data, with different aspects and options.

The experiments we described earlier have one thing in common: Researchers in all cases had full control over what participants saw. For example, students who participated in the original 1992 camera experiment were sitting in a quiet classroom and focused on a piece of paper that featured either two or three cameras. That's all. They couldn't talk to each other, surf the Web, check their iPhones (who even dreamt of an iPhone back then?), or do anything else that would distract them. One of the guiding principles in planning such studies is limiting what the participants see, how they see it, and how much information they have.

We cannot think of an environment that is farther away from a quiet lab than the World Wide Web.

When the camera experiment was repeated in 2012 in lab-like conditions (that is, people were limited in what they saw), things worked as in the original experiment. But things worked differently when people were free to see other options. A follow-up study with these participants showed that they had poorer recall for the attribute values of the options. In other words, it wasn't necessarily that they looked around, found a better camera, and decided to stick with it. It's probably more likely that they saw so much stuff that the noise "spoiled" the effect.

The truth is that even that experiment was more structured than what typically happens in real life. Participants were limited to Amazon and were asked to focus on Canon PowerShot cameras (or on Fellows shredders in the shredders experiment). Consumer searches in real life are often even less structured. When we recently typed the word "camera" in Google, we immediately saw ten cameras from different makers, ranging in price from $69 to

$945. What's more—hundreds of consumer reviews were accessible from that page. These reviews create two effects. The first is straightforward—even though reviews are not perfect quality indicators, their content helps consumers assess the quality of offers. But the second effect can be as powerful: This avalanche of information creates a lot of noise—a lot of distractions that create situations that are quite different from those in sanitized lab experiments and "spoil" the necessary conditions for marketers to influence.

This is the surprising power of noise—in the current information environment, influencing people is a bit like trying to hypnotize someone while riding a motorcycle at 100 mph. There are just too many distractions.

We are certainly not proposing that lab studies of consumer decision making no longer serve a useful purpose in the current environment. We argue that, by and large, our ability to generalize from tightly controlled experiments (with limited information) to consumer decision making in reality has been diminished. The gap between the lab and reality is getting wider. In particular, lab "effects" that depend on tightly controlled reference points may often not apply to a noisy environment that is characterized by unpredictable reference points and widely different contexts. This means that lab results can often lead to misleading conclusions that misrepresent what happens in reality.

Buying products in the twentieth century was an experience that was more conducive to influence by marketers. Even though you weren't as isolated as in a lab, you were usually in some controlled environment. You stood at the store in front of a limited number of dishwashers, or you looked at a catalog that came in the mail and focused on a few items on the page. You were usually confined to a small set. Things work very differently in today's shopping mall and certainly online.

There's an important exception worth noting. While many of those "irrationality" demonstrations are less relevant in the new environment, there's a key ingredient that must be present in the consumer environment in order for this "de-biasing" effect to happen. Here's a study that looked into this in the context of a standard framing effect. It is based on a well-known experiment that showed that people tend to reject an economic policy program when they are told that it will result in 5 percent unemployment, but to prefer the (same) program when they are told that it will result in 95 percent employment. Participants in this new experiment were asked to imagine that they were faced with the decision of adopting one of two economic policies, and here, too, people tended to reject the program when it was framed negatively (5 percent unemployment) and adopt it when it was framed positively (95 percent employment). Things started to get interesting when the researcher James Druckman from Northwestern University exposed participants to *heterogeneous* framings or asked to discuss the problem in small groups that consisted of some participants who were exposed to positive framing and some to negative. What happened then? The framing effect was eliminated.[10]

This is important. A key element to ensure that people are not susceptible to relative tactics is exposure to diverse sources, perspectives, options, and considerations. It's not enough to hear others' opinions. Susceptibility to influence by irrelevant reference points will decline only if others see different things or see things differently. People who belong to a cult will not be protected from their leader's influence if they never talk to others outside the cult. This means that assessing quality in a monolithic cultlike environment does not make judgments and decisions more absolute—they remain locked in the shared frame. Raving fans of a brand (or a political leader) who only listen to like-minded fans may be as susceptible to relative tactics as in the past. In short, when most others in a situation have the same information, are in the same "condition," face the same frame, or see the same option set, "irrationality" will prevail.

EXTRAPOLATIONS ON STEROIDS

Before we go on, we need to make a couple of general points about the field of behavioral decision making. The field has offered meaningful and important insights into how people make decisions, and as we have argued, some of the effects demonstrated in the field are declining because of a changing environment. But the truth is that there are also effects that were never that strong to begin with. Some of the more prominent examples that demonstrate "irrationality" had limited relevance under normal conditions even in the old times. Some studies reached broad conclusions that were based on extrapolations from rather narrow and unrepresentative tests. The boundary conditions and the limitations of the studies that are reported in the academic papers are usually lost in the popular press. All that is left is a great story for a cocktail party that doesn't necessarily represent what's really going on in the world.

For example, an influential early finding of a preference reversal: When you ask people to choose between two gambles (for example, a 50 percent chance to win $10 and 50 percent chance to lose $5, or a 5 percent chance to win $100 and 95 percent chance to lose $4), they usually choose the one with the better odds of winning. But if you ask them to price the gamble (how much would you sell each gamble for?), people usually price the one that offers the higher payoff option higher. This and similar findings, which have significant theoretical implications, have been relied upon to advance the idea that people generally don't have preferences, so they tend to "construct" preferences on the fly based on what they happen to consider at the moment. But how much can we really learn from this example about everyday preferences? Pricing gambles is not something that people normally (or ever) do, so no wonder they make mistakes.

Some of these effects get attention and make good conversation topics. They are intriguing, no doubt. Researchers, authors, and journalists all know that surprising results and counterintuitive effects make good stories and these are exactly the stories that often get more attention than they deserve and are prone to exaggerations.

Another point that has to be made in this context: People outside the field assume that these academic findings about decision errors are usually as reliable and robust as those in the natural sciences. Some indeed are robust and tend to replicate from one study to the next, but many are not. Some findings are very sensitive to a particular laboratory test methodology, and it's unfortunately not uncommon for researchers to try three different tests of an idea and report the one that works (or works best). Moreover, in theory, different methods for testing the same principle should lead to the same results, yet many of the reported findings are notoriously method-sensitive. So sometimes that great cocktail party story is based on shaky science. When the popular press reports on such findings, they usually neglect to mention that the intriguing effects operate under very specific, rather narrow conditions, and may not apply in most situations.

At the same time, we want to make sure that the message of our book is not exaggerated or misinterpreted. We will try to describe in later chapters when our argument applies and when it does not. Furthermore, it's important to note that not all effects that have been demonstrated in this or related fields will be affected by the new information environment. Consider, for example, the power of default choice. Fewer than 5 percent of people in Denmark choose to donate organs after they die, as opposed to 99.91 percent of the French. Is it that the French are more altruistic? No. As Eric Johnson and Daniel Goldstein showed, what determines this is the default choice. If you want to donate your organs in Denmark you have to be proactive. In France you don't have to do anything.[11] In recent years these types of effects have been used in clever ways to influence behavior, as described in the book *Nudge*, by Richard Thaler and Cass Sunstein. We do not expect the advantage of defaults and status quo to be significantly affected by the trends we describe here.[12]

IT'S ABOUT TECHNOLOGY

There are important insights that are based on robust research that simply don't apply in the evolving consumer environment as much as they did in the past. Consider anchoring, which is one of the best-documented, most robust judgment phenomena (shown back in 1974 by Tversky and Kahneman).[13] This effect can be very relevant to consumer behavior. For example, participants in an experiment that Itamar ran with Aimee Drolet, from the University of California, Los Angeles, were asked to write down the last two digits of their Social Security number. Next, they were presented with a picture of a toaster, and were asked to assume that the number they had just written down was the price in dollars of the toaster. Would they pay that amount? Some said yes, some said no. Next, participants were asked to write down the highest price they would be willing to pay for this toaster. Remarkably, people's decisions were clearly affected by the random number: Those with Social Security numbers that ended with 50–99 were willing to pay, on average, about $10 more than people whose Social Security number ended with 00–49.[14]

In the past, anchoring and so-called "reference prices" were often used to show how marketers can influence consumers' choice. There's a story, for example, about a manager of a store that sold Brunswick pool tables who conducted a little experiment. One week he directed customers who came into his store to the least expensive table first. The following week he started with the most expensive table first. The average sale on the first week was $550. On the second week it was $1,000.[15]

Anchoring is still a robust effect, though "noise" and the availability of multiple anchors can decrease the effect of any one anchor that a marketer may offer. In fact, price anchors can often favor lower prices, especially when price search engines display the lowest prices *first*, in which case these prices are more likely to serve as anchors that determine how higher prices are perceived.

The shift from relative to absolute derives largely from the new technologies and their effect on decision making and not from some advancement of our brain. There's a lot of talk these days about "the new consumer"—a smarter, skeptical person who's immune to marketing. We don't buy that view. People are fundamentally the same as they were fifty years ago and will be fifty years from now. They are becoming less susceptible to marketers' influence not because they are smarter or more logical. It is tools like the ones we mentioned earlier (and will discuss later) that are changing things (advanced search engines, reviews from other users, unprecedented access to experts, easy access to friends and acquaintances). This is important because, as we will show later, in the absence of such tools, relative thinking will prevail.

What's the main takeaway from this chapter? As you hear about fascinating findings about consumers' "irrationality," we suggest that you take them with a grain of salt. While lab experiments can demonstrate some neat effects, these experiments often depend on the researcher having full control over what participants see, which is radically different from today's shopping reality. There is very little control over what people see when they shop online, and as smartphones are increasingly used by consumers at brick-and-mortar stores, the gap between the lab and reality gets even wider. Over-extrapolated examples that portray the consumer as an irrational and bendable Gumby will probably continue to pop up in the press. There's always demand for the surprising and counterintuitive. But as more and more people take advantage of new tools, marketers start to realize that Gumby has a spine. Consumers are far from being as susceptible to influence as they are being portrayed.

3

NEW PATTERNS IN CONSUMER DECISION MAKING

LAMENTING INFORMATION OVERLOAD is nothing new. Historian Ann Blair found scholars complaining as early as 1545 about a "confusing and harmful abundance of books."[1] These days you hear so much about information overload and its paralyzing effects on decision making that sometimes you wonder how consumers make decisions at all. While we agree that people face unprecedented amounts of information (and that indeed some *are* overwhelmed by it), most consumers can handle the information just fine. Consumers are actually very good at identifying that slice of information that is most relevant to them. They can use information selectively and efficiently and benefit from it without being overwhelmed or overloaded. The scale of information abundance that we currently experience is a very new phenomenon in the history of the human race, and it will probably take a while before we fully comprehend its implications. The conclusion that it paralyzes decision making seems a bit hurried, and a bit detached from reality if you watch people shopping before Christmas.

In fact, we see new patterns in decision making that emerge with the abundance of high-quality information. We already covered the primary pattern—a fundamental shift from reliance on relative evaluations to reliance on absolute values. In a world with improved access to high-quality information, more and more decisions will be based on absolute values, resulting in better choices overall.

In this chapter we'll explore three additional interesting patterns: First, some consumers compulsively acquire information, which can turn the traditional decision making process on its head. Second, consumers are often compelled to use the information they acquired, which accelerates the adoption (or rejection) of new products. Third, with the abundance of "rational," spec-driven information, decisions about products and services are made more from the head and less from the heart.

Clearly, there's a wide range in how people react to the new information environment, so not all consumers experience these trends at the same intensity. There are those who can't or won't use new sources of information (we'll discuss them in Chapter 12). This chapter is about the growing segments of the population who do.

Let's start with the much-heralded concept of "choice overload"— the belief that giving people more options can cause them to make no choices at all. As we mentioned in Chapter 1, many observers have emphasized that people are overwhelmed by too much information on the Internet. This may be true for some people, but those who take advantage of new tools can actually narrow down and sort their choice set rather quickly. Think about your own experience on Amazon.com (and recall that 30 percent of U.S. consumers start their online purchase research on Amazon). Search for a camcorder on Amazon and you'll see a couple of dozen options. You can then quickly narrow them down to the most popular or the best-rated models. For each one you can tell the average rating and number of reviewers in about a second. Or consider a website such as Sephora.com, with its enormous selection of beauty products. A customer who's looking for makeup foundation can quickly zero in on what she wants through a set of menus or through keyword search. Sorting through reviews is becoming easier as well. A customer doesn't have to read through 659 pages of reviews of

Bare Minerals SPF 15 Matte Foundation. Instead, she can focus on only those reviews written by consumers with dark skin and brown eyes, for example, by clicking on these two filters. New searching and sorting technologies are likely to further develop and alleviate the problem, which probably hasn't been that severe to begin with. As you recall, a review article that combined the results of fifty experiments dealing with choice overload showed the effect to be quite fragile, concluding that the overall effect was almost zero.[2] Even if some consumers are initially overwhelmed by too many options, in many categories they rely on expert opinions and on recommendations from other users. This may be another case where there's a gap between what can be shown in the lab and what actually happens in real life. Consumers may be overwhelmed when facing twenty laptops, but if they are immediately drawn to the most popular models and to those with the highest ratings, the problem is largely resolved.

Let's look now at the three trends that are emerging as a result of our new information diet: "couch tracking," "faster verdict," and "more from the head."

COUCH TRACKING

"This is the #1 netbook on my radar now"
"I've been watching these tablets for a year"
"I have been following the HTC Holiday rumors for months"

These comments from Engadget and other forums represent the first decision pattern: Some consumers routinely acquire information that can completely transform the decision making process for these people. Traditional models of decision making have not paid much attention to this "on my radar" behavior. Aside from habitual, impulse, and "low involvement" purchases, the purchase process in traditional models is typically assumed to begin when the consumer recognizes a problem. Next, the consumer engages in information search and evaluates options, which leads to preferences and a purchase decision (or purchase delay). But today, when high-quality information is so readily and cheaply accessible, some people don't see the need to postpone information acquisition until a specific purchase intention is formed. Instead, like sports buffs keeping track of the game from their couches, millions of people keep track of products on an ongoing basis.

Granted, this is not the way people buy vacuum cleaners or laundry detergent. But this continuing information acquisition process—which we nickname couch tracking—represents an important shift for certain segments and certain categories.

It's not an insignificant phenomenon, and we expect it to become even more prevalent. Gadget websites get millions of visitors a month (we're talking about sites such as CNET, Gizmodo, Engadget, macrumors, The Verge, gadgetwise, PhoneDog). Add to this the millions of people who follow products on mainstream media or on retail websites such as Amazon. Many also follow these information sources through Facebook or Twitter. Some couch tracking is directed at particular brands. Companies like to think of these folks as "fans" or "loyal customers." They aren't necessarily. These brands may simply be on these consumers' radar. Pinterest is another relevant tool in that it makes it easy to maintain wish lists. Then there are online communities that focus on an area of interest, a product or a brand of interest. For example, members of nikonians.com are talking about Nikon cameras. They keep track of the scene regardless of any specific purchase intention. If you're a sports car enthusiast, there's sportscarforums.com. There are forums about bags, video games, motorcycles, boats, pets, snowmobiles . . . you name it. The main point is this: If you're reading any of these sources on an ongoing or even occasional basis, it means that more often than not, you're *not* in the market for the products you're reading about. You just want to know what's out there. You're couch tracking.

What does the rise of couch tracking mean to marketers? It means that preferences are often formed well in advance of any specific plan or intention to purchase. As a result, once an intention to buy is formed, the decision is pretty much already made. Accordingly, marketers should pay more attention to couch trackers rather than just focus on declared buyers. The idea of "being in the market" is changing. The sequential, phased decision process is becoming less common for certain segments. Instead, when these consumers get close to buying, in many cases they have already decided.

ACTIVE SEARCH AND FASTER VERDICTS

We react differently to information that we seek as opposed to information that we encountered incidentally. What's the difference? The very fact that we initiate the information acquisition—that we actively seek it—creates an interesting side effect. When we deliberately seek information, we are more likely to use it. Scholars like Amos Tversky, Eldar Shafir, and Anthony Bastardi have shown in a series of studies that when people engage in deliberate pursuit of information (whether this information is instrumental to their decision or not), they are inclined to use it.[3] The explanation is pretty straightforward: In essence, people infer from their own behavior that, if they looked or waited for that information, they must value it and should now take advantage of it.

While pre-purchase search is certainly not new, the amount, sources, cost, and quality of searches have significantly changed. The same factors that lead to the couch tracking phenomenon also mean that consumers nowadays acquire more information than they used to.[4] When much of our information diet consisted of incidental information (things that we didn't ask for, like TV commercials), we didn't feel as compelled to use it. Yet these days, when a higher percentage of decisions is a result of an active premeditated search, more decisions lead to action. And by "action" we don't necessarily mean buying. A decision not to buy is also a verdict. This may be one of the factors that contribute to the acceleration of adoption (or rejection) of new products. People hear about a product, they search for it, and since they deliberately searched, they feel that they need to act one way or another. The fate of products is determined faster as a result.

The decision making process is often compressed for another reason. If in the past some unplanned purchases were dropped because consumers felt they "need to do more research," today more people feel comfortable going from discovery to purchase, sometimes at a surprising speed. Decisions now sometimes happen in one sitting. Browsing through an online store, you discover a new camera, you see that it's number one under the "Camera & Photo" category, you get all the quality and user popularity information you need, and decide to purchase. The answer's out there, so there is less of a reason to wait. Marketers often talk about the decision process as a funnel that goes from awareness to comprehension, to preference formation and then to purchase. They also like to measure the number of consumers who are at each stage at a certain point in time, yet these measurements don't mean as much when people can skip steps so easily.

MORE FROM THE HEAD, LESS FROM THE HEART

Another shift in our information diet that largely goes unnoticed has to do with the emotional content of the information we consume. To understand what we mean, consider two scenarios: Under scenario A you walk into an art gallery unprepared and see some beautiful paintings. Simple—it's all about your raw impression of the paintings. Under scenario B, you read some background information about the exhibit *before* you go to that gallery: You read a detailed analysis of the paintings, resale value of the work displayed, the artist's bio, and how she fits in the current art world. Under scenario A your emotions don't face much competition from your cerebral side, so they are likely to play a bigger role in your decision. In contrast, under scenario B, everything you've read is competing with that most primal emotional reaction. Your emotions are still likely to play a role, but probably a reduced one.

Hanging out on newsgroups or reading consumers' contributions on review sites, you're much more likely to come across "rational" than "emotional" information. By "rational" we refer to the instrumental, essential value of the product, to things such as reliability, features and other specs, uses, resale values, and popularity. By "emotional" we refer to feelings like warmth or nostalgia. Now, it's true that people do use words like "love" or "hate" in reviews, but we need to make a distinction between mentioning a word and actually evoking that emotion. Advertisers usually know how to evoke emotions (especially on TV). On the other hand, reviewers, even when they try, are usually less skillful at that (probably with the exception of anger and frustration, which are evoked more easily). But most content generated by consumers tends to be fact-based anyway. In many cases emotional considerations are seen as private, idiosyncratic aspects that are not suitable for sharing with others.

These days there's less sugar in our information diet, and decisions influenced by reviews and the like tend to be made from the head and less from the heart. There's also less sugarcoating. People tend to be brutally honest on the Internet, which creates a "say it as it is" culture.[5] The language that consumers used to rely on in making decisions has changed dramatically. Thirty years ago, when you shopped for a camera, you relied on ads that talked about preserving the precious memories of your family or told you a camera will give you "the power to be your best." The language of reviews tends to be more specific, more matter-of-fact and focused on quality and the use of the camera. Consumers are less exposed to advertising puffery when most of their information comes from experts and fellow consumers. Emotional appeal can still be powerful, and we're not saying that "warm and fuzzy" is dead. It's just less effective when it faces meaningful competition from more "rational" sources. Think of yourself buying a car in the 1990s. Besides *Car and Driver* and *Consumer Reports*, the information environment was dominated by the marketer who injected as much emotional appeal as they wanted. Emotions still play an important role in buying a car, but if you immerse yourself in dozens of reviews before your next purchase, the relative role of these emotions is reduced.

While emotional response is often very important (for example, when considering which car to buy), for products and services that have specs (and we are not talking about spouses) quality is usually regarded by consumers as the most important consideration that should guide choices. Product preferences are usually expected to be based on objective quality rather than subjective feelings. It's no wonder, then, that with the explosion of information about quality, consumers gravitate toward it.

A PEEK AT PLANET ABSOLUTE

Peter Rojas is one of those who have created environments that facilitate the trends we just discussed. He's someone who really takes full advantage of the information out there. So much so that when we spoke to Rojas, it suddenly dawned on us that we may be talking to someone from our utopian Planet Absolute. The setting of the interview went along with that intergalactic feeling: We, the earthlings, were sitting at Emanuel's old dining table, and to support the iPad that we used for Skyping, we piled some books into a structure that we were hoping wouldn't collapse in the middle of the interview. Rojas was sitting in New York City wearing ultramodern headphones that gave him a somewhat futuristic look. It's fair to say that we're well-informed consumers when it comes to technology, but on occasion, we had a hard time keeping up with the stuff he was throwing at us. Rojas is exposed to insane amounts of information about technology, and to say that he's up-to-date is an understatement because he usually knows things through leaks well before they're announced.

Rojas's personal journey represents some of the changes that have taken place in consumer information. About ten years before our conversation with him, he was freelancing for *Wired* magazine. He was an experienced technology journalist who had written for the *New York Times*, *Fortune*, and the *Guardian*, and had been editor of *Red Herring*, a magazine that focused on the business of technology. In retrospect we know that this was the twilight of a top-down media world where companies could pretty much control when and where they released information to the public through the media. In 2002 Rojas started moving into blogging, which was a relatively new thing. He wrote a blog called Gizmodo, which was dedicated to gadgets. At the time, the thought that anyone outside the tech industry would be interested in a spy photo of a new phone wasn't obvious, but Rojas sensed that interest in technology and gadgets had gone way beyond just Silicon Valley. In 2004, he started a similar blog, Engadget, a site that took advantage of a wide network of readers in the industry who would feed it with tips, secret product specifications, and photos of prototypes.

Rojas is the first to point out that not everyone reads the news blogs he started. So who does? "I tend to think of them as people for whom following technology is just like other people follow sports," he told us. "They have their favorite teams, and they like the horse race. It's not just about what they're going to buy, it's also about the dynamics, who's up, who's down, what's coming down the pipe." In short, they are couch tracking.

In 2009 Rojas and Ryan Block started a site called gdgt.com (pronounced "gadget-dot-com"). As opposed to Engadget and Gizmodo, which were essentially news sites driven by a team of editors, gdgt.com is driven by the users. It's kind of a Wikipedia for gadgets crossed with a social network. If you follow Rojas, for example, you can click on his profile and see that he has 76 gadgets. Click on one of them—the Samsung Galaxy S III, for example— and you can read 115 reviews of this model, 17 discussion threads, or 33 questions that were answered by owners.

Spending some time on the site, it's easy to see the trends we discussed here. Choice overload doesn't seem to be a problem; things are easy to find and sort. For example, under the category of laptops, you can search for only those in a particular price range and processing power. Each gadget you find is displayed with a score that is based on reviews from professional tech sites as well as users. For those who want just the bottom line, gdgt displays up to three "Must Haves" per category. Couch trackers can tag a product as one that's on their radar by simply marking it with the "I want it" tag (the other tags are "I have it" or "I had it"). Heavy users of the site are into compulsive collection of information and are clearly compelled to have the latest and greatest. We're sure that gdgt members have emotions and that those play some role in their decisions, but you'd be hard-pressed to find emotions expressed in the content they create.[6]

As we pointed out, there's a wide range in how people react to the new information environment. Thinking about it as a continuum, the gdgt.com crowd represents the super-informed on one end. On the very other end, there are those who do not take advantage of the available information or are totally overwhelmed by it. The rest of us are somewhere in the middle, but as tools develop and handling information becomes even easier, it's just a matter of time before at least some of the behaviors we described are adopted by wider and wider circles.

In this chapter we examined three emerging trends in consumer decision making. First, we talked about "couch tracking," where consumers acquire information on an ongoing basis from the comfort of their couch. This can turn traditional models of decision making upside down: When these consumers gather information, they are not in the market, and when they are in the market, they have already decided. Second, we argued that consumers reach their verdict faster. When people deliberately seek information, they are more likely to use it, and since more decisions are a result of an active, premeditated search, consumers reach a verdict faster (adoption or rejection). Third, we said that decisions will be made more from the head and less from the heart. Although emotions will always play an important role in people's decisions, consumers today are more likely to come across "rational" information created by fellow consumers (who tend to focus in their content on things like reliability, features, price, popularity, and specs). Overall, the current abundance of information is a new phenomenon and it will take some time before we fully understand its implications. We certainly agree that people can be overwhelmed by too many disorganized options under certain conditions, but research suggests that the choice overload problem is not as serious as it has been portrayed. This is true especially as search and sorting tools steadily improve.

4

WHY WE'RE BULLISH ABOUT ABSOLUTE VALUES

THERE WAS NOTHING special about a review written by a Gary O'Reilly, who loved the book *The Mistress*, by British actress Martine McCutcheon. "It was funny and moving in parts and well worth the time spent on it," O'Reilly wrote, awarding the book five stars on Amazon's British site. Over the years O'Reilly has written a few more reviews, all positive and all for books from the publishing company Pan Macmillan. In summer 2012, the *Sunday Times* reported that Jeremy Trevathan, head of Pan Macmillan's adult division, admitted that he was O'Reilly.[1]

As we were working on this book, similarly alarming stories kept popping up. Here are three more: In 2012, David Streitfeld of the *New York Times* wrote about a man named Todd Jason Rutherford from Oklahoma who had started a website called GettingBookReviews.com with a simple offer for authors who wanted their books to be reviewed on Amazon.com. Pay $499, and twenty reviews will be written about your book. For $999, you'll get fifty reviews. It didn't take long before orders started pouring in and added up to $28,000 a month, according to the *Times*.[2] Another related story was aired on ABC's *20/20* in 2010 about how Hamas got an A-minus rating with the Better Business Bureau in Santa Monica, California. Beyond the obvious question of how an organization that the United States considers a terrorist group can operate in California (let alone get almost a perfect score), the program raised serious concerns when a blogger claimed that all it took to get this rating was for someone to call with a credit card and pay $425 to the Better Business Bureau.[3] Another story we came across was about a woman from Salford, England, who admitted writing negative reviews of a vegetarian restaurant that she had never visited. She just had a grudge against the owner. "Staff cold and unattentive. The vegan option wasn't vegan. There were hairs in my quiche," one of her reviews on TripAdvisor read.[4]

Stories about vendors that try to game the system, vindictive customers, or accusations of corrupted rating systems appear frequently in the press, raising justified concerns about the credibility of these information sources. There are companies that sell followers on Twitter, views on YouTube, or Likes on Facebook. (We came across a company that offers five hundred Facebook Likes for $19. If you go on the monthly plan, the price goes down to $15.) Indeed, there are many questions that are raised about online reviews and other forms of user-generated content: If reviews can be manipulated by unscrupulous marketers, how can they serve as proxies for quality? And can't competitors distort the picture to their advantage? What about disgruntled employees or consumers with unreasonable expectations?

These are serious concerns, which may call into question a core premise of our book. If enough attempts to game the system are successful, consumers' ability to assess the absolute value of products and services will be seriously reduced, and consumers will not enjoy the benefits of the new information environment. Under an extreme scenario in which manipulations go out of control and across the board, our book may be remembered as just an intriguing idea—a dream that never materialized.

Despite these valid concerns, we are bullish about the trends we describe in this book. In this chapter we explain why. Before we delve into the stories of Hamas in Santa Monica and fake review services, here's a summary of why these trends are almost inevitable:

- While it's easy to fake some reviews, gaming the system (without being caught) is harder than one thinks, especially as participation in rating systems grows.
- There are cases where manipulations are successful. In these cases, a gap between positive reviews and negative experiences is likely to generate frustration, which can erode consumer trust in a review site.
- When attempts to game the system are caught, the press and bloggers alert the public, which may further erode consumer trust in a review site.
- Losing consumer trust is bad business for a review site. As a result, the review site will either try to improve by curbing manipulation, or will lose users to alternative solutions.
- Reviews are far from being perfect, but the one solution that consumers are *not* turning to is to ignore reviews altogether and just rely on marketers as the main source for information regarding quality.
- If consumers lose trust in certain review sites, they are much more likely to migrate to review sites they *do* trust, to opinions of experts, and/or to recommendations from friends and acquaintances. All of these are much more accessible in the new, socially intensive information environment.

Let's start with the last two points. While we'll focus in this chapter on reviews written by strangers, it is important to reiterate that consumers' ability to better assess absolute values is also driven by unprecedented access to experts, friends, and acquaintances. A decade ago, most people's access to experts was limited to magazines or newspaper columns. Today, top experts are a few clicks away, and their recommendations are amplified through social media (as we write this, tweets regarding *Consumer Reports'* review of the iPhone 5 are spreading). It is also radically easier to get feedback from people you know. Post a question on Facebook or Twitter ("Can anyone recommend a good moving company?") and you are likely to get advice in minutes. Using Facebook's Graph Search you can find what people *you know* use or say about different products and services.[5] In Chapter 13 we'll look at new tools that facilitate the assessment of quality even further. The bottom line is this: If consumers will lose their trust in reviews (and currently, there are no signs of that), they are likely to seek information from more trusted sources and new tools. They are highly unlikely to turn to marketers as the main source for information regarding quality. Still, even though reviews written by strangers are just part of what drives the trends we discuss in this book, they are an important part, and most of the concerns we've heard surround them, so these reviews will be our main focus for the remainder of this chapter.

FAKING IS EASY. TIPPING THE SCALE IS USUALLY MUCH HARDER

Writing a fake review is very easy, and when there are not enough genuine reviews to counterbalance fake reviews, the latter can have some impact. But the more reviewers participate in a rating system, the harder it becomes to game the system. As participation in rating systems grows, trying to tip the scale without being caught will be more difficult. Even though there are disturbing cases in which manipulation is successful, in many cases manipulation attempts don't yield real results. We can't dismiss the problem, especially when there are only a few reviews, but we need to keep things in perspective, and we need to differentiate between the alarming ethical issues raised by these actions and the actual impact that some fake reviews have.

While it's simple for a product manager to post a few fake reviews about a new gadget without getting caught, it's harder to do it on a larger scale. A Tennessee company found out about this the hard way when they had to pay the Federal Trade Commission (FTC) $250,000 to settle charges that it used misleading online "consumer" and "independent" reviews.[6] Or consider the case of Jeremy Trevathan of Pan Macmillan, who posted a review of *The Mistress*, a book published by his own company. The harm caused to unsuspecting consumers who rely on fake reviews is obvious, and in some cases can lead to costly mistakes, but let's examine the impact of this review. A single review is just that—one review. In this case there were about fifty additional reviews, twenty-five of which gave the book one star, some calling it "a disaster" or "Painfully bad." So *The Mistress* had a 2.5-star average rating.[7] Of course, Trevathan could have asked employees and friends to write additional glowing reviews, but there was a risk associated with it— getting caught can hurt a marketer's reputation. Benjamin Franklin famously said that three people can keep a secret if two of them are dead. If dozens of people are involved, it's very hard to prevent leaks. Such group behavior is also easier to detect by algorithms employed by review sites.[8]

It would be naïve to think that manipulations never succeed. The *New York Times* story about Todd Rutherford and his paid reviews service mentioned the case of John Locke, who confirmed to the reporter that he had paid Todd Rutherford for three hundred reviews. According to the *Times*, Locke had sold a few thousand e-books before he signed up with GettingBookReviews.com. Then, in December 2010, after he commissioned Rutherford to order reviews for him, things picked up significantly and Locke sold fifteen thousand e-books. Locke attributed his success to other factors and said that reviews are the smallest part of being successful. He seems to be an effective promoter who connects with readers through his blog, tweets, and personalized emails. Pricing his e-books at ninety-nine cents didn't hurt, either. Eventually he had sold more than a million e-books through Amazon, becoming a poster child for self-publishing. It seems, however, that other authors who paid for reviews were not as successful as Locke. Not even close. When we checked the rankings of some of these books, one was at number 5,121,624 despite the fact that it had about thirty incredible reviews. Another book (with eighteen glowing five-star reviews) was ranked at 1,254,944. Evidently, Rutherford wasn't producing an endless stream of bestselling books. If Rutherford made $28,000 a month by providing positive reviews, it proves that some authors are willing to pay good money to see their books reviewed. It doesn't necessarily prove that readers are fooled by those reviews. We will later present research that links higher review rankings with higher revenues, but this doesn't mean that faking your way to success is easy, and it is certainly not a sustainable business model.

REVIEW SITES CAN CURB MANIPULATIONS

When a rating system consistently disappoints consumers in assessing the quality of products or services, it will have to improve, or consumers will look for alternative solutions. A failure to control fake reviews can eventually harm a review site. A reader from Chicago wrote in response to the *New York Times* story, "I enjoyed buying obscure and interesting books on Amazon that I couldn't find anywhere else. That changed in about 2009 when I started getting burned by 5 star books that were utter garbage once I started reading them myself."[9] A similar thing happened to business traveler Michelle Madhok with hotels she stayed at. "I read reviews of hotels that I've stayed at," she told a reporter, "and they're just wrong. I wonder if they've really stayed at the hotel." What happened as a result? She had become increasingly skeptical of online reviews.[10]

People who don't trust reviews are bad business for Yelp, TripAdvisor, and other review sites. Yelp, for example, relies on advertising as its main source of revenue. If people stop trusting the site, they will find alternative sources of information, and Yelp's main source of revenue will dry up. Similarly, people who don't trust reviews are bad business for Amazon, because reviews are a big attraction to the site. As a result of the *New York Times* article, Amazon removed some of Rutherford's reviews. In the months that followed, Amazon took some further measures to remove fake reviews (sometimes raising criticism for eliminating legitimate ones).[11] Google, which also has a stake in the reviews business, suspended Rutherford's advertising account, because the company does not approve of ads for favorable reviews.

In order to keep its audience, a suspect rating system is likely to try to regain people's trust. The question is: Can review sites curb manipulations? The short answer is yes. It's an endless cat-and-mouse game, but there are many examples for tactics that can cumulatively reduce successful manipulations. For example, in October 2012 Yelp ran a sting operation in which employees pretended to be reviewers, and offered reviews for sale to businesses. Yelp caught about a dozen companies in this operation and these companies had their Yelp page tagged for three months with an alert: "We caught someone red-handed trying to buy reviews for this business."[12] The results were highly publicized in the press and on TV and are likely to make some business owners think twice before they buy fake reviews.

Many review sites employ algorithms to weed out bogus reviews. Yelp, for example, displays about 80 percent of the reviews that are submitted. Review sites don't publicize their algorithms, for obvious reasons, but in general they are trying to detect anything unusual. One advantage that a rating system has in this battle is its knowledge of normal patterns. For example, one of the books that was backed by Rutherford's reviews was published in 2009, and had eighteen five-star reviews. A quick glance at the dates of these reviews reveals something odd: Sixteen of them were entered in a span of ten days in January 2011. It is highly unusual for a book to get such a sudden burst of reviews two years after it was published. This is clearly inconsistent with usual patterns and should have raised a red flag. Sites can also detect suspicious patterns in the content of reviews or with a specific user's behavior (a user who for months obsessively visits the same restaurant on a rating site is not displaying normal behavior; a review from such a user is suspicious).

Accepting reviews only from verified buyers is another method that is likely to work in certain domains. Think about two review sites that rate hotels: TripAdvisor and Expedia. In order to post a review on TripAdvisor, you don't need to prove that you stayed at the hotel you're reviewing. In contrast, to review a hotel on Expedia, you need to have actually stayed there. In which rating system do you expect to see more fake reviews? Myle Ott, a computer scientist from Cornell University, and his colleagues Claire Cardie and Jeff Hancock tested this question by comparing six online review sites that rate hotels: Expedia, Hotels.com, Orbitz, Priceline, TripAdvisor, and Yelp. They focused on the relative differences in the rate of deception between the sites, and their results suggest (as you might have guessed) that deception is more prevalent in sites with a low "signal cost," like TripAdvisor or Yelp, where the requirements for posting are minimal.[13]

The key point from Ott's work is that deception rates vary among sites and have to do with what the site does to prevent deception. After talking to people who manage rating sites, we have no doubt that much can be done to curb fake reviews and that not all sites are created equal when it comes to handling manipulations. Consider Angie's List. In order to post a review on Angie's List, you need to be a paid subscriber of the service, and although your name is not revealed to visitors of the site, it is known to the folks at Angie's List and to the contractor you're reviewing (so that he or she can respond to your review). Posting fake reviews is obviously harder on Angie's List than on a site where you can post anonymously and without any other commitment.[14]

How prevalent are fake reviews? There is no easy answer, though all the experts we asked agreed on two points: First, it's hard to tell. And second, sites can take measures to fight manipulation, so the answer can vary among sites. We read in the *New York Times* that Bing Liu, a computer scientist from the University of Illinois, estimates that about one-third of all consumer reviews on the Internet are fake. But when we asked him about it, he clarified that this percentage refers to fake reviews *before* any attempts to curb manipulations are done by a site.[15] Myle Ott from Cornell doubts that the exact percentage of fake reviews can be determined, and as we discussed, his research shows that rating sites can take measures to curb manipulation.[16] The research firm Gartner estimated that by 2014, 10–15 percent of social media reviews will be fake.[17] Jenny Sussin, one of the researchers behind the study, noted that Bazaarvoice (which manages the reviews for sites like Expedia, Walmart. com, Costco, and Best Buy) is a company that does a good job in detecting fake content. When we talked to Brett Hurt, cofounder of Bazaarvoice, he estimated that only 1 percent of all content gathered across client sites is rejected as inauthentic by the company's anti-fraud technology and team of authenticity analysts.

The bottom line is this: Manipulation *can* be curbed. Review sites have strong economic incentives to curb manipulations, and they increasingly address the problem.

CHECKS AND BALANCES

In the new environment the reviewers are under review as well. The true nature of things is likely, over time, to be revealed, and this applies not only to manipulation attempts by outsiders, but to the integrity of the rating sites themselves. The story of Hamas and the Better Business Bureau will illustrate this. Millions of people every year check the reliability of businesses through the Better Business Bureau, but in 2010 the organization itself came under fire on ABC's *20/20* when business owners accused the BBB of letting companies pay to improve their ratings. Wolfgang Puck, for example, argued that they are running a pay-to-play operation (one part of his food empire got an F): "If you become a member you're sure to get an A, but if you don't pay, it's very difficult to get an A," he said. Terri Hartman, manager of an antique hardware store in Los Angeles, said she was told by a BBB tele-marketer she had to pay a membership fee if the store's C grade was to be improved. (That grade was based on an old complaint that had been resolved.) Hartman said she paid the membership fee, and shortly after that the C was upgraded to an A+ and the old complaint no longer showed in the store's record.

The Hamas listing was actually a publicity stunt arranged by an anonymous blogger and a group of business owners who wanted to make a point. They listed Hamas with a nonexistent address in Santa Monica. They claimed that about twenty-four hours after paying $425 for membership, Hamas got an A- rating. In a similar act, the group said BBB awarded an A+ to a racist website. Again, they said all it took was a call with a credit card.[18]

Yelp has faced similar allegations in the past few years from busi-ness owners who say sales reps from the company put pressure on them to advertise, and link advertising to the display order of bad reviews. For example, Stacy Oltman, a restaurant manager from the Seattle area, told the *Seattle Times* she got a call from a Yelp salesperson who gave her a hint: "You have gotten a terrible review online. We would love to help you remove it." (Yelp maintains that businesses cannot pay to remove or reorder bad reviews.)[19]

So far, people have not been influenced too much by these sto-ries. The *20/20* story about Hamas was damaging to the Better Business Bureau, but the organization took some measures that seem to have improved the situation. Yelp's monthly visitors con-tinue to go up,[20] and in general, despite an ongoing stream of stories in the media, the public shows pretty high confidence in reviews written by other consumers. A Nielsen study conducted among 28,000 Internet respondents in fifty-six countries found that online consumer reviews are the second most trusted source of informa-tion about products, with 70 percent of respondents indicating they trust messages from this source "completely" or "somewhat" (a 15 percent increase in four years).[21] The only source that was trusted more was recommendations from friends and family.

If a tech company flies a blogger to a trade show across the world and pays for his hotel, he may be biased in the way he reports about their new products. This, again, may raise some doubts regarding consumers' ability to assess the quality of products. Yet here, too, there are checks and balances. Some bloggers (like many other people) love perks, but there's one thing they usually love even better: They love to have readers. And readers look for spin-free answers. If they start to sense that a blogger sticks too much to the party line of a certain company, they will look elsewhere. And these days, there's no short supply of "elsewhere." That is another reason why manipulating the outcome of reviews is harder than one might think. In order to game the system, a marketer would have to "bribe" most of the experts, all the reviewers, all the bloggers (or most of them), and that starts to get expensive, and is probably impossible anyhow. Another piece of the puzzle of checks and balances are governments and organizations that can fight manipulation attempts. In the United States, for example, the FTC requires bloggers to disclose any material connections (such as payment or free product) they share with a company.[22]

Of course, even with the best safeguards, reviews will continue to be imperfect quality indicators. As we said up front, knowing the absolute value (assuming it exists and is unambiguous) is the extreme utopian case that will not be achieved. So we are talking about getting closer to that extreme, and this seems to start happening. Peter Rojas, the founder of Engadget, Gizmodo, and gdgt. com, pointed out to us that reviewers—bloggers, journalists, and other expert reviewers—generally reach a broad consensus about a new gadget. "And it's not some conspiracy. It's just that the products tend to get the reviews they deserve," he added.[23] A report by a biased blogger (just like a fake review) is one piece of the puzzle. Any incorrect facts are pointed out quickly by readers, and opinions that go against the majority's point of view have to be well argued or they are dismissed.

Another proof that reviews help people assess the quality of products is the growing evidence that user reviews and expert reviews usually move in the same direction, a trend that cannot be explained simply based on the effects of experts on consumers. Michael Luca from Harvard found strong positive correlation between expert and consumer opinions on Rotten Tomatoes, a rating system of movies.[24] Luca also found a link between Yelp reviews of restaurants and hygiene grades (lower grades by city inspectors are associated with low ratings by Yelp reviewers). In another study, Luca and coauthors Loretti Dobrescu and Alberto Motta compared reviews of books on Amazon with reviews by professional critics and found that expert ratings are correlated with Amazon ratings (although experts tended to favor more established authors and award winners).[25] Tim and Nina Zagat (old hands in the battle against fake reviews; they started the New York City guide in 1979) told Emanuel in a 2007 interview that they employ food critics in different cities as one of their many methods to detect unreasonable ratings.[26]

Joanna Langfield is the owner of The Good Life, a small vegetarian restaurant in Shrewsbury, England. All was working fine when in the summer of 2011 the restaurant started getting very negative reviews on TripAdvisor and other review sites. "It started off quite extreme," she told a reporter. "Someone posted a review calling me 'arrogant' and making other nasty references. TripAdvisor actually took that one down." The reviews didn't stop, though, and TripAdvisor was not willing to remove other reviews. Langfield felt powerless.

Beyond the emotional stress, the damage to the vegetarian restaurant was real. Before Christmas, the restaurant owner got a statement from her accountant showing an unusual dip. According to Langfield, profits fell by about 25 percent.[27]

After a long time, a man who worked for one of the review sites gave police the IP address associated with the reviews which eventually led police to the person behind the posts. It was a woman whose husband was a former partner of Joanna Langfield. The woman received a police caution for harassment and published a public announcement in national newspapers in which she apologized for her action.

In the same way that people are not becoming smarter in this new era, they are not becoming more (or less) honest because they have access to Yelp or TripAdvisor. The stories that opened this chapter are ricochets from an endless battle that most likely will continue into the future in the same way that the battle against shoplifting, credit card fraud, or crime in general will never reach an end. The anguish of people (like Joanna Langfield) who are victims of such manipulations is very real, and we should all fight back and try to curb attempts to game the system. Yet we doubt that manipulations will ever disappear. There's always someone who stands to gain from distorting the truth—the marketer or his competitors—and there are angry or unreasonable people who will lie for a few bucks or for a variety of other reasons.

But such concerns and bumps on the road cannot reverse what is inevitable—user and expert reviews have the potential to provide essential information about quality, and help make better decisions. If trust in one review site will erode beyond a certain threshold, that site will have a strong incentive to take action. If they don't, consumers will migrate to sites they *do* trust, and increase their dependence on experts, friends, and acquaintances. Aside from objective, verifiable specs and facts, the one source that consumers are *not* turning to as the main source for information regarding quality are marketers. If anything, the opposite is happening: Consumers are looking for new and better ways to get closer to the absolute value of things (and as we discuss in Chapter 13, these tools keep coming). This is why we're bullish about the trends that we described in the first part of the book. Now let's turn to the second part, which examines how the shift from relative to absolute changes marketing forever.

11

How Marketing Changes Forever

5

WHEN BRANDS MEAN LESS

BACK IN FEBRUARY 2006, when a Yelp member named Brenna F. reviewed the Seattle restaurant Machiavelli, nobody thought twice about it. And if someone did, we doubt they imagined that it would have any impact on chain restaurants like McDonald's or Applebee's. Brenna gave Machiavelli three stars (out of five) and wrote: "Good pasta, reasonable prices, and cozy seating. Go here with friends, but not with a first date."

Ristorante Machiavelli is one of more than a thousand restaurants in the city of Seattle. You're unlikely to read about it in *Gourmet* magazine, and it doesn't have the advertising budget of a chain such as Olive Garden. But Yelp helped Machiavelli (and other small restaurants) gain something that, up until recently, was the exclusive asset of big brands.

After Brenna F. posted her review, it took almost two months before another person reviewed Machiavelli. Megan D. gave the restaurant four stars in April and pointed out that the portions were large. The third review was posted in August by Rachel B., who recommended the Caesar salad and the baked chicken. Slowly but surely, the trickle of reviews added up to create a clear picture of Machiavelli: You should expect a line (especially on weekend nights);

the spinach ravioli is worth trying. So are the tuna carpaccio, the olive bread, and the penne with roasted red pepper. Overall: good, straightforward Italian food at very reasonable prices. Machiavelli today has around four hundred reviews, and reading through just a few of them, you get a good idea of what to expect.

And this is where big chains are impacted. In the past, having "a good idea of what to expect" was one of their important advantages over small restaurants. You always know what to expect at Subway or McDonald's. But when you know what to expect at small restaurants through Yelp or Zagat, brand names are becoming relatively less important. In the old days, consumers often had a hard time assessing quality before making a decision and had to rely on cues such as the affiliation with a chain. This gave rise to much of what we know as marketing. When quality was hard to predict, a brand was a simple shortcut that told you what's likely to be good and what isn't. But when you can quickly tell how good or bad something is, based on more reliable sources than just the name, brand has a reduced role as a quality signal.

To further examine the link between Yelp reviews and brand names, let's discuss some research by Harvard professor Michael Luca. Luca became interested in the impact of reviews on business a few years ago when sites such as Yelp just started to pick up. Many were skeptical about this phenomenon, seeing reviews as a niche activity of a small group of people. It wasn't clear at all whether sites like Yelp had any impact on the bottom line. Luca picked the restaurant industry as a good domain to study this. To seriously examine the impact reviews have on business, he knew he needed to put his hands on restaurant revenue data from some big city. He contacted the state of New York but had no luck. He started going down the list of large U.S. cities and was turned down again and again. After months of disappointments, he finally found a city that was willing to cooperate—Seattle. Armed with revenue data for all Seattle restaurants, Luca got to work. Showing a correlation between ratings and revenues wasn't too hard, but this wasn't enough. The fact that restaurants that get high ratings also get high revenues isn't too surprising and may not be related to their presence on Yelp. He wanted to be able to demonstrate more than that.[1]

To examine any causal relationship between Yelp reviews and restaurant revenues, Luca took advantage of the way Yelp displays its results. He knew that Yelp (like other review sites) doesn't display the actual rating average, but they round it up or down. For example, if a restaurant has a 3.24 average, Yelp rounds it down and users see three stars. If a restaurant has a 3.25 average Yelp rounds it up and users see 3.5 stars. So focusing on restaurants just around those rounding thresholds could be insightful. A restaurant with a 3.25 average is virtually the same as a restaurant with a 3.24 average. If its revenues are significantly higher, this may suggest that it's related to its 3.5-star rating that users see on Yelp.

Indeed, Luca's research showed exactly that. There was a jump in revenues that followed those discontinuous changes in rating. Overall, every additional star on Yelp was associated with about 5 percent increase in revenue. Luca looked at the revenues of all restaurants in Seattle between 2003 and 2009, which allowed him to observe a market before and after the introduction of Yelp. What's most interesting in our context is this: He found that Yelp had a large impact on revenues for independent restaurants like Machiavelli, but chains experienced a decline in revenue relative to independent restaurants in the post-Yelp period. "Higher Yelp penetration leads to an increase in revenue for independent restaurants, but a decrease in revenue for chain restaurants," he wrote. With the rise of an alternative source for information, brands became relatively less important.[2]

There is another important effect of the growing reliance on experts, users, and various useful information services (such as price comparison sites) and the corresponding declining impact of brands. Brand names tend to exaggerate the real quality differences among products. If you focus on brand name when considering a headphone or even an artificial sweetener, your prior beliefs tend to categorize products with a broad brush and tend to amplify presumed differences between good and bad brands. And unless the brand you choose is extremely different from what you expected, you'll tend to confirm what "you knew all along" (consistent with the classic confirmation bias). User and expert reviews tend to level the playing field. True, reviewers may also be swayed by brand names to some degree. However, reviews are often based on actual experience. Moreover, to offer their target audience added value, reviewers may want to highlight things that differ from the layperson's expectations. In reality, quality differences are often much smaller than perceived brand differences would imply. Accordingly, reviews that are based on actual user experiences will likely reflect the limited quality differentiation among products. You may think that the music sound produced by Brand X is so much better, but reviews of Brand Y can cause you to rethink your brand-driven decision and take a closer look at Brand Y, which costs less and evidently sounds just as good.

Are we saying that this is the end of brands? Of course not. We're saying that the power of brand as a main cue for quality is diminishing. Brands still have some important roles that are not likely to go away, and as we discuss later, in categories such as those involving fashion, status, or little thought, the rate of change is likely to be slow. As David Aaker and other scholars have pointed out over the years, brand equity has four components: awareness, perceived quality, mental associations, and loyalty. Two elements out of the four are hit the hardest in the new era: perceived quality and loyalty (we discuss loyalty in the next chapter). And as we mentioned earlier, there are domains that are much less affected by the new information environment, and for those categories, *all* components of brands are still important. But for categories where consumers rely on the opinion of others, and especially where there's little ambivalence about things like features or performance, we expect this trend to reveal itself at full strength. In the age of full access, the impact of brand equity will diminish as a result of the growing reliance on more accurate quality information.

THE GOOD OLD DAYS

A key reason why brands were so powerful was that they served as a signal for quality. If a company had one product line that was known for its high quality, the company could easily use its brand to introduce other products and line extensions. A strong brand could even save a mediocre product, at least for a while. Here's an example: In the early 1980s, Emanuel worked on the Kodak account as a copywriter in Israel, and one morning the local distributors called an urgent meeting. A few weeks earlier they had received a sealed package from Kodak's headquarters in Rochester, New York, with clear instructions not to open it before a certain date. When the day came, they opened the package and saw a thin, neatly designed new camera that, the promotional material indicated, was going to revolutionize photography. Now, under a veil of secrecy, the distributors were showing the camera to the agency people. It was called the "The Kodak Disc." Instead of a roll of film, this camera was loaded with a flat disc with fifteen small exposures. It was incredibly easy to use. You didn't even have to advance the film, because the disk would automatically rotate after each shot.

Advertising people are easily excited and this was no exception. There were a lot of oohs and aahs in the room. . . . It was a neat gadget. With all the enthusiasm, though, not much attention was given to the pictures that the camera produced. They were okay, but a bit grainy.

Not long after that meeting, the product was launched worldwide with big fanfare. The ads emphasized ease of use, better success rate, and fun, all under the reassuring umbrella of the Kodak brand. The results? Very nice sales (in Israel as in the rest of the world). In the first year, Kodak shipped more than 8 million Disc cameras worldwide. Competitors rushed to the market and things looked promising.

Yet a few years later, the product was discontinued. It was those grainy pictures. In the end, they weren't good enough for most consumers. The Kodak brand stood for high quality, so people relied on it and bought the camera. But the Kodak brand could carry things only so far. Eventually enough people heard about those grainy pictures from friends, or noted the grainy results when shown family pictures.[3]

Could you imagine this product surviving for so long in today's environment? We doubt it. We could just see the product reviews by users: "I love this camera. Hate the pictures!" or "Why is Granny so grainy?"

Incidentally, one group of people that was quick to take advantage of the grainy pictures were salespeople at department stores. Always the masters of relative tactics, they used the Kodak Disc to sell 35mm cameras by placing their respective pictures side by side on the counter. "Usually when I show shoppers the better-quality 35mm picture, I can talk them into spending a little more to buy the 35mm camera," one sales clerk explained.[4]

One of the key functions of brands was to serve as a launchpad for line and brand extensions.[5] The main reason for relying on an established brand name is rather straightforward—facilitate acceptance of the extension based on the perceived equity of the core brand. This, of course, assumes that consumers judge the extension's value and quality based on its name; but if consumers rely less on the name and more on its absolute quality, the advantage of a brand or line extension strategy is becoming less significant and may tilt the balance of pros and cons in favor of using a new name for each product (possibly still linked to the parent company's name).

Of course, the virtues and roles of brands extend well beyond serving as quality signals, and these other, nonquality functions play an important role in certain categories and under certain consumer evaluation processes, such as when consumers do not have access to better information sources or product quality is a secondary consideration. For example, we don't expect brand names to lose their impact anytime soon in the fashion, cosmetics, and vodka categories, though you'll be surprised to see how many reviews and comments there are, for example, about the "SHANY Professional 13-Piece Cosmetic Brush Set with Pouch" (816 on Amazon as of April 26, 2013). However, in most categories, quality signaling is a key function of brands, the one that is supposed to drive consumers' expectations and willingness-to-pay, so there is little doubt about the typical impact of better information about absolute quality and the resulting (diminishing) effect of brand names.

BRAND VOLATILITY

An examination of leading brands during the twentieth century has revealed a remarkable stability in many categories. This might change in categories where quality is important and where people rely on other consumers and experts. Stability of leading brands was possible when brand names were a primary quality indicator and thus a key decision factor, especially in categories with limited product differentiation. But since brands usually have no monopoly on quality or features, it is highly unlikely that any brand will consistently rank at the top. As a result, the market performance and shares of brands where quality plays a key role will fluctuate much more than they did when brands were key decision drivers and actual quality was hard to figure out.

This will work differently across categories. As we discuss in later chapters, the key is the importance of quality in a category and whether people rely on other consumers and experts. Things also may work differently in categories where prestige, status, and emotional link to a brand play an important role. In domains where objective, spec-based quality is not the issue, we can expect lower fluctuations in brand equity. So fashion brands of handbags or scarves (of the likes of Louis Vuitton or Hermès) are on safer grounds. However, if quality is important and can be specified, even prestigious brands are not immune. Mercedes-Benz is a prestigious brand, which also receives excellent ratings from experts and consumers. But what if its quality ratings start to slip? We expect its popularity and prestige to decline accordingly. No claim to fame is safe.

Furthermore, we expect the weight of brand status and prestige in consumer decision making to decline in categories where consumers can assess quality. In class-conscious cultures such as in East Asia, especially in places where the progression of the shift from relative to absolute is slower, brand status will continue to play an important role, but that will change, too, as better information about quality becomes widely available.

Think of brands like Myspace, AOL, Xerox, Palm, or Toshiba, which at some point looked invincible. Toshiba held the number-one ranking in laptops until 2002. Not anymore.[6] It's hard to accept that what happened to these companies can happen to today's stars. But it will if something better comes along. Take a look at Nokia. In the last quarter of 2009, it had 40 percent of the cellular market, and the brand was admired in the industry. As this book goes to print, Nokia's market share is 17.9 percent and continues to slip.[7] And if you think that leading brands like Samsung, Apple, or Google are immune to this, think again. Jimmy Durante said it best when he sang: "Fame, if you win it, comes and goes in a minute."

When we presented the concept of this book in academia and industry, no proposition generated more resistance than the idea that brand (and correspondingly, brand loyalty) is becoming less important. Many think that, if anything, the abundance of information makes brands even more important. Their argument usually goes as follows: Consumers cannot handle all the information available on the Internet, so they give up and just select the brand they like most. Earlier we presented research regarding the robustness (or lack thereof) of the choice overload problem, but let's take a closer look at the idea that the amount of information that one might consider leads to greater brand reliance. We'd like to make three points: First, the suggestion that consumers have to either process much of the available information or just ignore it altogether (and simply select their favorite brand) grossly misrepresents the many better intermediate options available to them. Most consumers are likely to find the information equilibrium that fits them—the amount of information they feel can help them make better decisions. For many consumers, the readily available summaries will be helpful and sufficient. How much time or effort does it really take to see the average rating of a product by fellow consumers (on Amazon, for example)? And while some consumers may not need the in-depth product analyses contained in expert reviews, they can certainly manage the bottom-line list of pros and cons. It's true that consumers often look for shortcuts, and that in the past brands served as such shortcuts. It's simply that today there are new (and more diagnostic) shortcuts and quality indicators, such as star ratings, review summaries, and other bottom-line icons. In the past few years we've seen the ongoing development of additional tools that help consumers succinctly but rather accurately assess overall product quality or certain features of interest without having to delve into all the details and sources. (For a selection of those tools, go to this book's website, www.AbsoluteValueBook.com.)

Second, the notion that, time after time, consumers continue to disregard the information available to them and keep selecting blindly, based mainly on the brand name and its past glory, greatly underestimates people's ability to learn and desire to make good decisions. And third, the limitations of brand-based choices could not be more transparent on the Internet—while some brands do get, on average, better reviews than other brands, one cannot ignore the evidence that, holding the brand constant, there is usually great variability across products under the same brand umbrella. For example, while Microsoft has had great product successes, it has also had well-publicized failures. Choosing based on the brand without paying attention to the specific evaluations often leads to regrettable mistakes. Thus the position that brands will remain as or more powerful as quality signals can be rejected based on at least three key factors: First, this argument oversimplifies the ever-expanding set of information sources available to consumers. Second, it greatly overestimates the information overload problem. Third, it ignores the existence (and the ongoing improvement) of search, sorting, and summation tools that can usually address the information problem quite efficiently.

Of course, in some cases brands will remain influential as quality proxies (in addition to their other functions). First, there are product categories where people don't bother to search for information, and in these domains brands will continue to serve as a proxy for quality. Second, there are segments that don't yet take advantage of the available information, and for these audiences, brand will continue to be important. Keep in mind, though, that things can change rather quickly: New technologies may introduce absolute evaluations in domains that seemed to be immune to the shift. Similarly, a segment that wasn't equipped with assessment tools may adopt them. We'll discuss all these issues in Part III.

Brand equity is just one element that will have a diminished role in consumer decision making. Related concepts that have been used to analyze brand performance, such as brand identity and brand personality, will correspondingly become less important. Such stable brand descriptors deserve a great deal of attention if consumers' product judgments are made largely based on the product name; but once absolute quality can be assessed more directly and accurately, the name and its associated identity and personality will play a smaller role. Moreover, because different products using a given name often vary in quality (broadly defined) and market acceptance, we expect to see faster dilution of brand meaning as consumers learn to evaluate each product based on its own merit. Thus better information and high quality variability across products may cause brands to suffer from a growing multiple personality disorder.

THE DECLINE OF OTHER QUALITY PROXIES

Brand is not the only cue that consumers use as a quality proxy when better information is not available. There are a few others and they will decline in importance as well. Country of origin is one of them. If a watch is made in Switzerland, a car in Germany, or an espresso machine in Italy, "it must be the best." At least that's how the thinking goes.

Country of origin can be a pretty good signal at the absence of detailed information. But it can't be too accurate as a predictor of quality. We found more than two dozen manufacturers of espresso machines in Italy,[8] and it is unreasonable to believe that every single model that these companies produce is better than all the other models manufactured in Germany, the United States, or other countries. Here's an example: DeLonghi is a respectable brand and Italian espresso machines indeed have a great reputation. But let's take a look at one particular model—the DeLonghi BCO120T Combination Coffee/Espresso Machine. Out of 130 people who reviewed the product on Amazon.com, 101 gave it one or two stars, many complaining that the product leaked or simply stopped working after a few weeks or months.[9] A woman from Ohio wrote a typical one-star review. She said the coffeemaker stopped working after seven months. DeLonghi repaired it but the problem repeated itself four months later.[10] Another customer reported that the machine "leaks so much dang water that I literally can mop my floor with the amount of water that ends up all over the place."[11] You don't have to read all eighty-six one-star reviews to realize that this model might have a problem. So even though it's made in Italy, you're not likely to rely on this quality cue when you have access to the actual experience of other consumers.

One of the strongest quality cues that is on the decline is price. When quality was hard to assess, price was a convenient shortcut for quality. "If it's expensive, it's probably good" or "You get what you pay for" (which is typically used to explain why you should pay more). Such statements represent rules of thumb that are supposedly based on some unidentified past lesson, but here, too, we see the impact of the new environment. The story of NōKA Chocolate may illustrate this point. NōKA Chocolate appeared on the scene around 2004 and immediately gained attention because of its shocking prices. At \$309–\$2,080 per pound, NōKA was perhaps trying to position itself as the Rolls-Royce of dark chocolate. But then a Dallas-based food blog published a detailed ten-part series that questioned the company's marketing claims, evaluated its products, and argued that the chocolate is not worth the price the company charges.[12] When we searched online to learn more about the brand, we quickly came across blog entries such as "NOKA chocolate exposed!" and "Noka Chocolate Is A Scam."[13] And as of July 2013, the company's website has not been active for some time. The high price didn't seem to do the trick. The fancy logo didn't do it, either. Nor did that little line over the *o* that alluded to faraway places. Even the fact that Neiman Marcus picked the product at some point didn't seem to save it. On the other hand, the blog that reported that NōKA was actually produced in a strip mall in Texas was read by about 750,000 people in just a few months.[14]

Two clarifications to avoid confusion: First, the conclusion that price is less important as a quality cue does not mean, of course, that price has a weaker effect on purchase decisions. In fact, the opposite is true in many cases. Once you can assess the absolute values of products, it becomes easier to determine if the value gap between products justifies the observed price difference. In other words, once you can assess absolute values more precisely, you can actually determine if you get what you pay for. As a result, consumers may often become more price sensitive. Our second point is that we're not claiming that price as a quality proxy will completely vanish. Price and other quality cues will of course continue to have at least some effect on the quality perceptions of at least a portion of all consumers, especially if there is some uncertainty about the available quality indicators. Consider, for example, red wine. Wine lovers can get the taste ratings of the highly influential Robert Parker and other wine raters such as *Wine Spectator* and *Wine Enthusiast*. But wine is a matter of taste, and with all due respect to the wine expertise of Robert Parker and his *Wine Advocate* magazine staff, his ratings may often not correspond to the way we taste the same wines. So despite the evidence that prices are a pretty unreliable (and often costly) quality proxy, we can expect many wine shoppers to use it at least to some extent.

OPPORTUNITY KNOCKS

As we pointed out earlier, the decline in brands as quality proxies means lower barriers to entry for newcomers. Remember Jonney Shih, the chairman of ASUS, who's taking advantage of this in the high-tech sector? Meet Mark Rosenzweig. He and his company, Euro-Pro, do something similar in small kitchen appliances and vacuum cleaners. Rosenzweig's family used to be in the sewing machine business in Canada. A few years ago he established Euro-Pro in Boston. Okay, maybe his story is not as exciting as that of one of his competitors, Sir James Dyson, who says he developed 5,126 prototypes before he made the first Dyson vacuum cleaner (*and* he was knighted by the queen). But Rosenzweig sells vacuum cleaners. Lots of them.

How exactly does the new information environment help Mark Rosenzweig and Euro-Pro? It can work in several ways. Sometimes the product search starts online. A customer (let's call her Julie) decides to buy a new vacuum cleaner and she has a general idea of what she's looking for—one of those upright models with no bags. She may also have a couple of brands in mind—say Hoover and Dyson. So Julie goes to Walmart.com and starts browsing. In the process she comes across a vacuum cleaner that she's never heard about before, called the Shark Navigator (made by Euro-Pro). Although the product is not cheap, its price compared to a Dyson seems reasonable, and the product has more than five hundred customer reviews, with an average rating of almost five stars. She reads some reviews from users (some of them used to own a Dyson) who rave about the product. Julie also sees photos posted by some users (for example, a picture of how much dirt someone's old vacuum collected versus how much dust the Shark sucked in). All this clearly makes her much less hesitant to get a Shark. She knows what she's getting into.

Another scenario may start at a brick-and-mortar store. A customer goes to Target to get a blender. Next to some familiar brands (like Cuisinart or KitchenAid) he sees a blender called Ninja, made by Euro-Pro. Maybe he remembers seeing a commercial for the product. He pulls his smartphone and looks up some reviews on the retailer's website, or on one of many apps that aggregate consumer reviews. He might check out the *Consumer Reports* app and learn that the $60 Ninja Blender gets a rating of 91 (ahead of all other products in its category).[15] He is sold.

Other customers may start the search with the Shark or the Ninja brands in mind. Euro-Pro does advertise extensively in print, TV commercials, and infomercials, and some customers respond to these ads by further searching for the brand. Here, too, the abundance of consumer reviews helps reassure potential buyers, especially since Euro-Pro is competing against heritage brands such as Hoover and Cuisinart.

It's not that brand is not important. As we pointed out earlier, brand equity has value in terms of name recognition, sometimes emotional attachment, prestige or status, and continuity. Our point is that it plays a *reduced* role as a proxy for quality, which enables new entries. Dyson itself is actually a beneficiary of the same trend. For years observers believed that with entrenched brands like Hoover, the vacuum cleaner market in the United States was almost impossible to penetrate. Dyson broke this in 2002, and others followed. Euro-Pro is not taking over the vacuum cleaner industry, and Dyson is doing very well, but it's also clear that the Shark Navigator is emerging as an alternative because customers can easily get a sense regarding its performance and durability. When we talked to him, Rosenzweig emphasized that brand is extremely important to his company. What's unique in these new times is that he as a newcomer can rapidly take market share from established players.[16] It seems to work. He told us that Euro-Pro is approaching $1 billion in sales and the Shark has captured more than 50 percent of the market for bagless upright vacuums in its price category. Incidentally, another executive in the same industry takes a totally different position on the importance of brand. In fact, he opposes the concept of brand so much that you're not allowed to use the term at the company's headquarters. "There's only one word that's banned in our company: brand," James Dyson said at a 2012 conference. "We're only as good as our latest product. I don't believe in brand at all."

The main point is that both Dyson and Rosenzweig have benefited from lower barriers to entry, which are the result of the reduced role of brand as a proxy for quality. This benefit isn't reserved to small companies or newcomers. Consider Sony. It isn't a secret that Sony hasn't released a hit for years (and hasn't turned a profit between 2008 and 2013).[17] Yet in 2012, Sony got a nice reminder that when you offer the right product, you can succeed even in a domain with which you're less associated. When the company introduced the Sony RX100 camera, the market quickly recognized it as a superior product for a consumer who wants an upscale, feature-filled pocket camera. Users loved it. Experts raved about it. The *New York Times* called it "the best pocket camera ever made."[18] Despite its high price ($650, which is extremely high for a pocket camera), it's been at a top sales ranking in the photo category on Amazon (for a while, *the* top-selling camera). Maybe not a turning point for Sony, but another example of the fact that for better or for worse, it's about product.

A DIFFERENT LOOK AT DIVERSIFICATION

The new information environment can also change your outlook on diversification. By and large, conventional wisdom in marketing is that you need to stick to your knitting. According to that view, consumers associate your brand with certain skills, and they will have a hard time accepting products that don't fit this perception.

In other words, if everyone knows that you're good at making TVs, you can venture into a related category like DVD players, but you have no business going into an unrelated field like washing machines.[19]

The new reality changes this, too.

Take a look at LG. They make TVs, DVD players, dishwashers, refrigerators, cell phones, and many other things. Now, suppose that you own a DVD player from LG, and while shopping for a washer and dryer you come across a washer/dryer combo from them. "Hmm . . . I didn't know LG makes washers and dryers," you say to yourself. In the past this might have ended right here. "Their DVD player is quite good, but this doesn't mean they know anything about laundry," you'd conclude, and retreat to brands like Whirlpool or Maytag, which are perceived as based on expertise in this category.

Today, you can read reviews and comparisons or go on YouTube and watch people talk about their LG washers and dryers. When we did that, we found dozens of related videos, some simple demos from recent proud owners who were compelled to share their new LG with the rest of the world, and some more formal reviews of a particular LG washer. In any case, when we were done watching, we certainly had a better feel for these machines. Your preliminary perception as a consumer regarding LG's skills is much less relevant when you can go online and get the skinny on the quality of the product. (You can visit our book's website for some links to these videos.) Here's another example: A consumer was looking for a Bluetooth stereo headset for years, with limited success. "I've tried numerous models, some good, some bad (some real bad)," he writes. Then one day, while browsing on Amazon, he came across the LG Tone Wireless headset. "I didn't know LG even made them," he said. But LG does make them, and the headphones had more than five hundred rave reviews with an average of 4.5 stars. Again, the perception of LG's skill set in this consumer's mind has become much less relevant. He bought the LG Tone and added his own five-star review the following week.

Sticking to the old philosophy of diversification according to perceived skills would not have brought Amazon.com to where it is today. Think, for a moment, about Amazon in 1995—it was an online bookstore and it stayed that way for about three years. They sold books and they were good at it. Adding music and video in 1998 wasn't such a stretch, but adding kitchen appliances, jewelry, gourmet food, and apparel in the next few years certainly was. It raised some legitimate questions: Why would I want to buy my next dress at a bookstore? What do these people know about jewelry or espresso machines?

Yet people started browsing the stores, and reading reviews from customers who had experienced Amazon in these domains. Here were real people who ordered products and got them on time, returned items that didn't fit, and, in general, raved about the convenience of shopping online. Suddenly the idea of buying a dress from a bookstore didn't seem that strange anymore. And Amazon didn't stop there. They ventured into online video, online storage, and other areas. Amazon has come a long way from selling just books.[20] Just imagine what would have happened if Jeff Bezos had listened to marketing consultants who had told him that Amazon should diversify only in ways that match the current perceptions of his company's skills.

Diversification strategy is a complex topic that involves many other factors. Spreading yourself too thin is one obvious danger and there are others that are beyond the scope of this book. But sticking to the exact expectations that your customers have from your brand should be less of a concern. It's much less relevant these days.

While working on the ASUS case, we were looking for an example for the thought process that consumers go through when they consider that brand. Surfing the Web, we came across a blog post titled "Why I Bought a No-Name Computer From a Components Firm." It's a great little anecdote, but it was the name of its author that surprised us. It was written by David Aaker, who's perhaps identified more than anyone else with the concept of brand equity.

Here's how he describes the process: In 2011 Aaker had to replace his wife's computer. He was told by the computer doctor that the PC had a nasty virus and had been obsolete for years anyway. The two brands that immediately popped up in Aaker's mind were Dell and HP—two companies whose products he used in the past.

"But minutes later, I decided to buy an ASUS computer even though I had never heard of it," Aaker wrote.

How could that be? Aaker followed the advice of the local expert, the computer doctor, who told him that he had just installed an ASUS for another client and that he liked their price, specs, and service. The computer guy also told Aaker that ASUS has been the motherboard supplier for leading computer brands. Still a bit suspicious, Aaker called his son-in-law (the family's computer expert), who confirmed the expert's opinion. Those in the know, who can easily assess the quality of ASUS, made their verdict. Aaker got an ASUS and Jonney Shih made another sale without spending a dime on advertising. When David Aaker buys a no-name computer, you know that something's happening to branding.[21]

6

SATISFACTION, LOYALTY, AND THE FUTURE OF PAST EXPERIENCE

LARS LASMUSSEN WAS standing onstage showing the new software that he and his team had been developing in Sydney, Australia, for the past two years. The Danish-born PhD was no stranger to the audience of software developers. This was the man who back in 2003 cofounded a company called Where 2 Technologies, which was acquired shortly after by Google to create Google Maps.[1] With the success of Google Maps under his belt, Rasmussen was now showing his new program, and was occasionally interrupted by applause from the crowd. Rasmussen was now working for Google, which was going to launch the new software in a few months. And since Google enjoyed tremendous goodwill from millions around the world, hopes for the software ran high.

But today, the past doesn't matter as much as it used to. Not Google's past triumphs. Not Rasmussen's past successes. The software he showed that day would be suspended a few months later. Actors have been saying for decades that "you're only as good as your last gig." These days, even your last gig doesn't matter that much anymore. Fortunately or not, it's the absolute value of your current product that drives its success.

In the past, when assessing quality was difficult, we heavily relied on our past experiences as consumers. When good information was hard to get, relying on our previous positive experience with a brand made sense. If we liked the Sony Walkman, we used this to infer that Sony also made good CD players. If we liked their CD player, that meant that Sony probably made good laptops. . . . But in a world with good, low-cost information, we can easily start from scratch each time. The fact that Sony made great products in the past is very nice, but we no longer need to use this information to judge whatever else Sony introduces. This has major implications for the significance of satisfaction and loyalty.

Let's go back for a moment to Planet Absolute—that utopian world where the sidewalks are paved with accurate quality information. You press a button and know the absolute value of things, and how well those values fit your preferences. Suppose you drove a Brand X car on that planet and you had a wonderful experience driving and owning it. On a scale of 0 to 10, you'd give it a 9—you were highly satisfied. After a couple of years of driving this car, you decide to buy a new one. If all you had was this internal rating of 9, this information would have been extremely valuable to you. But on Planet Absolute you can press that magic button and know for sure what your experience quality will be with the current Brand X models and whether any other car you're considering might provide a better experience. So you care less about your past experience. The answers for all cars (not just the one you drove) are simply out there.

This is starting to happen on Planet Earth, too. Think of the way we make decisions about rental movies these days. The fact that we can get good information about movies through services such as Rotten Tomatoes or IMDb means that our satisfaction with the past work of the movie creators is less relevant. Suppose you're considering renting the movie *Swept Away*, directed by Guy Ritchie, who also directed one of your favorite films—*Snatch*. Without additional information, your past experience with *Snatch* would drive you to rent *Swept Away*. But when you check Rotten Tomatoes, you see that *Swept Away* got an average rating of 5 from film critics (not 5 stars . . . that is 5 out of 100!). The audience was a tad more generous with the movie, giving it an average rating of 27 percent, which is still very poor. After you read just a few short reviews (a typical one: "Don't count on being swept away by this contrived, predictable shipwrecked romance"), you're much less likely to rely on your experience with *Snatch* in making a decision regarding *Swept Away*. Studios will probably continue to push movies by highlighting the past achievements of their creators ("From the producers of . . ." or "from the director of . . ."), but these tactics will have a diminishing impact.

We both like the cars we drive. Itamar likes his sporty Audi (a lot) and Emanuel likes his good old Volvo. Yet how much weight will our prior experience play when we buy new cars? Not much. It's just so easy to get a good idea about what it means to own other cars. Audi and Volvo will have to compete for our business while getting little credit for our prior good experience.

LOYALTY OR OPEN MARRIAGE?

Marketers love to talk about loyalty and long-term relationships with customers, but these days, more and more consumers see their relationships with companies as an open marriage. Here are just a couple of examples: A 2012 Deloitte study demonstrated a sharp decline in loyalty to hotel chains, with only 8 percent of survey respondents saying that they always stay at the same hotel brand. While there might be different factors that underlie this trend, at least part of it is driven by consumers' ability to use tools like price comparison sites, review sites, and other sources to assess the absolute value of each hotel before deciding where to stay.[2]

Here's another example: Executives at Research in Motion (RIM) (now "BlackBerry"), used to often talk about their millions of passionate and loyal customers. They weren't making this up. Millions of people around the world loved their BlackBerry device at one point or another. Some loyal users were so addicted to their gadgets that they would refer to them as "crackberries."[3] And yet all this goodwill didn't help much when RIM wasn't keeping up with Apple and Android phones. In surveys conducted in the past couple of years, a significant percentage of BlackBerry users said that they were going to switch.[4] Not long before this book went to print, RIM released the BlackBerry 10 and it remains to be seen if it can stop the decline. Yet it's clear that many BlackBerry users did not stick around just because they were "loyal."

Something about the gap between managers and consumers in the way they view loyalty can be learned from the following study: In 2012, the CMO Council conducted a global study among marketing executives in the mobile industry. High on their list of goals, these executives listed building stronger affinity with existing customers and growing loyalty and advocacy. The same organization conducted a study among mobile subscribers and asked them to characterize themselves as customers. Only 29 percent saw themselves as loyalists. Most subscribers described themselves using phrases such as "Show me better service, better packages, or better phone upgrades and I am switching" or "I don't care who I do business with, just as long as my phone works" or "I will go where the latest and greatest technology is."[5]

We don't blame marketers for valuing loyalty so much. It seems only fair that a company will be rewarded for its past good deeds. It instills a positive message for the entire organization, and the profit impact calculations are impressive; it also has other significant potential benefits, such as a predictable cash stream, customers who are less price sensitive, reduced marketing costs, and serving as a barrier from entry to competitors.[6] Not surprisingly, textbooks, articles, loyalty gurus, and others have repeated the mantra that loyalty is the key to profitability; various statistics have been used, such as the impact of addressing a complaint on repeat purchase and the lower cost of retaining customers than acquiring new customers. Furthermore, books, executive education programs, and consultants have taught managers how to compute customers' lifetime value, which is supposed to guide the amount of money and effort a company can afford to spend on new customer acquisition.

Despite the allure of such arguments, they are becoming less compelling and less relevant. Once the arrangement becomes more like an open marriage, whereby a customer looks for the best available option for each new purchase, theoretical lifetime value calculations are just that, mostly theoretical. Long-term relationships (especially when switching costs are low) become the exception. There is no point making marketing decisions based on lifetime value calculations if that potential is unlikely to be realized. Relying on customers' lifetime value makes the most sense when customers tend to spend an extended period of time with the company.

The decline in loyalty is most pronounced in categories characterized by separable, discrete purchases, such as cars and cameras, particularly where switching costs are manageable. It is slower when continuous relationships are involved (working with a bank, accountant, and in many B2B services), and when it is expensive and/or time consuming to move to a different vendor. But these days loyalty for stand-alone products has already become less common and less robust, because the available information makes it much easier to rely on more accurate, product-specific quality assessments. When it was harder to obtain accurate information, relying on your previous positive experience with a brand made sense, but when the answer is out there, you don't necessarily need to stick with your past choices. In fact, from a consumer's perspective, loyalty can often be an inferior input, because quality and performance can vary greatly across products by the same company. This means that even if consumers had a good experience with other products by the same brand, each new purchase decision needs to be earned based on the product's actual capabilities.

It also means that measuring consumers' loyalty and its value to the company, especially where each product purchase (for example, a computer or a camera) is an infrequent event, is less meaningful and informative than it used to be. Consider, for example, the popular Net Promoter Score (NPS). A key ingredient in this method is measuring the percent of "promoters" who are defined as "loyal enthusiasts who keep buying from a company and urge their friends to do the same."[7] But the notion that people can be divided into chronic company promoters (or detractors) is misguided in a world where consumers increasingly evaluate specific products on their merit. A customer may be a promoter of one Samsung phone but be a detractor for the next model. Holistic brand or company measures are becoming less useful.

OPPORTUNITY KNOCKS

As with the decline of brand equity, the decline in the impact of consumer loyalty can present significant opportunities. If you feel a decline of loyalty among your customers, your competitors probably face the same problem (especially if, like most companies, quality and the relative competitive advantage or disadvantage of their products is uneven across their product lines). When consumers can easily assess the absolute value of products, more purchase decisions are in play. Targeting your competitors' current customers can be more effective than it used to be. If you offer a better solution than your competitors, don't hesitate to show it to their followers (not a new strategy, of course, but it may become more effective). If indeed your product is superior in ways consumers care about, its merit will become apparent to them faster than in the past.

We also have some good news to marketers whose last product was less than perfect: You may be getting a better second chance. The decline of past experience signifies a somewhat more forgiving era. Not that we recommend that you screw up. In fact, if you do, the market has no mercy, as is evident from numerous failures of products that didn't deliver, and the verdict these days is faster (as we explained in Chapter 3). Also, people are likely to remember your mistakes longer than your achievements since the impact of a negative experience is much greater than that of a positive one.

Having said all that, consumers' diminishing reliance on past experience *can* help marketers. Here's an example: Suppose that you ate at a new French restaurant in your town, and you had a so-so experience. A few months later you search Zagat for a place to eat and you come across that restaurant again. Based on your past experience, your decision would be not to go to that place again. But then you notice that the average rating of that restaurant has gone up. You take a peek at some reviews and notice that people rave about the coq au vin and crème brûlée (neither of which you tried when you were there). Some other people say that the chef's tasting menu is amazing and really the best way to go. Your past ("so-so") experience is facing some competition and you may actually decide to give this place a second chance.

This can happen on a much larger scale, as illustrated in the case of Hyundai. The first car from Hyundai to be imported into the United States was the Hyundai Excel. David Letterman had a joke that illustrates the public's reaction to the car: As part of the Top Ten Hilarious "Mischief Night" Pranks to Play in Space, No. 8 read: "Paste a 'Hyundai' logo on the main control panel." There were numerous similar jokes. It was a pretty bad car. The company kept struggling with quality for several years, but over time quality became the focus and Hyundai's reputation for product quality increased. A ten-year/100,000-mile warranty on engines and transmissions helped as well, and their U.S. sales rose an average of 14 percent a year.[8]

The most dramatic leap came in 2004, when in a study by J. D. Power, new-car buyers ranked Hyundai higher in initial quality than any domestic or European manufacturer.[9] It was Hyundai's good fortune that by then close to 70 percent of the U.S. population was already on the Internet and had access to this news (among new-car buyers the Internet penetration was probably even higher). Today Hyundai is one of the leading brands in the United States and its plant in Alabama can't build cars fast enough. Despite a rough start, Hyundai got a second chance from the North American consumer. When customers can quickly get a good idea of how good (or bad) a new product is, a company has a better chance to reverse its course.

Bottom line: The decline of past experience goes both ways. The bad news is that you can never rest on your laurels. The good news is that more decisions are in play and you have better second chances.

ON SATISFACTION

Let's shift gears for a moment for a fun exercise. Think of it as a field trip that will help us clarify some concepts related to satisfaction. Start by going to Yelp or Zagat (or any other restaurant review site) and find a restaurant in your area where you've never eaten before. Find one that you think you'd like. Read five or more reviews. If you feel that this isn't the right restaurant for you, read a few reviews about a different restaurant, until you find one that looks really good. Now comes the hard part of the exercise—go to that restaurant and have a good meal. If anyone tells you that you can't go (your boss, your significant other), tell them that you're on a scientific mission, and if you feel generous, invite them along.

You're back? Good. We hope you enjoyed it.

Actually, there is a high likelihood (no certainty) that you did. Because we suspect that after reading some reviews about the restaurant you picked, you had a pretty good idea of what to expect. You most likely had more accurate expectations than if you relied solely on the restaurant's website. You were also not very likely to make major mistakes, because if you came across reviews that raised some serious red flags, you switched to a different restaurant as we instructed you (and as most people would do). Since you knew what to expect in terms of the service, the food, and the general atmosphere at the restaurant, your expectations and your actual experience were likely to be pretty close. When people assess their satisfaction, what they consider and feel is just the vague comparison between expectations and experience. Since better information sources lead to more accurate expectations, the gaps between expectations and actual experiences should generally be smaller. Of course, some of our less fortunate readers will experience disappointing service or dishes, and you may have detected some inaccurate information in the reviews you read—reviews are not perfect quality predictors—but on average, better information should lead to fewer unpleasant surprises. An important outcome of the new information environment is that consumers are likely, on average, to have better (objective) experiences and fewer big disappointments.

Should we then expect satisfaction ratings to steadily go up? Not necessarily.

To illustrate why, let's look at another example: Suppose you buy a camera to take some pictures at a big family event. Once you set your expectations based on all the user and expert reviews, the fact that the camera delivers on its promise means that you are satisfied. Satisfied, but not delighted—you knew it was a good camera all along, so it's not a big surprise. You now have a better product and can do a better job thanks to the information you had before buying, but you don't necessarily show it in your camera satisfaction ratings.

Similar in some ways to happiness ratings, which tend not to change when there are general changes (such as rise in income) that apply to most others, having the tools to make better decisions is unlikely to produce a general increase in satisfaction ratings.[10] But as we indicated, the gaps should be getting smaller and satisfaction ratings should correspondingly become less variable and less extreme (though without a mean shift).

What narrows the expectation-experience gap further is a stronger confirmation bias. This bias refers to people's general tendency to confirm their prior hypotheses and expectations. For example, when you're told that a movie is great, this usually affects your experience (unless the gap between the actual experience and your expectations is very large, in which case you get a contrast effect).

So what you felt about that filet mignon you ate at the restaurant was affected by the expectations formed by the reviews you read. Confirmation bias exists also when your expectations are formed by advertising, but it is reasonable to expect that this bias should be more potent when your expectations were formed by the opinions of more trusted sources. As more information today is gathered from reviews and other sources that are perceived as trusted (as opposed to advertising, which is usually perceived as less reliable), this confirmation bias is likely to be stronger.

Of course, we are not proposing that loyalty and satisfaction are no longer relevant. First, it's a slow, gradual process. Quality is still associated with uncertainty, and emotional attachment to brands will not go away though its impact on purchase decisions is declining. Second, everything we're talking about applies to categories where many people *do* take advantage of the available information regarding quality. In categories where this is not the case, past satisfaction and loyalty can still play an important role in certain decisions. For example, for low-involvement purchases, where consumers look for shortcuts and don't wish to thoroughly evaluate options from scratch, loyalty can still be valuable for a company. But in categories that are affected by the shift in decision making, it's becoming harder to ensure customers' loyalty. The same goes for satisfaction. Having satisfied customers is obviously still the objective of every company. It's just that having these happy customers today doesn't guarantee your success tomorrow.

Third, at the present time and in the foreseeable future, there will be some customer segments that don't take advantage of the available information. In these cases, loyalty and past experience will continue to play their traditional roles as quality proxies. Yet these segments are likely to shrink over time since information is so easily obtained. For example, brand loyalty used to be more significant for cell phones just five years ago. Today, more and more consumers—and not only the savviest ones—look around before buying a new phone, even if they liked their last handset. It's just so easy to watch a video review on PhoneDog.com or to ask your friends what they're using. Finally, a note to avoid confusion: When we talk about loyalty, we're not talking about loyalty programs. The mere fact that loyalty is less used as a cue for quality does not mean that loyalty programs (for example, of airlines) are less relevant—many loyalty programs offer real value.

We opened this chapter with Lars Rasmussen, who was introducing a new piece of software to a cheering audience. The software he was showing was Google Wave. It was supposed to replace email, and serve as a one-stop shop for all electronic communications—from instant messaging to group collaboration. We actually had some hopes to make use of it in writing this book. We started using Google Wave in late 2009, but we didn't get far. It was too confusing and complicated for us. And we weren't alone. This was the experience of many early users, which they quickly shared with the rest of the world. We have great respect for Lars Rasmussen and for Google for their past achievements, but those past achievements didn't make us stay with Wave. We went back to email. In 2010 Google suspended the project. Our point here is not to analyze why Wave was discontinued, but to point out that the past achievements of its creators were irrelevant to the way it was evaluated in the marketplace.[11]

The main takeaway from this chapter: Success is driven by the merit of your current product and much less by your customers' past experience. This can go both ways. It means that you can never rest on your laurels. But it also means that more decisions are in play and that you might get a better second chance. It also suggests that loyalty is overrated. Businesspeople tend to believe in loyalty and long-term relationships with customers (and some of this certainly exists), but more and more consumers see their relationships with companies as an open marriage: If something better comes along, they will go with the better option.

There's something almost cruel and seemingly unfair about this disregard for the past—for better or for worse, your past record doesn't matter as much as it used to. But there's also something fair about it. Should we expect you to like this book—*Absolute Value*—because of our past work? Of course not. Emanuel's previous books and Itamar's past articles may play a role in the way you assess our present work, but in the end, our past writings are irrelevant. This is the age of *now*.

7

ABSOLUTE DIFFUSION:
FROM PINEHURST TO PINTEREST

THERE'S A GROVE of pine trees in west central Iowa surrounded by fields of corn and soybean. It's located about five miles south of Carroll (population ten thousand). There used to be a house near the grove, and some farm buildings—a barn, a silo, a couple of sheds. They're all gone now.

The place is called Pinehurst Farm. If we could magically transport ourselves in time and visit Pinehurst in the 1930s, we would find ourselves in the middle of a bustling farm—tractors, hogs, cows, chickens. The family that lived here was a pretty typical Midwest farming family, and in our context we're mostly interested in how they learned about new stuff. We know that they subscribed to *Popular Mechanics* and *Wallaces' Farmer*. Once a week they would get into their car for a shopping trip to nearby Carroll. Occasionally the family would meet their neighbors and exchange information. There were also some relatives from Omaha who would come to visit from time to time.[1]

Few people who drive by today pay any attention to that grove of pine trees, but the way we think about the adoption of new technologies is rooted in the information environment at Pinehurst

Farm. The family that used to live here was the Rogers family, and their son—Everett M. Rogers—is identified more than anyone else with diffusion theory. Rogers, a brilliant scholar, developed extensive theories that show how information spreads in society. These theories go way beyond Midwest farming, but at their core they are based on an information environment that is radically different than the one that is emerging around us.

Perhaps the key difference is the speed at which uncertainty is resolved. With the limited information sources available at Pinehurst Farm, almost any new product or idea presented a huge question mark. There were only a few people around you could ask about a new farming practice, a new tractor, a new gadget. Determining the quality of something new was really hard. The same level of uncertainty about many products was maintained for decades, and really started changing only about a decade ago. You may remember, for example, what was involved in buying new software in the early 1990s: You'd go through issues of *PC Magazine* or *MacUser*. You'd ask friends and colleagues with the hope that they were using the same software. Assessing the quality of new stuff was still hard.

Compare this to a decision regarding an app you're considering downloading. You go to the app store, take a quick look at the overall rating, a glance at the number of users who rated the app, and you get the general idea. Sometimes this is enough (Houzz, with more than 22,000 reviews and a five-star average, is likely to be a good app). Browsing through some actual reviews (sampling from the negative ones, too) helps you refine your decision. This way, for example, it's easy to conclude that Angry Birds (with close to five stars from 1,453 users) is probably a better choice than some game with a two-star average from a few dozen users.

Diffusion theory is rooted in the existence of uncertainty. Of course, uncertainty is not going to completely disappear, but in the new information environment, we can expect faster uncertainty resolution regarding the product quality, regarding preference fit, and regarding product acceptance by relevant others. In minutes you can tell how good Angry Birds is, whether it might fit what you usually like, and how popular it is.

Before we continue, we want to make a personal note. We owe a lot to Everett Rogers, especially Emanuel, who views Rogers as his mentor. Rogers was a champion of Emanuel's first book and even wrote the foreword.[2] Beyond that, Rogers is actually responsible for us—Emanuel and Itamar—meeting in the first place. (We'll tell that story in a moment.) This chapter is an examination of some elements of diffusion theory that are affected by the changing information environment. There are many diffusion principles that go unchanged.[3]

This isn't just an academic issue. The acceleration of uncertainty resolution has important implications for companies, especially in the technology sector. A lot of marketing thinking is still based on an information environment characterized by high levels of uncertainty. A key example is the classic adoption model, which still guides many strategies. This model (which also has its roots in a study of adoption among Iowa farmers)[4] classifies the population into five adoption categories: innovators, early adopters, early majority, late majority, and laggards. This is the way many observers still view the technology adoption life cycle: At first a few innovators who are willing to take risks will adopt an innovation. They will be followed by the early adopters, then the first mainstream group, the early majority, will start to adopt the innovation, followed by the late majority. Finally the laggards will adopt the innovation (or choose not to).

The different adopter categories are rooted, at least in part, in different personalities, and people's attitudes toward technology. This won't change. There will always be people who are fascinated by new technologies, those who see it more pragmatically and those who are reluctant to get new stuff. What *has* changed is the rate at which information is available to each of these groups. The sharp distinction among adopter categories was most meaningful when the increase in information availability was very slow. If you were someone with a pragmatic attitude toward new technologies, it took a long time until someone with the same attitude—a neighbor or a friend—adopted the innovation and was able to tell you about it in terms that you understood and could relate to. This is the complete opposite of what's going on today, where a lot of information is available very quickly—enough information that helps anyone make an informed decision not long after a new product is released.

While people still differ in their attitude toward technology, the extent that they are willing (and can afford) to take risks, and their innovativeness, they can now find rather quickly people like themselves who have adopted the product. An early adopter can find other early adopters, while a pragmatist from the early majority can find reviews and opinions of other pragmatists not long thereafter.

And it's not only about strangers who write reviews. We want to make sure this important point doesn't go unnoticed. Existing diffusion theory emerged in a world in which friends, family, and neighbors drove imitation and adoption. Although these strong ties still play an important role in diffusion, in today's world consumers acquire more and more information from "weak ties." Many readers are probably familiar with Mark Granovetter's "strength of weak ties," but for the benefit of those who aren't, here's the theory in a nutshell. Granovetter showed that your closest friends and family—those who move in the same social circles as you do—are likely to be exposed to the same sources of information as you are. Therefore, they don't usually bring you fresh news. On the other hand, people outside this group are much more likely to hear things that you do not. In this way, weak ties with distant acquaintances are most apt to bring in information that is new. This was true when Granovetter did his original research decades ago, but likely even more true today.[5]

The Web is mostly about weak ties. We still talk a lot with our strong ties (family and close friends) and this communication seems to be much more prevalent, but when it comes to the dissemination of *new* information in a connected world, weak ties are critical.[6]

This explosion in weak ties dramatically increases the chance that you'll find among the people you know someone with similar attitudes toward innovations. In other words, if you're a pragmatist who needs to speak to other pragmatists before you'll adopt, there's a much higher chance that you'll come across some of them today than there was twenty years ago. The Internet doesn't only allow you to find like-minded strangers who write about an innovation. It lets you see which of your connections on Facebook, Twitter, LinkedIn, etc., have already adopted. Some of these acquaintances may talk about the innovation in terms that won't necessarily resonate with you, but there is a good chance that it won't take long before you find—in your vast network of weak ties—some pragmatists like you. Incidentally, oftentimes this doesn't happen through active search that you conduct. As your acquaintances on these social networking sites talk about their lives, they also relay information about things like the apps they downloaded, the latest camera they're considering, or a new laptop they just bought.

The bottom line is this: These days, finding people like you—whether they're strangers or acquaintances—who have adopted an innovation is much simpler than it was in the past.

Before we go on, this seems like a good place to tell the story of how Everett Rogers helped us meet (which relates to weak ties). In 1999, a fellow Stanford professor told Itamar about an upcoming book called *The Anatomy of Buzz* (Emanuel's first book). This is how we met. We got together for lunch and discovered that, beyond our mutual professional interests, we share a common past: We grew up about a mile from each other and attended the same high school in Tel Aviv around the same time. In the 1980s we both lived with our families around Berkeley, California. But we had never met until that common acquaintance created the connection after we both moved to the Palo Alto area. In other words, for decades we lived in neighboring social clusters without knowing of each other. It was that weak tie who connected us, and he happened to be Mark Granovetter, father of the "strength of weak ties" theory. Granovetter was a neighbor of Itamar's, and Emanuel interviewed him for his book. And who introduced Emanuel to Mark Granovetter? The boy from Pinehurst Farm, Everett Rogers.

PRACTICAL IMPLICATIONS

Why does it all matter? What harm can there be in marketers classifying their audience into adopter categories? We believe that thinking about adopter categories when they are less meaningful can lead to the wrong strategic decisions.

Here's an example: In the early 1990s Geoffrey Moore brought the adoption model to the attention of technology marketers by arguing that there is a chasm between the early adopters (who are interested in the technology) and the early majority, a mainstream group that is more pragmatic about technology. As we mentioned, these pragmatists essentially want to hear from other pragmatists that the gadget they're considering is working and will solve their problem. The chasm idea struck a chord with tech marketers who became very interested in how to "cross the chasm," in other words, go into the mainstream.[7]

But what if there's no chasm anymore? Or what if the chasm is much less of a problem than it used to be? We agree with Moore's point that the chasm existed because there was a gap of communication between the innovators (who talk about the technology) and the early majority (who are interested in its practicality). But what happens when anyone can go online pretty early after (or even before) an innovation is released, and find like-minded acquaintances or strangers who talk about the new product? Pragmatists from the early majority don't need to wait until their next-door neighbor or someone at work adopts the innovation. Even if you used to behave as a late adopter in the old days, you may adopt new things much earlier now because your need for reassurance by like-minded people is satisfied earlier. You simply find them on the Internet instead of among your close friends.

Yet tech companies still think in terms of a chasm. They still try to cross it. Moore argues that one way to do this is through a strategy he calls Bowling Alley. The idea is to find—within the early majority—some niches or segments that desperately need the product. Once they adopt the product, they will tell other pragmatists in other segments and so, segment after segment—like pins in a bowling alley—the technology will spread.

The implication is that marketers should target—and customize their product for—certain very specific segments or niches, but marketing strategies like Bowling Alley may be less effective and even cause delay in today's environment.

Consider the case of tablet computing. Everybody is familiar with Apple's iPad, but not everyone remembers that Microsoft introduced a tablet way before Apple (back in 2002).[8] The tablet PC initiative was a top priority at Microsoft, which partnered with several OEMs to manufacture the hardware. The device looked like a thicker iPad running Windows XP and all the applications that were used on desktop or laptop PCs at the time. In addition, using a digital pen, you could write on the tablet and manipulate your notes as if you typed them in. It was also wireless, and despite some wrinkles, it was considered a pretty good innovation.

Microsoft launched its Tablet PC in a strategy that followed the Bowling Alley idea. Instead of releasing the technology and letting interested segments adopt it organically, Microsoft chose to target vertical markets such as health care, insurance, real estate, and legal, where the use of the tablet made sense (at least to the folks at Microsoft).

Five years later, Apple introduced the iPad without predetermining (or limiting) who was going to use it. Indeed, the iPad was initially adopted by many who would never have been classified as innovators or early adopters. Lots of seniors adopted the iPad. People heard about it, went online, saw that this thing works for what they need it to do, and got their iPad right away. Comparing the two companies, author Keir Thomas observed that Microsoft was limiting the user by pushing them into particular scenarios. In contrast, Apple products are built around giving users freedom.[9]

It's possible, of course, that Apple was better in execution and user interface and that Microsoft tablet technology was still crude and not mature enough. But it's also clear that Microsoft's decision to market and tailor the tablet to specific applications and users guided the design and marketing message, which is exactly our point. The need to target small niches and vertical markets in order to penetrate the early majority has simply declined.

There's another potential pitfall that marketers should avoid when it comes to adopter categories in the new era. If you believe that your product will first be adopted by chronic innovators, and that it will take some time before early adopters or the early majority will start adopting it, you might release a product that doesn't fit mainstream users. Innovators can be more forgiving when it comes to user interface, for example. They are usually into the technology and love to have lots of features. If you design your product to appeal to innovators and early adopters, you may introduce products that will not be accepted by mainstream users. Suppose your company is in the fitness monitoring business. If you operated in the 1990s, the user interface in your first version could perhaps be a bit clunky. At your design meetings you would put most of the emphasis on features. User interface? "These folks will live with anything we throw their way as long as it has lots of features," you think to yourself. "We'll cross the chasm in version 2.0." (Of course, we're exaggerating a bit, but you get the idea.)

Today, it doesn't work this way because on day one your early users—who could come from anywhere—will start posting reviews online. Today's environment allows for easy communication within adoption segments and across (blurring) adoption segments. So whether new products succeed or fail depends on their merit, which is revealed, for better or worse, rather quickly. Bottom line: The target market for new innovative products should be defined more broadly, not just chronic "innovators." Your first version can be adopted by anyone because information about it is so readily accessible.

Another shift relates to the factors that determine acceptance and diffusion rate of innovations. Past research has highlighted five key innovation characteristics as the drivers of adoption rate: relative advantage, compatibility, observability, communicability, and trialability. As summarized in Rogers's treatise, these factors have been shown to underlie the success or failure of innovations and the speed of diffusion. When innovations were spreading locally from neighbor to neighbor, observability was important. You bought a new tractor after you saw the new John Deere your neighbor was riding. A lot of this is still going on, of course. But observability has become less of an issue because the Web has made almost everything observable. Same goes for communicability. Although an individual consumer may have trouble communicating the benefits of an innovation, the loads of communicators on the Web are likely to generate an effective way to explain it. Similarly, the ability to try a product on a limited basis without major investments is less important than in the past because the information available on the Web and from friends offers effective substitutes for personal experience with the product.

The one adoption driver that is clearly going to *increase* in importance is the relative advantage of an innovation. It's simply because the advantage of a product (compared to previous or competing ones) can be identified more clearly and quickly. The term "relative advantage" may be confusing in the context of this book because it actually refers to the absolute advantage, but it's simply the term Rogers and others used when referring to the advantage of one product (the innovation) compared to the products that innovation is aimed to replace.

Compatibility with a user's prior experiences will also remain a significant driver of adoption rates. But it may decline in importance when one has access to technology that effectively demonstrates how the product is used. It is easier to try something new and seemingly incompatible when one can readily see (for example, on YouTube) its benefits and the ease of adoption. The basic premise remains the same: The increasing impact of absolute values means that consumers will be better able to evaluate products for what they are, rather than just how they compare with other options they happen to see. This trend is expected to enhance the compatibility between people's revealed preferences or choices and their inherent preference. Instead of continuing to use the same defaults and proven products, you can more easily experience new approaches and learn about them from others. For example, before the iPhone was introduced, many people thought they would never get used to a cell phone without a mechanical keyboard. But as soon as the iPhone was introduced, users spread the word that the iPhone interface was actually user-friendly and the transition away from a mechanical keyboard was easy.

FROM PINEHURST TO PINTEREST

Less than a hundred miles east of Pinehurst Farm lies the city of Des Moines, where a young man by the name of Ben Silbermann grew up in the 1980s. As a kid, Silbermann assumed that he'd be a doctor like both of his parents, but after graduating from Yale, he became attracted to the tech scene, feeling that something really big was happening in the world and that he wanted to be part of it. After a consulting job in Washington, D.C., he moved to California, where he worked for Google for a while, but the political science major didn't find himself in this engineering-oriented company. Silbermann left Google in 2008 (probably the worst timing, since it was just when the entire economy seemed to be collapsing). He started working with some friends on new ideas. They worked in his living room and virtually in every coffee shop between Mountain View and San Francisco.

After some initial product ideas that didn't go far, Silbermann and his friends Paul Sciarra and Evan Sharp found a product concept that they were excited about and they started to pitch it to venture capitalists in Silicon Valley. It was a website where users could create "boards" around areas of interest. When the user sees an image on the Web that they want to keep or share, they click a

"Pin It" button and assign the image to one of their boards. The name of the site was Pinterest. No VC was interested in funding the start-up.

Somehow Silbermann and his friends managed to develop the product and launched it in early 2010. Silicon Valley, the innovators, and the early adopters responded with a big collective yawn. But Silbermann and his friends showed Pinterest to some lifestyle bloggers, crafters, and hobbyists, and to the folks he grew up with back in Iowa, and something interesting started to happen. "The early people were from the area where I grew up, in Des Moines, and the site grew very organically from there," Silbermann told the *New York Times*.[10]

Bowling Alley? Silbermann did go to a show of interior designers who adopted the product rather enthusiastically, but most of the other people adopted the product organically. In early 2012 Pinterest hit 11.7 million unique monthly U.S. visitors, thus crossing the 10 million mark faster than any other standalone site in history, according to comScore and TechCrunch.[11]

Reflecting on his experience at a forum for entrepreneurs in San Francisco, Silbermann noted: "I've talked to a lot of really smart people in Silicon Valley about this idea of early adopters. . . . I think that products will find their markets more smoothly and this idea that it's gated through Silicon Valley . . . I don't think it's as relevant anymore."[12]

In April 2012, one study ranked Pinterest as the number-three social media website, behind Facebook and Twitter. In February 2013 comScore reported that Pinterest had 48.7 million users globally. This, of course, doesn't say it can't collapse as fast as it rose. But, Iowa, you've come a long way since the slow days of Pinehurst Farm.[13]

Incidentally, Everett Rogers's father was clearly what his son would describe as a laggard: Avoiding buying anything new was part of daily life on Pinehurst Farm. (When you needed a nail, you first looked for an old rusty nail that you could straiten and reuse.) Everett Rogers himself was no early adopter, either. "I just write about innovations. I don't necessarily use them," he told Emanuel back in 1998 to explain why he doesn't check his email. People will still differ in how they feel about technology (and new things in general). Some will always be fascinated by the latest and greatest, some will see technology more pragmatically, and some will always be a bit more reluctant to adopt new products. The difference is that today, all these people can quickly find someone with the same attitude who already owns the product and talks about it in familiar terms. When uncertainty is resolved quickly, there is much less of a need to think about distinct adoption categories. When adoption categories are less important, so are strategies, such as "Bowling Alley," that derive from category thinking. It also means that your product should be ready from day one to all types of users, not only those who are most tech savvy. As uncertainty about quality is resolved faster, the rules of diffusion are changing.

8

POINTLESS POSITIONING AND PERSUASION

HERE'S A COMMERCIAL that you may have seen in 2011: Mark, Tom, and Travis of the rock band Blink-182 are working in the garden, when suddenly their bodies start to glow in light blue. Perplexed by what's happening, Travis Barker (the band's drummer) asks:

"Why are we glowing blue?"

A young woman, obviously a fan, who's just about to take their picture from across the fence, explains:

"Hey, don't be nervous. It's just because my new phone has the 'Facebook Share' button. When there's something to share, it glows."

"Oh, that's a reasonable explanation," guitarist Tom DeLonge mumbles as the voice-over wraps up: "Share it faster with HTC Status from AT&T. The only phone with a 'Facebook Share' button that glows anytime you take a photo, video, or anything else worth sharing."[1]

This commercial is obviously trying to position this new phone as "the Facebook phone." Positioning is rooted in the idea that product perceptions are driven by product presentation relative to other options. Instead of evaluating the product based on its actual value, you presumably evaluate it under the influence of the marketer's communications strategy. So it is not the product's absolute values that matter, but rather, it is the prescribed relative values—the product's recommended position relative to other products. It's difficult for us as consumers to decide which car rental company is the best. When Avis positioned itself against the competition ("We Are No 2. We Try Harder"), it made sense to our comparison-hungry minds. Al Ries and Jack Trout, who many years ago wrote the book on positioning, described it as a battle that's going on in the consumer's mind. Their idea was that each marketer has to find an area that is not occupied in the consumer's mind and capture it (that is, be the first brand that comes to mind when the consumer thinks about a certain attribute). In the automotive industry, for example, Volvo captured "safety," Ferrari got "speed," Lincoln stood for "luxury," and Toyota captured "reliability."

Following this logic, the idea of positioning a phone around Facebook made some sense. No other phone "owned" the position of "the Facebook phone" and the marketers perhaps imagined millions of young Facebook addicts (and Blink-182 fans) who would kill to have this phone. In the past this might have worked just fine. But this phone was introduced in an era when things work a bit differently. These days "finding a unique angle" isn't enough. It has to be real. And in reality you can easily share on Facebook from all smartphones and everybody knows that.

That "Facebook phone" was dubbed by some the "Failbook phone." User reviews were pretty bad and teens reacted to the new device with a big "whatevs" (today's version of the 1990s' "Whatever"). They simply didn't buy into the positioning that the marketers tried to establish in their minds. Nice positioning statements compiled in corporate meeting rooms are less likely to be adopted by the market these days. Marketers can save themselves a lot of money by avoiding doomed-to-failure positioning attempts.[2]

Don't get us wrong: If your product has a real advantage over your competitors, you *should* highlight this differentiating factor. But when marketers talk about differentiating, they often talk about finding a unique angle that no one has yet covered. Trying to make a product appear unique by adding fluff or emphasizing a feature or claimed differentiator that is of limited use or relevance to most doesn't work as well as it used to.

That is just part of the problem. Even when you think your product *is* differentiated enough, positioning is less effective than it used to be, because a new product is likely to be evaluated based on its absolute values. In contrast, the manner in which it is portrayed or positioned by the marketer is likely to have much less influence on consumers' perceptions and choices. In 2013, HTC, in collaboration with Facebook, launched another phone—the HTC First—positioned as the Facebook phone. This one had somewhat closer integration with Facebook, which may appeal to some consumers (although as this book goes to print, this phone too doesn't seem to be successful). The main problem is that positioning won't protect the product from the usual expert and user scrutiny. One review of the HTC First, for example, recognized the special Facebook-related features but immediately continued, "However, as smart-phones go, the First is decidedly average, and it has a substandard camera. . . ."[3]

Here's another TV commercial that helps illustrate this point. This one, too, involves an HTC phone but this time with Verizon. A guy walks out of the subway in New York City. We hear cars honking and other street noise, but when he puts on his earphones, the background noise is gone. He presses a button on his phone and listens to a rap song. As he walks on the sidewalk, a parked car explodes right behind him, trash cans shoot into the air, but he's totally consumed by the music. Doesn't seem to be bothered. Even as a police car flips in midair, with a yellow cab following suit, the dude just walks around listening to his music. To those who didn't get the message, a voice-over delivers the punch line: "Experience your sound like never before. The HTC Rezound with Beats Audio built in on the Verizon 4G Lte network."

In this commercial (and in other promotional efforts) the marketers were apparently trying to position the HTC Rezound as the "sound phone." Again, in the past, this should have worked just fine, especially since HTC had something unique to offer. About a year before the phone was launched, HTC had bought a majority stake in Beats Electronics, a digital sound company known for its Beats by Dr. Dre headphones. The HTC Rezound was the first to incorporate Beats audio.[4]

But what happened in reality? Reviewers on the Web evaluated the HTC Rezound like any other cell phone. We've read dozens of reviews of this phone, both by experts and by users, and most have not isolated sound as the single attribute to pay attention to. For example, PhoneDog, a popular YouTube channel that reviews mobile devices, dedicated a long video review to the phone. It wasn't a bad review; it's just that most of it wasn't around the special sound capabilities. Almost all reviews gave pretty equal coverage to attributes like thickness, display, speed, and so on. When evaluated on all these attributes, the HTC Rezound was not superior to the Droid Razr or the Galaxy Nexus, which were introduced at about the same time without the music positioning.

In the old days, when consumers were much more influenced by information from marketers, it was possible to make them compare a product primarily on one attribute, as the marketers were attempting to do with this campaign. Executed effectively, it was possible to convince the consumer that your brand stood for some unique concept; but when consumers use diverse and detailed sources of information, chances are slim that they will all focus on one feature and neglect other pertinent considerations.[5]

Volvo was the symbol of safety for a long time, but once consumers found out from reliable sources that other cars are just as safe, Volvo's claim to fame dissipated. "We Are No 2. We Try Harder" was a brilliant slogan, but its impact must be lower when a traveler can get detailed information about the actual rental experience: How long is an average wait for the shuttle at the airport? Are they pushy or friendly at the counter? Are there any surprises when you return the car and it's time to pay the bill? The tools that are available at the present are not there yet in terms of providing accurate, branch-specific information. But when a traveler will be able to peek in advance at the answers to these questions, smart positioning slogans will not make much of a difference. It's not that positioning is completely useless (especially for products such as laundry detergents, where the quality is hard to evaluate), but it's much less useful than it used to be, and this trend will accelerate as marketers' ability to affect consumers' perceptions continues to decline.

ORGANIC SEGMENTATION

It's tempting to imagine that businesses succeed as a result of well-executed positioning and segmentation strategies, but the truth is that segments these days often cannot be foreseen and, instead, evolve organically. Think about Twitter, for example. Twitter (like many other Web companies) did not have a positioning or segmentation strategy. They offered a service and certain "target" segments emerged and positioned it as they liked. Twitter can be different things to different people.[6] Granted, this type of "organic segmentation" doesn't always happen and we are not suggesting that marketers introduce products without putting any thought into who's going to use them. Planning products to appeal to certain segments continues to be important, and segmentation before and after a product launch is imperative. Still, it's worth exploring three points about segmentation as they relate to positioning.

First, marketers should realize that they have less control than before over the actual segments that buy their products. When marketers controlled their information, they could decide who would get their catalog or brochure and (more or less) what they should think about it. In contrast, when information is everywhere, anyone can pick it up and go with it. There are still some things that marketers can do to steer particular groups toward their offerings (for example: Nike can seed a new shoe in certain demographics, or sell it through exclusive distribution channels). Yet organic (demand-driven) segmentation and positioning of the type seen with Twitter are going to occur more often than in the past. Marketers should still plan for certain segments but also be ready to be surprised and quickly adjust as the product is adopted in the marketplace. Nintendo did a good job in this regard when they introduced the Wii. The primary target of video games until then was 4 to 40-year-olds (depending on the genre). Then came the Wii, and a surprising new segment emerged—the elderly. Detecting that older people just *loved* Wii Sports (and especially Wii Bowling), Nintendo was fast to embrace this segment, for example, by actively promoting the game to AARP members.[7]

Second, organic segmentation also means that, counter to the common belief in marketing, you *can* sometimes be all things to all people. In the past, marketers were supposed to predefine different benefit segments and tailor products for them. The rule was that you should not use the same product for multiple segments, because that would create an ambiguous position. Today, as long as the product can satisfy wants, many of which cannot be identified a priori, chances are that suitable consumer segments will emerge organically, regardless of the seller's preconceived ideas. In Chapter 7, we described the adoption of Pinterest and the Apple iPad, which very much followed this pattern. Consumers' access to granular and detailed information can help organic segmentation in more traditional markets, too. Suppose you own a hotel. If you follow the "don't be all things to all people" idea, your hotel should be clearly positioned as either a business hotel, a family hotel, or a romantic hideaway. Advocates of strict positioning would tell you that if you try to be all three, your message will be muddled. But in reality, many hotels have always been able to maintain "multiple personalities." And it's even easier today because a traveler can see the hotel exclusively from a particular angle. A business traveler who goes to TripAdvisor can read only those reviews of your hotel written by fellow business travelers. A couple planning their honeymoon can focus on those reviews written by other couples. Parents traveling with kids can read reviews written by families. In the past, if these parents saw that your hotel was "for the business traveler," they would be apprehensive. Today they can get an accurate picture of what it means to stay at your hotel with kids.

Third, a related segmentation strategy that is losing its effectiveness is selling very similar products under different tags. Known as "versioning" in the marketing literature, some consumers refer to it as "crippleware," "defective by design," or "damaged good." Fifteen years ago you could position two nearly identical laptops under two different labels. One would be "the business laptop" and another one would be considered "the consumer laptop." The difference would usually be a feature that has been disabled in the low-end model. Today there are two problems with that. First, versioning is less likely to work because both businesses and consumers can quickly figure out the similarity between the laptops and get the better deal regardless of the label marketers put on it. The second issue is that versioning is often seen by people as unfair, and since the fairness of an exchange can play a significant role in how consumers evaluate an offer, this can lead to a bigger problem. Researchers Andrew Gershoff, Ran Kivetz, and Anat Keinan showed in a series of experiments that versioning may be indeed perceived as unfair and unethical and lead to decreased purchase intentions for a brand.[8] Beyond product versioning, what might be called "price versioning" may also become more transparent for consumers and therefore less effective. For example, in 2013 AT&T Wireless changed the price of the HTC First—the first-ever "Facebook Phone"—from $99 to $0.99. The pricing change reflected the apparent new target segment of the phone: lower-end wireless users. However, observers quickly pointed out that, once the corresponding change in the cost of the data plan is considered, the price reduction is less than it might first seem.[9]

POINTLESS PERSUASION

You surely remember the scene from *Annie Hall*: Woody Allen stands in line at a movie theater while an opinionated man behind him explains to his girlfriend the works of Fellini, Samuel Beckett, and Marshall McLuhan. When Allen can no longer stand the endless drivel, he tells the man that he doesn't know anything about Marshall McLuhan. But the fellow sounds pretty convincing when he lays out his credentials: "Oh really? I happen to teach a class at Columbia called 'TV, Media, and Culture,' so I think that my insights into Mr. McLuhan have a great deal of validity," he argues. When the guy says he teaches at Columbia, he's using a pretty common influence tactic, one based on source credibility theory. Symbols of authority such as titles or clothing can help in persuasion. This is why salespeople wear well-tailored business suits, and why the actor who recommends a new drug on a TV commercial is wearing a white lab coat.[10]

Yet not much of the man's persuasive power is left after what happens next. Woody grabs Marshall McLuhan himself from behind a pole, and McLuhan turns to the man: "I heard what you're saying. You know nothing of my work." Even someone with the finest rhetorical skills would understand that it's pointless to now try to persuade his listeners that he's right. Marshall McLuhan knows Marshall McLuhan.

The persuader's power is reduced (in this case annihilated) at the presence of a reliable source. And this is happening more and more in marketing. Advertisers and salespeople are armed with numerous persuasive techniques that can be quite effective in isolation. We're not going to list them all here, but let's just mention a couple (in addition to authority, which we just discussed). One is liking: The more we like someone, the more we want to say yes to them.[11] (Salespeople live by this.) And such emotional responses often precede and affect evaluation of reasons. Reciprocation is another common influence technique: Give your prospects something small at the onset, and they will feel indebted to you.

Yet the effectiveness of these techniques takes a dive when they compete with facts delivered by credible sources. These tricks of the trade have one thing in common: They are not about the merit of the product but about something else. A big part of advertising and personal selling can be seen as the art of relative persuasion—finding shiny objects that would sway customers to prefer one product over all the others. Instead of letting you make your choice by assessing your likely experience with a product, the salesman or the advertiser tries to have you base your decision on something unrelated—an athlete endorser, a man wearing a white lab coat, a good example, or an enticing story, the fact that the salesman gave you a T-shirt or complimented you on your hair. . . . Those influence methods may still work. The only problem is that companies no longer serve as *the* source for quality information, so these persuasion techniques don't matter as much as they used to. Consumers rarely pull a "Marshall McLuhan" on companies (although this happens, too). It usually happens in a less dramatic way. There's simply a better act in town that consumers turn to—their peers.

What are the implications to marketers? Where consumers rely on more credible sources, companies should focus less on persuasion attempts or on trying to shape people's preferences. There isn't much of a point in trying to persuade consumers that the tablet your company makes is better than the one made by your competitors. There are still good reasons to point out important features and advocate your company's design (especially to those who will review your product), but by and large, your company's ability to persuade is greatly reduced. Don't fire your marketing department just yet, though. They still can make a difference in generating interest among consumers, a task that is becoming more difficult in the noisy world in which we live. We'll discuss this later, too, but it's worth mentioning right away that generating interest in the categories most affected by the trends we discuss here can rarely be achieved by pouring tons of money into advertising. The reason is that consumers in these categories are focused on *new* sources of information (experts or other users), not the marketer. The best interest is generated when these sources will draw the consumer's attention to your product.

What does all this mean to advertising agencies, sales forces, and other persuasion agents?

As persuasive advertising and personal selling are becoming less important, one might expect marketing institutions and departments to change accordingly. For example, marketing communication agencies will have to adapt to focus less on persuasion or preference formation and more on generating interest, or they may face increasing challenges in justifying their added value. Simultaneously, PR agencies and other organizations that can help generate interest in ways that make sense in this new era are likely to further develop.

Companies may also expect a shift in the importance of their sales forces. In the past, salespeople served as a major source for information, helped reassure customers of their choices, and did a lot of hand-holding, functions that are less essential in certain areas. These days there are more efficient ways to transmit information than through salespeople. While relationship will continue to be important, and there are so far no indications that B2B companies downsize their sales forces, one would expect the impact of relationships on vendor choice to decline over time.

Positioning statements represent perhaps the ultimate "relative" tactic. Instead of evaluating the product based on its actual value, the consumer is supposed to evaluate it relative to other options that the marketer chose to highlight. It's easy to see why it doesn't work as well in today's environment, where consumers rely on multiple information sources that are not under anyone's control. The same applies to companies' attempts to "reposition" their brand through a new logo or a catchy phrase. Changing people's perception, which has always been exceptionally difficult, is even more difficult today. It's pointless to try to reposition a company without actual change on the ground. What you say (or how you say it) is less important today. It's more about what you *do*. The name of the game is merit.

In Part I, we discussed the shift from relative evaluations to absolute values, which is driven by the emerging socially intensive information environment. In Part II we saw how this changes marketing forever. Now let's move on to Part III, where we discuss a new framework that should help marketers make more effective decisions.

III

A New Framework

9

THE INFLUENCE MIX

WE DOUBT THAT many readers of this book frequently visit certain fan pages on Facebook, such as those dedicated to paper towel brands like Bounty or Brawny. So if you've ever wondered what's happening on those pages when you're not looking, here's a quick snapshot from a random week in the winter of 2012. On the Bounty page, the moderator asked fans: "Have an endless to do list? If only Bounty could wipe away some chores. What do you want to wipe away this week?" Nineteen people had something to say about that. At the Brawny Towels page, a different question was presented: "Eat a Red Apple Day is tomorrow. Name one of the messiest recipes that calls for apples!" Thirty-four people responded (applesauce seemed to be the winner).

With marketers' rush to social media, we often see strategies that are adopted across categories without much attention to how well they are aligned with the way consumers make decisions in a certain domain. Inviting fans to "join the conversation" can be perfect in some categories, but the potential impact of engaging consumers in a conversation about paper towels is limited at best.

Things work differently in different categories. The shifts we describe in this book will not happen evenly across the board.

There are areas where they are in full swing, then there are areas where they are progressing very slowly, and there are domains they will most likely never reach. We don't expect these trends to apply in the same way to cars and paper towels, to well-connected and to less connected consumers, and to decisions made with or without time pressure. In this chapter we introduce a framework—the Influence Mix—that lays the foundation for this discussion. Simply put, this framework should help marketers determine the relevance of the trends we've described to their particular situation. From brands losing their role as proxies for quality to the declining effectiveness of persuasion techniques—the extent to which these trends apply to a particular firm depends on its customers' Influence Mix.

We start with a simple idea: A person's decision to buy is affected by a mix of three related sources:

- The individual's *Prior* preferences, beliefs, and experiences (P)
- Others. *Other* people and information services (O)
- *Marketers* (M)

For example, when you buy a new cell phone, you're influenced by your prior attitudes, habits, and pre-stored information (P), by your friends, reviewers, and experts (O), and by the cell phone marketer (M). Let's briefly discuss the main characteristics of each of these sources.

P—Often Vague and Unstable

Prior preferences refer to all the consumer's pre-stored information, attitudes, beliefs, and feelings about something. As consumers, we like to think that our preferences are well defined and clear, but this is often not the case. As we explained in Chapter 2, because preferences (especially for less frequently purchased products) are often vague and not so stable, they can be influenced by the context (or the options that happen to be in front of you), how you are asked to express your preferences, and the description of options.

Although we have argued that these arbitrary influences become less effective and controllable in the new environment, there is still plenty of evidence that preferences can be influenced. Such vagueness and instability are inherent to preferences and are unlikely to change regardless of the amount of available information. P also has a stable, "harder" part, which we will discuss later in this chapter, but if we have to leave you with a couple of keywords regarding P, we would say that, more often than not, these words would be "vague" or "unstable."

O—Often Trusted and Diverse

O is an umbrella notation that we use for "other people" and information services. It includes all the information sources other than P or M: reviews from other users, expert opinions, price comparison tools, and other emerging technologies or sources. When making purchase decisions, consumers want to make good decisions and avoid risk. And O is often regarded as the most useful source. In some cases (as many consumers have learned from experience) information from O can be just as biased as information from M, but even when that is the case, many consumers perceive the opinions of O as more credible. They love the feeling of "going behind the back" of M to get the real scoop from O. A big asset of O is in its richness and the nuanced information it provides, which derives in part from the large and diverse sample size. When you look at a hotel on a review site, you see it through the eyes of dozens, sometimes hundreds of reviewers. These reviews are based on different times people visited the hotel, the particular employees who happened to serve them, and each reviewer's specific point of view. O includes a wide range of information providers and influencers, which are quite diverse in terms of their characteristics, how they are perceived, and their roles across product and service categories and consumer segments. Within the different O contributors there is kind of a division of labor, with each party doing what it can do best. For example, while regular users tend to emphasize their experience, experts such as *Consumer Reports* or CNET emphasize what they do better—comparison of specs and objective performance.

M—"The Usual Suspect"

It won't come as a surprise to most readers that consumers don't trust marketers as much as marketers would like them to. At its core, this doesn't originate from marketers being dishonest but from the fact that they have an obvious vested interest. Given this inherent mistrust, it may sound surprising that people even look at ads, engage with brands on Facebook, or visit company websites, but this can be easily explained. For one, consumers are often fine with getting basic information from brands; they trust marketers when it comes to specifications, color, availability, or special deals. (The number-one reason for why consumers "like" brands on Facebook is to be eligible for special offers.)[1] But when it comes to assessment of the quality of a product, marketers are not seen as objective as experts or other consumers.

WHEN "VAGUE" MEETS "TRUSTED"

We think of the Influence Mix as a zero-sum game. For any given decision, the greater the reliance on one source, the lower the need for other sources. So a rise in the weight of one factor must come at the expense of another. For example, if the impact of O on your camera purchase goes up, the influence of M and/or P must be lower. To be clear, we're not talking about a Rock, Paper, Scissors game among P, O, and M, with one source coming on top. It's simply that the three sources are compensatory and together drive decisions, so an increase in one diminishes (but usually doesn't eliminate) the importance of another.

Reliance on information sources is, of course, a function of their costs and benefits, and in the past decade we've seen a significant rise in benefits and a simultaneous decline in costs of information from O, which has drastically increased the relative contribution of this source.[2] The main winner is O and the main loser is M because in most cases O is a direct, dominating substitute for M. Marketers' self-interest makes them inherently suspect, whereas O (despite its limitations) offers much richer and more credible information about products.

What about P? Why doesn't P take over the mix more often? To understand the answer, a few more words are due about its vagueness. There's a great scene in the Marx Brothers movie *Duck Soup* in which Chico tries to pass himself off as Groucho. He places a fake mustache under his nose and sticks a cigar in his mouth, but one of the characters, Mrs. Gloria Teasdale, is skeptical because she just saw the real Groucho leave the room. To persuade her that he indeed is Groucho, Chico delivers a killer argument: "Well, who you gonna believe, me or your own eyes?"[3] As it turns out, this line is not as absurd as it might sound. There are experiments that show that sometimes we are willing to rely so much on other people, that we are willing to push aside not only our preferences, but the evidence in front of us.[4] And plenty of research shows that people's beliefs and preferences are often ill-defined, so information from O may overshadow prior beliefs and perceptions.

We can think of the impact of O in terms of the classic economic distinction between "search goods" and "experience goods."[5] The quality of search goods and their attributes, such as the beauty of flowers, can be inspected and determined before purchase, whereas experience goods and their attributes, such as cars, movies, and new types of food, can be assessed accurately only after gaining personal experience.[6] Now, if reliable O provides accurate information about quality, then more and more products become effectively like search goods, for which quality can be assessed before purchase. In fact, in many (but certainly not all) cases, the information available before purchase is a better predictor of an individual's long-term consumption experience than that person's own initial personal experience with the product. For example, a car may have an unexpected problem during the first week of ownership, but its reliability ratings, for example, in J. D. Power and *Consumer Reports,* are likely to be better predictors of the consumer's long-term experience with that car.

If you're looking for a summary of how influence is transforming in many categories, here it is: Since P is vague and unstable, other sources usually capture "decision share" from it. In the past, M gladly played this role, but with the rise in availability of O (which is perceived as more informative and reliable), O is taking over.

NOT SO FAST, MY FRIEND

It's important to understand that while the last paragraph reflects the general trend, there are cases in which P or M still dominates the mix. If you're a parent, we're sure you're well aware that O has its limits. Your children don't automatically like brussels sprouts or broccoli just because they see you eat them and hear from you how good they are. People can have strong preferences that dominate their decisions. Consider how the authors of this book feel about dark chocolate. Emanuel cannot stand it. Itamar, on the other hand, considers 90 percent cocoa content chocolate a healthy delicacy and has communicated his love for this confection to Emanuel many times (some would say, too many times). But this O influence has not left a dent on Emanuel's preferences. Ads or articles that highlight the health benefits of dark chocolate have not been successful, either. In other words, Emanuel's deeply rooted, well-rehearsed (negative) preferences for this product don't leave much room for O or M influence. There are cases where P is clear and transparent, and in those cases it dominates the decision.

Think about how you feel about cilantro, licorice candy, or jazz. Your preferences for these things are probably stable and very clear to you. Could someone simply trick you into liking or disliking these things? Probably not. You either like jazz or you don't. The existence of stable preferences sounds pretty obvious, but for the past few decades, researchers in the area of behavioral decision theory have raised serious doubts about the existence of any such stable preferences (except for repeat, habitual decisions and brand loyalty). Instead, the common belief in the field has been that preferences are typically constructed when decisions are made, and then they usually dissipate. Yet in some cases, stable preferences play a bigger role than they get credit for.

Incidentally, the roots of theses stable preferences may surprise you. The results of a study that Itamar recently conducted with Aner Sela from the University of Florida suggest that people's preferences for jazz, chocolate, sci-fi movies, compromises, and (maybe) hybrid cars appear to have a large heritable component. No, people don't have a Prius gene, but the study suggests that a certain combination of heritable traits leads a large group of consumers to behave in a similar way. What does this mean? It means that part of your liking (or disliking) of dark chocolate doesn't come from your experience with chocolate and from M and O influence. Rather, it may be in your DNA. (Notice the words "part" and "may." Nobody is arguing that chocolate preferences are totally genetic. And it will take years before we fully understand the exact meaning of these results.)

When you walk into the supermarket, many of your routine or habitual purchases are dominated by P. Getting milk, bread, and eggs into your shopping cart is a matter of habit and is affected mainly by your prior preferences, leaving little room for M or O influence. Of course, at some point P may have been shaped by M and O. Your long-term preferences for chocolate are also influenced by chocolate inputs in the environment—both the actual chocolate and the abstract concept of chocolate. Everything people around you said about chocolate. All those Hershey's or Cadbury commercials you've seen over the years. So advertising (M) and your friends (O) can, over time, help shape your preferences (P). These external forces can also affect whether your hidden preference tendencies will see the light of day. For instance, while many video game players had the potential to enjoy a motion-sensitive remote, without the creative idea of the Wii inventor that preference would not have come to light.

Our main point is this: With all due respect to O, marketers should understand its proper role in each category. While people may, once in a while, talk about paper towels, their choice is not significantly influenced by their peers in this domain. Even in categories that people discuss more often, the chatter doesn't always mean that O dominates the decision. Here's an example: Around the turn of the millennium, everybody was talking about Krispy Kreme doughnuts. Nicole Kidman reportedly referred to them as "God's gift to doughnut lovers" and, according to *Fast Company*, Willard Scott of NBC revealed that he worships in "the church of Krispy Kreme." At first, this may seem to imply that the Influence Mix was dominated by O, but think about the way consumers make decisions in this domain. While it's true that people tell their friends about a new doughnut place (and we've seen a few doughnut shops with more than a thousand reviews on Yelp), by and large people don't decide on getting a doughnut by reading reviews, listening to Nicole Kidman, or conducting extensive research. Having lots of people buzz about your product can certainly be a good thing, but it doesn't automatically mean that O is a major component in consumers' decisions. When it comes to doughnuts, decisions are influenced by things like prior preferences, store location, and promotional activities, which means that managers like those at Krispy Kreme should not be blinded by the buzz about their brand (which is bound to die out, as it did around 2004 for Krispy Kreme) and should continue to invest in marketing activities such as coupons and other promotions.[7]

When O or P don't play a major role in a purchase decision, it means that room is left for M influence. Think about buying a toothbrush, for example. Standing at the drugstore in front of an aisle of toothbrushes, a shopper is likely to be influenced by whatever is at her eye level, the packaging of the product, and by brand. So makers of toothbrushes are likely to operate under different rules than carmakers, for example. Yet too often we hear sweeping generalizations about "marketing" regardless of the product category.

SO WHAT'S YOUR CUSTOMERS' MIX?

Marketers must understand their customers' current and future Influence Mix, that is, the importance of P, O, and M for their customers' purchase decisions, given the product category, their customers' characteristics (which, of course, vary by customer segment), and the brand position. As a framework, the Influence Mix can help marketers analyze how the weights of the three sources are likely to evolve over time and, accordingly, how much and where to invest their marketing dollars. Put a different way, your Influence Mix can help you understand the significance of absolute evaluations in your case, and, in turn, this may determine whether your company should use its traditional marketing framework or adopt a whole new way of looking at things.

The critical questions for you to ask are: To what extent do my customers currently depend on O and on specific O types or ingredients in making their purchase decision, and to what extent might they depend on O in the future? Since we're not dealing with a yes/no question, we present the answer on a continuum. The trends described in this book are relevant to you to the extent that information sources other than P or M are being used by your customers. The closer your customers are located to the O-Dependent end of this continuum, the more significant these trends are in your situation.

O-Independent   O-Dependent

If you operate in a completely O-Independent domain (the left side of the continuum), this means that most of your customers do not rely on O at all in their purchase decision, and even among those exposed to O, the impact of that information on purchase decisions is negligible. If you sell clothes hangers, your customers are just around the "O-Independent" end on the left. At the other end of the continuum—the O-Dependent end—you can find customers for products and services where the purchase decision is more influenced by O. For example, the decision to join a social networking site such as Facebook is heavily influenced by other people because the service itself is all about interacting with others. For most companies, the answer is somewhere in between these two extreme cases. Here are some of the general factors that affect your customers' location on this continuum:

- *Decision importance*

  Consumers are less likely to invest their time in researching things that are less important to them. Buying a laptop is much more important than buying paper towels, so a lot of what we said earlier applies to the first and not to the latter. For example, the decline of brand as a quality proxy applies less to Bounty and more to Dell. Important decisions move your customers to the right.

- *Quality and differentiation*

  The percentage of consumers who bother to take advantage of available quality information also depends on the importance of product quality information and, relatedly, on product differentiation. For example, when it comes to a not-so-important commodity like paper clips, quality information is not particularly important, both because paper clips are not very important for most consumers and because quality differentiation is limited.

- *Risk and uncertainty*

  Decisions involving greater risk tend to move things toward the O-Dependent end. The risk can be monetary or psychological. That's why you should expect more O for new products. Risk also relates to product complexity. Both novice and expert purchasers of more technically complex products are likely to rely on O. Risk, uncertainty, and complexity tend to move your customers to the right of the continuum.

- *The rate of change in your category*
Change leads to uncertainty, risk, and a need to keep up with the latest, so if you operate in an industry with frequent new entrants, changes in market share, and new features and capabilities, it is likely that your customers depend on O. Changes in your category move your customers to the right.

- *Usefulness of O*
The ability to assess quality and fit by listening to others differs from category to category. When a friend tells you that her new printer is amazingly reliable, this is a matter of experience and this information is likely to be useful to you. However, if this friend tells you about a new dress she bought, this information may or may not be useful. It's a matter of taste. (You may still seek information from those who are in your taste segment, but P is likely to play a significant role in your final decision.)

- *Network externalities*
The benefits of buying a popular product are significant in the technology sector. If you buy a phone that nobody else uses, it may be hard to find accessories. So you want to find out what others use. Conversely, this is not a consideration when you buy furniture, for example. In fact, sometimes popularity has a negative effect (for example, for some consumers, wearing the same perfume as others or owning the same furniture is a negative).

- *Public consumption*
We can expect the impact of O to be greater with respect to publicly consumed products. Everyone sees what car you drive, what phone you use, so O is a consideration in their purchase.

Public consumption moves customers to the right on the continuum.

Your customers' location on the O-influence continuum may vary across your products and, for a given product, across customer segments. In fact, you may find that segmenting your customers based on their location on the continuum is a more useful segmentation variable than most other traditional segmentation bases (such as demographics, psychographics, benefits, etc.). In Chapter 11, which is dedicated to market research, we'll discuss what can be done to assess your customers' location on the continuum.

How does a category's life cycle stage affect customers' location along the influence continuum? Risk and quality variability obviously tend to be greater in early stages of a category development, which suggests that early adopters will pay close attention to the available O to reduce the risk. But these days buyers can also easily benefit from O when the category matures. Consider microwave ovens, which reached the maturity phase a long time ago. At this point, the impact of a brand name is much smaller, whereas value for the money and specs and features are more important. So people do seek information from current users and experts about the best overall options, recognizing that brand names are poor proxies and may not represent the companies that actually make the products. Also, as the category matures, we would expect the quantity and reliability of O to increase, which should lead to greater reliance on O.

NOT SET IN STONE

Your customers' location on the continuum is not set in stone and should be seen as the current state in an evolving trend. Since the rise of O is an ongoing process and is very much driven by technology, it's possible that new tools will allow O to take over in domains that are currently dominated by M or P. That's why marketers should be on the lookout for game-changing technologies (and changes in consumer behavior) that might lead to new types of information sources and O-influencers. The trends we discuss here may be vaguely relevant to a company today but increasingly important only a few years later. For example, if large communication screens that let us chat with family and friends become ubiquitous in our kitchens, O's importance may increase for products we use when cooking. Here's a hypothetical example that may become a reality someday in the future: Picture a home device that measures the free radicals in your blood. Lots of marketers claim that their products reduce free radicals by providing antioxidants. An accurate and inexpensive device will reduce M's influence in the mix as the device will replace the marketer in assessing this claim.

The information vehicles consumers rely on affect the mix as well. Lots of people still watch TV, and TVs are perfectly suited for M's influence. You sit in front of a large screen watching your favorite program when a commercial comes on. In contrast, mobile phones, which have taken the world by storm, are inherently less M-friendly. The screen is small and the user switching options are easy and numerous. Consumers are less likely to stare at a commercial on their cell phone than on their TV, so this technology further contributes to the decline in M's ability to influence.

Channels of distribution and of customer acquisition are important drivers of your customers' location on the continuum as well. Certain channels are more conducive to O, whereas others are much less so. This has important practical implications. Think of car insurance, for example: Such services are sold often one-on-one or by phone, making reviews less accessible. If a company such as Amazon were to start offering car insurance, we'd expect to see more reviews that have greater impact. In other words, it would make O more accessible. If you are an established player like Geico or State Farm, with high brand equity and a high advertising budget, you have no reason to promote or rush into such comparison-friendly channels. If, on the other hand, you are a newcomer, you should promote O-friendly channels that make options more comparable and thus limit the role of brand equity and loyalty. We suggest that, sooner or later, the big brands won't be able to fight the inherent impact of O, and the most efficient channels will prevail.

In general, your customers' location on the continuum can move as O information becomes more widely available, and we can expect (and observe) greater reliance on it. Products that were considered "low involvement" in the past can move toward "high involvement" as information becomes more accessible and diagnostic. For example, it used to be difficult to find out the nutritional value of food in fast-food restaurants. Today you can look it up on the Web or use apps like HealthyOut or Fast Food Calorie Lookup and get the answer in seconds. So, for certain segments, pre-purchase search is becoming more extensive and common in the fast-food category, moving them to the O-Dependent side.

IN A HURRY?

Here's a fun exercise. On the next Black Friday, set your alarm clock to 3 A.M., drive to your nearest department store, and stand in line with some other folks who are half asleep. Then, when the store staff opens the doors, rush in with everyone else. Okay, maybe it's not that much fun. You can save yourself the trip and watch some videos from previous Black Fridays on YouTube. (We provide some links from the book's website.) Whether you go there yourself or watch the video, you'll be observing people making decisions under time pressure: people grabbing boxes into their shopping carts just because there's a SALE sign over the display, people blindly following the crowd, people buying "bargains" that aren't really. And most likely, you'll see this happen with typical O-Dependent categories such as consumer electronics. Our point is this: The degree to which a consumer relies on O depends not only on the category but also on various contextual or situational factors. Some of the same people who grab products indiscriminately on Black Friday may take full advantage of information when they shop under different conditions (for example, online), but with not much time to decide they are susceptible to relative influences, relying on the general belief that "if it's on sale on Black Friday, it must be a bargain."[8]

Here's another example of a situational factor that determines the degree to which a decision is O-Dependent. We came across a product review on Amazon that really confused us. It was a review for a particular model of a self-cleaning litter box, written by a woman named Teresa. To say that Teresa didn't like the product would be an understatement. She said it was expensive, the lid did not close properly, and the gears got clogged with her cat's litter, so she had to clean them with Q-tips. Just six months after she bought it, the machine started making horrible noises so Teresa turned it off. "It was a complete disappointment," Teresa wrote in her review, and gave the product one star out of five.[9] What confused us was the fact that before she bought the product, 240 (!) other customers gave the same product a one-star review. They all begged potential buyers not to follow in their footsteps, with headlines such as: "Junk! Save Your Money!!!" or "Don't waste your money on this model!" And yet Teresa shelled out almost $150 for this item.

Why would anyone buy a product that "stinks literally and figuratively" (as one of Teresa's fellow reviewers put it)? Why would anyone buy a product with more than two hundred one-star reviews?

When a decision is made at the point of purchase without much prior deliberation, then brand name, price, an enticing product description, and other quality proxies still exert great influence. This is what happened with Teresa: It was an impulse purchase at a brick-and-mortar store. She didn't see all those negative online reviews before she bought. Confined to the local context, she was susceptible to much more M influence. (Maybe the product was at her eye level, perhaps she was familiar with the brand, maybe it was sold at a discount.) It was only when she decided, out of frustration, to write her own review that she discovered she was not the first to have such an experience with this particular model.

Point of purchase at brick-and-mortar stores will still be a place where consumers are susceptible to relative influence. Smartphones are likely, over time, to reduce this effect (even on Black Friday, where we see people using apps like ShopSavvy to check prices), but this won't happen overnight. So marketers of inferior products can (unfortunately) get away with mediocre products by focusing their efforts on point-of-purchase promotions in brick-and-mortar stores. It's also worth noting that choice overload can be a problem in this context. Unlike the Web, where sorting tools are available, in a store environment (for example, the cereal aisle at the supermarket) too many options can indeed be overwhelming and harder to choose from.

There are other situations where consumers are confined to the local context. Casinos are designed with no windows or clocks on the walls so that you're less aware of how late it is and are more likely to pay attention to what the casino owners want you to focus on.[10] If you're on a flight with no Internet access, you may be enticed to buy not-so-useful products from the in-flight catalog. On one especially long flight, Emanuel ordered a system of weights you hold between your teeth to supposedly tone the definition of your jawline (He was disappointed). When you're in a foreign country, you have limited access to information because of language barriers. Itamar recently paid $85 for long underwear (an American brand!) in Beijing. (It was minus-15 Celsius, or about minus-5 Fahrenheit, which also introduced some urgency to the situation.)

A STRONG BRAND CAN PARTIALLY CONTROL THE IMPACT OF O

Who is more O-Dependent, Apple or a lesser-known brand? Instinctively you may answer Apple because "everybody's talking about Apple." The answer, however, is more complex. Before taking a risk by acquiring a lesser-known brand, consumers are likely to pay close attention to what previous adopters are saying. What matters is the perceived risk associated with the particular brand. High-risk options tend to be closer to the O–Dependent end. A company like Apple may be somewhat protected from the impact of O but not to the degree that some observers believe. There is no doubt that Apple and a few other brands don't need to do much in order to get attention—any new Apple product is an event. If a new Apple product then gets favorable reviews from users and experts, success is virtually guaranteed. In fact, assuming the product is not a total disappointment, Apple loyalists may buy it even if the reviews are not so favorable. But while Apple (at this time) and a few other brands may be protected from O to some degree, most brands don't have that luxury—each new product must pass the O test. In a way, you can see a (very) strong brand as a credit line you build with customers. Consistent top performance may create such a level of confidence among your customers that they don't feel the need to check with other sources. Realistically, though, this credit line is something that only a handful of brands can enjoy, and even for them, it can be short-lived.

Don't expect to be able to determine that your customers' decisions are based on, say, 30 percent P, 60 percent O, and 10 percent M. The Influence Mix is an analytical framework, not a precise measurement tool. Separating the three sources can be sometimes tricky, in part because their relative contributions depend on your time perspective (and one component depends on the others). As we pointed out, much of people's P has been acquired over time from O and M. Accordingly, whether a particular piece of information, a judgment, or a decision criterion falls under P depends on the applicable time frame. We focus here on the mix during the purchase process. But even though precise accounting of the relative contributions of information sources cannot be accomplished, it is possible to make broad qualitative observations regarding trends in their relative impact. Based on these qualitative observations, marketers can balance their marketing efforts to where they are likely to have the greatest impact.

In this chapter, we offered a framework that should help businesses determine the relevance of the trends we've described to their particular situation. The extent to which these trends apply to a particular firm depends on its customers' Influence Mix. The big trend that we've been pointing out throughout this book is higher O-influence among consumers. But let's not get carried away. What's true for cars or tablets doesn't necessarily apply to other categories. Marketers should avoid blindly following trends and adopt the philosophy du jour. Instead, they should align their activities with the way consumers make decisions in their specific situation. Having said that, the way consumers make decisions in a particular domain may change. So marketers should be on the lookout for game-changing technologies (and consumer behavior) that might lead to new types of information sources and O-influencers. Your customers' location on the continuum is not set in stone. Since the rise of O is an ongoing process and is very much driven by technology, it's possible that new tools will allow O to take over in domains that are currently dominated by M or by P.

10

COMMUNICATION:
MATCH YOUR CUSTOMERS' INFLUENCE MIX

PERHAPS THE BIGGEST area of confusion among marketers these days is understanding what is changing and what is not. Most marketers recognize that the times are changing, but many have not adjusted their strategies accordingly. Others have adopted "consumer empowerment" and "spend your marketing dollars where your customers spend their spare time" mantras, which they apply indiscriminately. We advocate a more nuanced approach. Marketers can greatly benefit from developing a deeper understanding of where they may have an impact on consumers and where their efforts are less likely to work. Their communication program for each product and target segment should follow their customers' location on the influence continuum.

To start with, marketers need to figure out their customers' Influence Mix and where their customers are, by segment, in terms of their dependence on O. They then need to determine the corresponding "effective mix." Quite simply, marketers' effective mix is derived from the key sources of influence on their customers' decisions. For example, sophisticated camera buyers may rely primarily on sites created by fellow photographers and experts. These customers may pay little attention to advertisements in social media, on TV, and other marketer-controlled media. If so, the effective mix should reflect this influence mix.

In general, those marketers operating in primarily O-*Independent* categories can hang on to some old rules, but be on the lookout for game-changing customer behavior and technologies. We'll discuss those toward the end of this chapter. Let's start with the growing number of marketers who find their customers closer to the O-Dependent end of the continuum.

NEW RULES. NEW ROLES

Throughout this book, we've been discussing the new rules that apply to O-Dependent domains. Let's recap some of the key conclusions:

- In an increasing number of categories, brands are losing their role as proxies for quality.
- A consumer's past satisfaction is not as important as it used to be in making purchase decisions.
- Consumers' loyalty is declining and is a weaker driver of future purchases.
- Positioning and persuasion techniques are less effective than in the past.
- Sales tactics that try to capitalize on consumer "irrationality" and preference instability don't work as effectively as one would expect from reading books and articles on the subject.
- Emotional appeals face tougher competition from the abundant "rational" information.
- The verdict about new products is reached faster, which makes the traditional classification of adopter types less relevant.

In a world dominated by these new rules, marketers will play new roles that can be radically different from the ones they played in the past. Marketers should stop thinking of themselves as the drivers of consumers' purchase decisions and embrace their role as followers. Another way to put it: Because their customers shifted their attention from M to O, these marketers need to focus on O as well, especially where they can do something about it. Your customers' Influence Mix essentially determines the effectiveness (or ineffectiveness) of various marketing tools. While understanding the mix can help in many areas, it has the most immediate implications to the way companies gain insight about the market (the topic of the next chapter) and to the way they communicate with the world, which we'll discuss here.

Yes, there are marketers who genuinely recognize the shift, but by and large, marketers still see themselves as having a major impact on consumers' perceptions, preferences, and purchase decisions. If you open most marketing textbooks or attend an executive education program today, you'll essentially see guidelines that are supposed to put the marketer in the driver's seat. According to most textbooks, if marketers properly segment, target, position, and tailor their tools, consumers will likely buy their products. These texts may still apply to the O–Independent side of the continuum but they are much less relevant for the growing group of products and services on the O–Dependent side. Having said that, this does not mean that marketers have no role in communication. Although their role has been reduced, marketers should still understand where they can make the greatest contribution and what that contribution may be.

GENERATING INTEREST
(NOT TOP-OF-MIND AWARENESS)

The death of advertising has been pronounced many times. Regis McKenna predicted the obsolescence of advertising more than twenty years ago.[1] Al and Laura Ries put it succinctly in *The Fall of Advertising and the Rise of PR*: "Advertising is Dead. Long Live PR."[2] While we agree that the power of advertising has been reduced, we doubt that it will ever disappear. The key is to understand advertising's very specific role in O-Dependent domains. In a nutshell, advertisers should focus on generating interest, not on creating top-of-mind awareness or on persuasion. This distinction is important to understand.

The established assumption whereby brands must be in the consumer's consideration set in order to have a chance to be considered when a decision is made is less relevant today. Easy access to information and the rapid changes in the marketplace mean that consumers tend to seek up-to-date information and the latest best options when a decision is about to be made.[3] In other words, consideration sets are actively created when it counts, and are less likely to be constructed based on the names that come to mind. Furthermore, merely making a name top-of-mind doesn't do much in categories where consumers rely on experts or other users to figure out which options deserve to be considered. Top-of-mind advertising is commonly used on the Web, with (increasingly intrusive) banner ads and the like. We also see more movie and TV product placements, such as American Airlines and Hilton in George Clooney's 2009 movie *Up in the Air* and a variety of Sony products in the James Bond movie *Casino Royale*. Marketers who use this practice hope that seeing their brand again and again will make consumers more likely to think of their brand when it's time to buy. Banner ads and product placements may still serve as reminders, but when it's time to buy, consumers will rely on more trusted sources, which will likely override any residual effect of exposure to banner ads. Yet many marketers blindly follow the rule that they have to be where consumers are. If consumers are on Facebook, they have to spend their advertising dollars on Facebook, whether or not they are effective—just to be "top-of-mind."

Instead of top-of-mind ads that focus on a brand name, the goal of advertising should be to generate interest in the product's advantages. This can happen at two stages: before or, most important, when and where a decision is made. Let's start with the latter. Advertisers should place ads closer to the "moment of truth" (for example, use search engine or retail website ads). That is, marketers should focus on absolute advertising regarding features that count, and that information should be readily accessible and easy to comprehend at the point of purchase (for example, on the Web page where the product is sold).

Advertising can also be most effective when it's successful in generating enough interest for the consumer to add it to his "watch list" (see our discussion of "couch tracking" in Chapter 3), which enhances the long-term likelihood that this will lead to purchase. Consider the following YouTube video: NBA star LeBron James is eating breakfast with his family as his son is playing with his dad's phone (a Samsung Galaxy Note II). "What're you doing over there?" James asks suspiciously. "Nothing . . . ," the boy says smiling. We, the viewers, can see that junior is using the phone's stylus to decorate a photo of his father with a bright red Afro. When he hands his dad's phone back to its lawful owner, the family gets a good laugh. Cut to a text message from Magic Johnson: "Congrats, young fella. Nothing like the first one. Enjoy the big night!" Cut to James video-chatting with a class at some school that is holding a big sign: "Congratulations, LeBron!" At a local food truck in Miami, LeBron is posing for a picture with fans. Next he's at a local barbershop getting a shave. As the barber works on the star's hairline (which has been subject to some mockery), LeBron and friends watch a video of the dunk sensation Porter Maberry (who's five foot five but dunks like a seven foot seven). Finally, LeBron arrives at the basketball arena for the highlight of the day—members of the Miami Heat team receive their championship rings. He folds the elegant flip cover and puts his phone in his pocket.

When Samsung went to market with its Samsung Galaxy Note II, they produced this ninety-second video.[4] Last time we checked, this video had more than 40 million hits on YouTube. A similar version was aired on TV and got nice attention from viewers.[5] The interest is driven by James, but it's not a "top-of-mind" ad that tries to drill in the brand name with the hope that you'll remember it one day. It's an ad that shows you a new phone with the hope it'll invoke your interest and get you to look for more information. Unique features are of course important for triggering interest. Stylus, video chat, the Galaxy Note II's screen size, flip cover—all get their screen time. Of course, if user and expert reviews were negative, the interest generated wouldn't lead anywhere, but in this case the high interest was coupled with high ratings from users, which has been reflected in sales.

This doesn't mean that the only way to generate interest is to sign up deals with NBA stars or have a giant advertising budget. Here's a campaign that utilized totally different tools and is for a much less glamorous product than a smartphone. Still, it focused on generating interest in a product, and not on simply creating awareness. The Scotch Thermal Laminator is a small machine (the size of a small printer) that allows users to protect documents. This isn't a product that is likely to get much attention on tech blogs or at the physical channel where it is usually hidden on some bottom shelf. Using Amazon's Vine program (in which reviewers are invited to post opinions about products), 3M sent the Laminator to the top reviewers on Amazon.[6] When you look at a laminator and its specifications, it's a pretty boring piece of machinery. Reviews can bring a product like this to life. This is what happened once the reviews came in: Parents talked about how they use it to immortalize their kids' artwork; teachers described how helpful it is in the classroom; someone explained how this lets him read his Bible study papers in the hot tub. . . . Once people have such a tool, they start laminating everything: aging sheet music, family documents, ID cards, recipes. . . . How did 3M use this to generate further interest? Once the product had several hundred reviews, 3M partnered with a large office retailer and emailed its customers some information from these reviews with a special offer. In other words, it created interest by bringing O to people's attention. "It made the Laminator into one of the fastest growing SKU's in our consumer business" Raj Rao, vice president of Global eTransformation at 3M, told us.[7]

COMMUNICATING THROUGH O

By definition, consumers in O-Dependent domains are focused on O, which makes it increasingly difficult for marketers to influence them directly. It's difficult to get consumers' interest and even more difficult to persuade them or shape their preferences. Marketers in an increasing number of categories should understand, therefore, that their primary role is shifting from persuasion to communicating with consumers *through* O.

Social media is important in our context, but in very specific ways that don't necessarily correspond with what you frequently hear these days. There are two misconceptions that marketers have in the way they view social media. First, many marketers view social media as yet another instrument in their arsenal of persuasion tools. Our Influence Mix framework may shed some light on the limitations of this view. Social media sites like Twitter or Facebook can be used to transmit information from either O or M. When they are used by consumers to communicate with each other (for example, when a consumer tweets about her new car) we consider this O. In contrast, when a company uses a social media site (for example, when GM tweets about a new model or posts a video on YouTube), we view this as M. This distinction is important because M—even when it uses social media—is still likely to be perceived as biased because of its vested interest. We'll elaborate in a moment, but the main point is this: Trying to persuade consumers that your product is the best has become less effective even if it's done via social media. Marketers should not lose sight of their ultimate goal, which is to stimulate genuine consumer content that will help consumers evaluate their likely experience with a product.

The second misconception is that some observers still frame social media under old concepts that are becoming less relevant. For example, we hear a lot about using social media for brand building or for fostering loyalty. Some suggest that social media lets consumers become even more loyal as they start advocating for a brand. It won't come as a surprise to our readers that we have some reservations. While there are some consumers who are active advocates and who bond with a brand (and yes, there are a few brands like Harley-Davidson where this advocacy and loyalty may be shared among many customers), by and large, consumers will rely less on brand and loyalty when making a decision, and instead will be likely to look around for the best product recommended by experts and other users. Those who are most likely to take advantage of special offers on a brand's page are those who are already fans or those looking for special offers. We also hear about using social media to create an emotional connection with consumers. One should be cautious here, too. As we pointed out, when consumers listen mostly to O (which tends to communicate "rational" reasons to buy), there's less of a chance that they'll be affected by long-term emotional ties to a company, even if these ties were created through social media. As we said earlier, emotions often play an important role in buying decisions and they can certainly be evoked through social media. Our point is that when consumers are immersed in rational information, the relative role of these emotions is reduced.

In the old days, the three main tasks of marketing communication were: generate interest, build preference for the product, and encourage purchase. (Of course, this is a simplified view, but it will serve us here.) Marketers are limited in generating interest in O-Dependent categories because consumers are focused on O. This is even more acute when it comes to preference formation. As we discussed, it's almost pointless to try to persuade people that they should prefer your product when they can (and do) easily turn to more reliable sources. So where can marketers make a difference in regards to preference formation? Increasingly, their key task on this front will be to make sure that each consumer can easily find O content that is relevant, recent, and helpful. To remove any doubt, we are not talking about planting fake reviews or any other similar methods. We are talking about open, transparent recruitment of honest opinions from experts or from actual consumers who have experienced a product or a service.

This is also the place to point out that not all "O" is created equal. The best O content helps the consumer get closer to knowing her likely experience with a product. The impact of a "Like" on Facebook in that sense is not the same as a thorough product review by a respected blogger. A re-tweet of some company promotion is not the same as a video review on YouTube that presents the pros and cons of a new smartphone. Of course, when consumers relay a message from M (such as a re-tweet or sharing a link to video), there's an implicit endorsement that somewhat reduces M's perceived bias. But the impact of such brief and public endorsements tends to be weaker than some other forms of communication.

MODERATING REVIEWS (AND WHY EVEN BAD ONES CAN HELP)

Marketers play a smaller role when it comes to preference formation, but one that should not be ignored. Names such as Reevoo, Bazaarvoice, or PowerReviews may not be familiar to all readers, yet the activities of these companies can help us understand what actions marketers can take on this front.[8] Let's take a quick look at one such company—Bazaarvoice. What does Bazaarvoice do exactly? First, they handle the collection and moderation of reviews for companies such as 3M, Lego, LG, Microsoft, and Samsung. Then they syndicate this content to retail sites around the world. So when you read product reviews on Walmart.com, BestBuy.com, or Costco.com, the vendor behind the scenes is Bazaarvoice.

Having plenty of reviews for each product or service is valuable to the consumer for several reasons. First, a large sample increases the chance that the reviews reflect the consumer's likely experience. Second, the likelihood that a few manipulated reviews will affect the overall ratings decreases as the number of reviews increases. Third, having recent reviews reassures the customer that they are likely to experience a similar level of service to what was described by other customers (a hotel that was last reviewed two years ago leaves a potential guest with too many questions). And fourth, in order for a consumer to find reviews that are relevant to her specific requirements, she needs to start with a large set. Bazaarvoice software allows a customer to sort the reviews by different attributes, so, for example, a customer who's looking for makeup can focus on reviews written by people with similar hair or eye color.

Companies such as Reevoo or Bazaarvoice solicit reviews from verified buyers to maximize the number of reviews that are based on actual experience. While the reviews are screened for profanity and other forms of offensive language, negative reviews are not filtered out. Brett Hurt, the cofounder of Bazaarvoice, told us that, perhaps surprisingly, they find that including negative reviews can actually drive sales. First, negative reviews signal to consumers that they are shopping in an authentic environment. This means that they can trust the positive reviews for the product (or other products on the site). Second, people's preferences differ, so one person's negative can be another person's positive. For example, a novice photographer who's shopping for a digital camera may read some reviews by serious hobbyists who slam a certain model for lacking power features. This may convey to the novice user that this is exactly the camera he's looking for.[9]

This is a good place to explain something important about the way people use reviews to learn about their likely experience. Reviews can have an impact even if the consumer disagrees with the comments or the criteria—it can make positive comments appear negative for the reader and vice versa. Specifically, Itamar's research showed that if you see someone disliking a product for reasons that do not apply to you (the reviewer criticizes the camera's manual override capabilities, but you have no intention of using the manual override feature anyway and are content to keep it on auto), you will often evaluate the product more favorably than if you had not been exposed to that review. And similarly, if you see a reviewer who selected a product for a reason that does not apply to you, you'll tend to find that product less attractive. These principles were demonstrated in various product categories. With respect to the effect of reviews, these findings show that the key factor determining the effect of a given review on a consumer is the fit between the content of the review and supporting reasons and the consumer exposed to the review.[10]

The bottom line regarding a marketer's role in preference formation is this: Marketers play a small role here, yet it is one that should not be overlooked. Soliciting, monitoring, and syndicating reviews (and other content) increases the chance that a marketer will get a fair representation by O and that a consumer will get a good idea regarding her likely experience with a product. And obviously we don't mean to say that marketers should be passive. They certainly should highlight the performance advantage of the product in interesting ways, especially to those whose opinions are likely to become public and be consulted by others. Still, even with the most slick communication, the fate of the product will be determined by the product's merit.

When it comes to marketers' role as communicators, we discussed here two parallel trends. One is a shift from creating top-of-mind awareness to generating interest. Another one is a shift from persuasion to communicating with consumers *through* O. The latter is one of the basic principles of word-of-mouth marketing that is beyond the scope of this book. (Emanuel and others have written extensively about this topic.) It also relates to the increasingly important role of public relations. In this respect we do agree with Al and Laura Ries: PR indeed is increasingly important (but this does not mean that advertising is dead, or that it can only be used to maintain brands that have been created by publicity).[11] With the unprecedented access to experts, public relations' efforts to capture the interest of such experts are increasingly important. Again, the specifics of PR are beyond our scope here.

One last point about marketers' role in the future. One thing that won't change is their role in triggering action. In an earlier chapter we said that consumers are likely to reach a faster verdict because when they initiate the information acquisition, they value that information and are inclined to use it. Consumers also have less of a reason to wait when the answer's out there. Still, procrastination is a powerful human trait (as anyone who would glance at our to-do list would conclude), so triggers for action can still make a difference. Incentives and triggers to action are important as ever, even in O–Dependent categories.

FOR MARKETERS OPERATING ON THE O-INDEPENDENT END OF THE CONTINUUM

We dedicated most of this chapter to the O–Dependent side of the continuum and will discuss the other end of the continuum very briefly. The reason is simple: Thousands of books and articles have been written about the old rules of marketing over the years, so there is no point in elaborating on them here. But we'd like to briefly outline the rules that will continue to affect *O-Independent* products and services:

- Brands still play a role as proxies for quality.
- Consumers still rely on their past satisfaction.
- Consumers may stay loyal to a brand.
- Positioning and persuasion techniques can work.
- Emotional appeals are as effective as in the past.
- Consumer preferences are susceptible to various seemingly irrational influences and manipulations.

These rules are well-known and self-explanatory. Our main message to marketers who operate in O–Independent domains is that they shouldn't blindly follow trends that apply to O–Dependent marketers. Again, their communication program should follow the location of their customers on the influence continuum and the derived effective mix. And yet, we still see efforts that don't take into consideration the natural decision process. Poppa D's Nuts is an Orlando, Florida–based start-up that makes butter-toffee peanuts. Their initial marketing focus? Facebook and Twitter. Terrific, but does social media buzz help sell nuts? When *USA Today* talked to the company, they had sold thirty bags at eighteen dollars each.[12] While O can play *some* role in selling snacks, the decision to buy butter-toffee peanuts is clearly dominated by M and P. Having Poppa D's Nuts in stores is really the name of the game (and we were happy to read that now Poppa D's Nuts are available in sports arenas, bars, and some 7-Elevens).[13] Misreading the Influence Mix is not limited to small companies, as we discussed with paper towel activities on Facebook. Or consider the "Lysol Community," an online forum where you're invited to "share your stories, ideas, and tips for cleaning and disinfecting your home." We're sure that some people are into disinfecting. In the face of growing consumers' concerns about the environment they live in, the Lysol community may very well provide a useful service to a certain segment of the population (even if the idea may seem frivolous to some other consumers), but *most consumers* are not likely to "join the conversation" about Lysol, and will not be influenced by their peers in their choice of a household disinfectant.[14] A lot of the talk about consumer empowerment is much less relevant in O-Independent domains, so marketers who operate at that end of the continuum but still believe that "the consumer is in control" may be missing some opportunities. On the O-Independent end, consumers are not much more in control than they were twenty years ago. (Incidentally, this doesn't mean that the consumer is or was a malleable Gumby. Marketing power has been exaggerated for decades.)

The main takeaway from this chapter is this: A company's effective communication program should derive from its customers' Influence Mix and from the location of its customers on the O-influence continuum. Marketers in O-Independent domains can live by some old rules. Things are very different in O-Dependent domains: When it comes to preference formation, there isn't much marketers can do directly. Their role is limited to making sure there's enough (preferably positive) content from O. In generating interest, marketers can play a more significant role in communicating with consumers directly through traditional advertising or social media. Still, since consumers in O–dependent domains are oriented toward O, the best and fastest way to evoke their interest is through O. As far as triggering action, we don't foresee a significant shift. Marketers can still benefit from incentives, promotions, coupons, and other triggers for action.

In addition to their roles in communication, marketers will continue to play an important role in gaining insight regarding a company's future offerings. Here, too, the strategy for achieving this should derive from the location of potential segments on the O–influence continuum. Marketers in O–Independent domains can continue to use some traditional market research, while those operating in O–Dependent areas will have to think differently, which is the focus of our next chapter.

11

MARKET RESEARCH:
FROM PREDICTING TO TRACKING

IN 2007, TEN thousand people around the globe were asked about portable devices—digital cameras, cell phones, MP3 players, and so on. It was part of a massive study conducted by the global media company Universal McCann. One of the hottest topics at the time was the first iPhone, which was announced in January but hadn't yet been released.[1] Once the researchers who conducted the study tallied the results, they reached an interesting conclusion: Convergent products like the iPhone are desired by consumers in countries such as Mexico or India, but not in affluent countries. "There is no real need for a convergent product in the U.S., Germany and Japan," the study stated.[2]

A researcher who was involved in the study explained that users in affluent countries would not be motivated to replace their existing gadgets. "The simple truth: convergence is a compromise driven by financial limitations, not aspiration. In the markets where multiple devices are affordable, the vast majority would prefer that to one device fits all," he told the *Guardian*.[3]

There's a growing feeling among marketers that something is not working with market research. Marketers spend billions of dollars on research every year, but the results are mixed at best. Some of the problems are not new and relate to the basic challenge of using research to predict what consumers will want (especially with respect to products that are radically different). But the problem gets even more difficult for O–Dependent products. There are several issues, but at the most fundamental level, O–Dependent marketers face one additional key problem: Market research usually tries to measure P, but decisions are increasingly based on O.

Participants in market research studies typically indicate their preferences without first checking any other information sources. But as we have discussed, this is very different than the way people shop in reality today. In the Universal McCann study, for example, people were asked to say how much they agree with the statement "I like the idea of having one portable device to fulfill all my needs." Indeed, there was a significant difference between the percentage of people who completely agreed with this statement in Mexico (79 percent) and in the United States (31 percent). So in theory, people in the United States were much less excited about the idea of a phone that's also a camera and a music player.

But it was a different story when people got closer to making a decision. They heard about the iPhone in the media (declaring it a revolutionary device).[4] They saw reports on TV of people standing in line all night to get their hands on the first iPhone. And they started reading blogs and reviews from real users. As iPhones started rolling into the marketplace, the abstract idea of "having one portable device to fulfill all my needs" was replaced by actual reports from people who used it. Users started to experience—and share—the advantage of having 24/7 access to a camera, or not having to carry an iPod in addition to a cell phone.

It's easy to blame the market research firm for this, but this is not our point. We are trying to explain the inherent difficulties in assessing consumers' reaction in this new era. First, as we just discussed, more decisions today are impacted by O, whereas market research measures P. But let's go beyond that: As we discussed, consumers have limited insight into their real preferences. This is especially true with respect to products that are radically different. Universal McCann correctly reported what they found. What market researchers often underestimate, though, is the degree to which consumers are myopic and have difficulty imagining or anticipating a new and very different reality. (Consumers tend to assume they'll continue to like what they like now, and show no appetite for things that look very different.) What makes the task of a market research firm even trickier is that just as consumers' expectations may be wrong (as was the case with the iPhone), there are many cases where industry expectations about what consumers will buy are wrong.

Even when market research techniques are administered in groups (for example, focus groups), it is not their purpose and they are incapable of predicting the behavior of consumers under the influence of other people. For example, focus groups (their known limitations aside) don't reflect other sources that consumers access in today's reality, such as expert opinions, reviews, and other information services. A question that naturally arises is how predictive is individual, disconnected market research when individuals' future perceptions, preferences, and actions are greatly influenced by information that will be acquired from O.

Consider, for example, conjoint analysis, which is often used to estimate how consumers value different product features.[5] Think of a guy named Jim who agreed to participate in such a study. He is presented with several product combinations and is asked to make some choices: Do you prefer a Samsung laptop with 2 GB of RAM, 80 GB hard drive, and 15.6-inch screen? Or would you rather have an HP with 4 GB of RAM, 60 GB hard drive, and 11.6-inch screen? After many similar questions that require Jim to make such choices, the market research firm uses sophisticated statistical techniques to derive the relative importance of different attributes.

This is all very nice. But what happens in reality when Jim is ready to buy his next laptop? He goes on CNET, Amazon, Decide. com, BestBuy.com, gdgt.com, or similar sites to read what others have to say. He's naturally attracted to the laptops with the highest ratings and scores (which are usually the first thing you see on these sites). When he starts reading reviews, he may be sidetracked by a new feature or consideration. A friend on Facebook posts something about her new laptop that takes Jim in yet a different direction. In short . . . O kicks in and takes over.

The problem is that conjoint and other preference measurement techniques ask people to make choices or rate options based on their current beliefs, without engaging in the kinds of information acquisition they would do in reality if they were actually buying the product. Not to mention that O-sourced information is often much more dynamic and constantly being updated, so even if a researcher were trying to somehow account for the present effect of O, that may become largely irrelevant and out of date by the time actual purchase decisions are made. Also, beyond the unpredictability of O's influence, decisions made under the influence of O are much "noisier" and unpredictable than hypothetical decisions made strictly by an individual consumer on her own when completing a questionnaire. While a limited set of studied features might be reasonably representative of the factors that an individual consumer will consider, a larger set of reviewers and information sources introduces various unpredictable factors (for example, "coolness," popularity, highlighting of seemingly insignificant features) that will be difficult to capture in conjoint measurement.

The impact of noise and hard-to-anticipate information sources created by the ability to predict purchase decisions is not unique to conjoint analysis and similarly limits the usefulness of other common research techniques such as brand equity measures or pricing studies. While predicting individual decisions that are made in isolation is not a simple task, predicting the joint evaluations of many consumers and the influences of other information sources is likely to be order of magnitude more challenging.

A MAJOR SHIFT

It's a cold evening in Cambridge, Massachusetts. People are leaving the Kendall Square Cinema after the 5:30 P.M. showing of *Lincoln*. As they walk out to the parking lot, snippets of their conversations are heard, and immediately fade away into the freezing air: "The acting was brilliant, but I was glad it was over." "You're kidding?" "Day-Lewis was amazing, but . . ."

A few feet away, in a redbrick building adjacent to the cinema, there's an office of a local start-up that works with conversations as its raw material—not the ephemeral kind from the walkway next door, but the online kind that stays out there for a long time and can be mined and analyzed. The start-up, Bluefin Labs, has forty of the top U.S. TV networks among its clients, including CBS, NBC, and Fox. Up to a few years ago, these networks were limited to techniques such as standard surveys, focus groups, and to data regarding the reach of shows. Now they can also know what resonates with people in real time based on what's being said on Twitter and other social media. In addition to TV networks, Bluefin is used by advertisers to see what ads resonate with consumers and to analyze their reaction. Advertisers will probably continue to test their commercials before airing them, but once a commercial is on the air, Bluefin lets them detect how it fares in real life, which can be quite different. A few days into the 2012 Olympic Games, for example, it became apparent that a commercial for one of Bluefin's clients was generating significant adverse commentary. When tested in isolation before it was ever aired, this commercial tested fine, but when it was shown in the context of the Olympics, it raised negative sentiment, which was starting to gain momentum on social media. The client was able to quickly replace the problematic ad.[6]

The redbrick walls at Bluefin are reminiscent of the industrial past of the building (which used to be a hose factory). Now, instead of workers sweating over heavy machinery soaked in the smell of rubber, the large halls are occupied by industrious young techies searching for insight in big data. Deb Roy, the Massachusetts Institute of Technology professor who cofounded the company, is known for a study he conducted about language development. He and his wife installed video cameras throughout their house, and for three years recorded everything that went on in the house from the moment their son was born. Having such rich data allowed Roy to uncover surprising insights about why certain words are learned before others. For example, the likelihood that his son would say a new word had a strong correlation with how unique it is in space. So the word "bye," which is closely associated with the entrance to the house, was more likely to be learned early than a word that is said in multiple locations around the house.

In the M★A★S★H conference room (meeting rooms are named after TV shows) a large screen displays what clients at TV networks see in real time—a listing of all shows on the air (even those of competitors). Clicking on a program shows a minute-by-minute level of social media conversation and its sentiment. A client can see which programs get the highest engagement and, within each show, what causes spikes in conversations. In other words, they can take an ongoing, comprehensive, and exceptionally detailed look at O.[7] The software is fed by two sources of data. First, there are the millions of comments that are made by viewers about TV shows.[8] Second, there's a video stream consisting of everything on U.S. television. Their software links what's said publicly on social media to specific moments or events within TV programs (an event can be a play in a game, or a scene within a show, or an ad). Digging further, the user can see what other shows, brands, or topics are of interest to those who engage with a particular TV program.[9]

Bluefin is one of many companies in the social analytics space that try to gain insight by keeping their hands on the pulse of O. Companies such as Salesforce.com, Visible Technologies, Synthesio, and Attensity offer more general listening platforms that go beyond just the TV industry and allow marketers in a variety of domains to make sense of what's being said on social media. This area is still maturing and obviously it doesn't offer any magic solutions, yet the general direction makes sense. While the use of traditional market research to derive long-term forecasts of consumer demand has become more challenging, the current environment does provide marketers more sophisticated and precise tools to track and respond to consumers' decisions as they occur. It is reasonable to expect that future market research will focus more on within-context predictions and short-term marketer responses and less on long-term preference forecasting.

What happened with the iPhone study is likely to repeat itself. It is hard to predict the success of a product ahead of time by measuring individual consumers' preferences and then try to use these preferences to predict consumers' future decisions. Increasingly, the name of the game will be: watch competitors' initiatives, assess consumer reaction to those initiatives, and react as fast as possible. In the case of the iPhone, the major players varied pretty radically in how well they read consumers' reaction and, consequently, how fast they reacted. Google, Samsung, HTC, Microsoft, Nokia, and RIM each reacted at a different pace. Samsung, for example, was pretty quick to respond, while Nokia's CEO admitted as late as 2011 that his company missed big trends and still did not have an answer. "The first iPhone shipped in 2007, and we still don't have a product that is close to their experience," he said.[10] Nokia should have paid attention to O and acted accordingly. In the case of ASUS's Eee PC, the major competitors seemed to have reacted rather swiftly. As you recall, Jonney Shih and his team surprised the PC industry with an inexpensive device. Conventional market research was not too likely to predict its popularity, especially since it was adopted by segments they did not target. Acer, for example, even though it initially downplayed the potential of the cheap device, was quick to develop its own netbook. HP, Dell, and Lenovo followed quickly and in fall 2008 all major manufacturers had a netbook to offer.[11]

We're likely to see more of that. Trying to predict where things are going has become more challenging. While traditional consumer research can still tell a marketer if their next toothpaste will do better with purple or black stripes, it is not of great help for more radical, unfamiliar changes. There is no effective way to use market research to predict consumer reaction to major changes or new concepts. When assessing new concepts, consumers tend to be locked into what they are used to and believe today, which makes them less receptive to very different concepts and more receptive to small improvements over the current state. Similarly, experts who try to predict the success or failure of radically new products are unlikely to be much more accurate than consumers. (Among other things, experts have famously made bad predictions regarding the success of the telephone, the Internet, and television.) What marketers are often left with is trying to quickly figure out where things are going and what consumers and competitors appear to follow. And then try to offer a better solution. Instead of predicting vague consumer preferences (which may change anyway when it's time to buy), these days one of the few things a marketer can do is follow O and play along to make the best of a situation they no longer control.

But as we noted earlier, the current environment does not mean the end of market research, just a shift in focus with some silver linings. The current environment and technology make it much easier for marketing researchers to run experiments, adjust, and run the next experiment. Even when absolute values are easier to identify, the manner in which options are displayed and described can make some difference. We are not talking about long-term decisions such as which products to sell, but many small improvements (which can add up). For example, a site such as CarsDirect.com may run an experiment to test the effect, if any, of the cars they highlight on their website, the other cars shown, and the ease of accessing related blogs and reviews. The company could try different display formats by randomly assigning some consumers to different page versions. If differences emerge, the company may replicate the experiment on another day or at a different location, possibly making further adjustments. Once the company determines that the differences in consumer response are stable and robust, the optimal design can be implemented more broadly. This is likely to be an ongoing process whereby the company continues to try different things using trial and error, making adjustments, and then running the next experiment. The cost of such experiments is rather small, and the ability to apply lessons quickly can have an impact on profitability.

MEASURING SATISFACTION

Another evolving area in consumer research is the measurement of customer satisfaction. Conventional wisdom holds that once the consumer has had a chance to experience the product or service, a marketer may follow up with a survey to see how satisfied she was. But think about what we showed in Chapter 6: As better information sources lead to more accurate expectations, the gap between expectations and actual experiences should generally be smaller. In other words, expectations are becoming more predictive of experience and post-sale satisfaction. This could suggest that measuring expectations prior to the experience can actually be more effective, more timely, and more actionable than measuring satisfaction afterward. However, for the same reasons that measuring preferences has become more challenging (due to growing O influence), measuring current (often vague) expectations may not produce accurate predictions of actual satisfaction. More important, using market research to measure both expectations and satisfaction has limited value in a world where up-to-the-minute satisfaction and evaluations ratings of actual users who share their views are so plentiful and easily accessible to marketers.

So marketers can cut their market research budgets and, rather than waste their time on measuring individual consumer's preferences, expectations, satisfaction, and loyalty, rely on readily available public information. For example, a marketer of high-price, sophisticated cameras can visit websites frequented by the relevant prospective buyers and see what they like, want, and dislike. And instead of asking owners of bread makers about their evaluations and recommendations (after gaining experience), one can simply sample and quantify the evaluations available on key websites where bread makers are sold and reviewed. In other words, measure reviews and other content created by O because it's ultimately what impacts the expectations and experiences of those considering a product or a service. Another advantage of this approach is its timeliness: Reviews and tools such as Twitter can give an up-to-the minute picture of consumer opinion, whereas survey results can lag behind and quickly become obsolete. For example, a mobile phone that looked perfect when a survey was done may look inferior shortly after some new options are introduced. Measurement of the ultimate customer satisfaction will then often become a lower priority and even redundant.

Bazaarvoice is an interesting company in this context. We earlier discussed the role a company of its kind plays in collecting, moderating, and syndicating reviews. But it also helps marketers gain insight from this content. On any given day, hundreds of Bazaarvoice employees read online reviews and tag the content. For example, if a customer reviews a Samsung TV and comments that the remote control requires a certain feature, it will be tagged with a product suggestion code. When you consider the fact that this is done with thousands of reviews in twenty-seven different languages, you start to appreciate the wealth of structured data that becomes available to a marketer. At the most basic level, a manager at Samsung can focus easily on all reviews of a certain model that are tagged with a product suggestion code to detect things that can be improved.[12] Once marketers start to mine the data and look for patterns, they can find interesting trends regarding desired features, additional accessories that might be bundled with a product, or other unexpected things.

At a very practical level, manufacturing defects and other problems can be spotted pretty quickly. For example, not long ago Kohl's spotted a sharp shift from positive to negative reviews for one of its products. Further investigation detected a problem with a particular production batch.[13] In the same way, a couple of years ago

3M detected a sudden outcry about the Scotch Brite Soap Dispensing Dishwand. ("What has happened to your dishwand??" a typical review read. "The little blue cap on the wand will not stay on and all the soap leaks out.") 3M found an error in the production specs, they pulled the product from the stores, and fixed the problem. Another example: One of Samsung's refrigerators must be plugged in for six hours before the ice machine works. By monitoring the product reviews, Samsung noticed that many customers thought the machine was broken, which led to a high return rate. The product manager distributed to stores a short video explaining the ice machine feature. Return rates decreased. The social analytics company Synthesio helped the global hotel chain Accor build a listening tool that helps the company track its online reputation. Among other benefits, it helped the chain identify (and fix) a problem with guest keys that were demagnetized by smartphones.[14] These types of problems could have been eventually identified in the past by analyzing complaints to call centers or through satisfaction surveys. Today they can be brought to management attention faster.

We're not talking only about detecting malfunctions. Reviews, user groups, and other forums can quickly highlight user perception that a product does not perform as expected or that its features are inferior. Conversely, reviews can help a company identify rising stars in its product line. At L.L.Bean, for example, a weekly report that goes to management with sales results and back order status also summarizes last week's reviews by product category, the trend line for each category, and the percentage of products that got four or five stars. A separate report highlights "winners and losers"— specific items that are doing especially well and those that were poorly reviewed. All negative reviews (one or two stars) are distributed on a daily basis to the product managers who are expected to respond by thanking the customer for the feedback, apologizing (when appropriate), offering an alternative, and reinforcing the L.L.Bean guarantee. If an item gets more than six bad reviews, this starts a discussion within the company: Is the product description inaccurate or does the product have a real problem? If it turns out that the problem is consistent and the product has no redeeming value, the inventory is liquidated, donated to charity, or (in extreme cases) destroyed.[15]

MARKET RESEARCH TO DETERMINE LOCATION ON THE CONTINUUM

Predicting the location of your customers on the influence continuum requires marketers to assess two fundamental factors: diagnosticity and accessibility.[16]

Diagnosticity is the more important driver (and it also affects accessibility). It refers to the degree to which O is informative (or diagnostic) about your personal product experience. Consider two categories, for example: cameras and investment management. Cameras are fixed items (the product you're reading about in a review is the same product you'll use) and chances are that there won't be great differences between the average of the reviewers' experiences and yours. In contrast, you may read a review of an investment firm that is based on a reviewer's experience with an excellent financial adviser. Yet the adviser who's assigned to you by the same company is not as good, so in this case O is not diagnostic of your personal experience. When there is great variability in a service, O is not likely to be a good predictor.

Market research to determine the diagnosticity of O in a certain category calls for finding out from consumers how useful and informative O is or can be (even if it's not currently available). One way to find out is to ask consumers through surveys and interviews. The other is to conduct experiments in which one group chooses a product or a service based on current information sources, and another group that also has extensive (but realistic) O sources; the comparison can allow a marketer to determine the potential net impact of O. Considering that O encompasses a variety of different sources, such an experiment can be conducted separately for specific O sources.

We generally believe that where there is a need (that is, where O is capable of providing useful information), it will become available over time. So, if you determined that O can be useful in a category, you can expect it to become more widely available over time, even if it's currently not available.

Assessing the current accessibility to O can be achieved by observing what's available out there and by analyzing consumer information search and purchase behavior—determine where people buy, how they buy, what information sources they consider, the sheer number of available reviews and expert evaluations, and so on. Are consumers making decisions on their own or are they reading reviews first? Do they consult with other users on social networking sites? How do they react to information they get from other consumers? Look at both the percent of potential customers who consider information from others, and for those who do, what is the impact of that information on their decisions.

Keep in mind that the availability of reviews, while helpful, is not enough to indicate reliance on O. Nowadays you can find some user-generated content and online reviews for almost any product. We even found some reviews of paper clips on Amazon.com ("It's a paperclip, yay, it works as described"). Yet the existence of these reviews doesn't mean that O is important in the purchase decision. There are also categories where people are more likely to talk about than to seek information. Consider fashion accessories. A woman is very likely to show a new scarf or a hat to her friends, but not necessarily seek information prior to purchasing such an accessory.[17]

Let's look at a quick hypothetical example for how one would go about conducting research to locate a service category on the O-influence continuum. Alison is an analyst who's been asked to assess customers' location on the continuum for a car insurance company. Her first step is to take inventory of what's available out there in terms of reviews and other quality-oriented user-generated content. She starts searching and cannot easily find too many meaningful reviews. She does find some general articles on how to go about buying car insurance, but when it comes to actual quality assessment of specific companies or agents, there isn't much out there. The next step for Alison is to determine the existing sources of information that people currently use. Through a survey and by observing consumers, she determines that at the present time, potential purchasers go to the providers' websites, compare rates, call agents; some talk to their friends. Her conclusion is that, at this time, the process is not very O-Dependent.

Alison's next step is to find out how useful O information could be if it were available. She conducts an experiment with four groups. One group has access to a couple of review sites currently available. For the second group, she creates a fictitious database with much more detailed and specific customer reviews. These reviews rate companies on their service before and after an accident and go into details for specific needs such as teenage drivers. Alison may also divide that group into two subgroups based on the content (more or less favorable) of the reviews. A third group is provided with detailed information and service specs from the insurance company. And a fourth group is provided with all three information sources and can review any or all of them. Alison may also test how the information reviewed by each group affects their preferences between the company being described and other insurance companies as well as the level of recall of provided information. Alison concludes that customers certainly respond well to more granular information from other customers, and this group is most likely to adopt preferences corresponding to the provided information and remember more of what they reviewed. She remarks that it will take a while before tools that provide such data will become available.

Such research may need to be done separately for different products, in particular if there is reason to believe that consumer decision making and information value differ across products. Also, each of your customers may use a slightly different combination of sources, so when we talk about your customers' location on the continuum we're talking about an average of prospective purchasers. In some cases, though, you may identify distinct groups of customers that are located on different places on the continuum. For example, you may find one segment of your customers that heavily relies on review sites before purchase, while another segment that uses your website as the main source of information. We will deal with this type of segmentation in the next chapter.

Questions, questions, questions. Some marketers will continue to chase the dream of figuring out the true preference of consumers and then giving them exactly what they want. They will continue to track slight changes in brand perceptions, segment migrations, and so on. There are a couple of problems with this approach. First, consumer preferences and perceptions tend to be vague. So the idea that if you only dig deeper by asking more and more questions, you'll learn about the consumer's true preferences, usually leads to "findings" that are not particularly meaningful or reliable. For example, some companies practice the "laddering technique," which promises to get at people's core values and preferences using a sequence of pre-specified questions. This approach essentially assumes that the true values are hidden deep inside, and if we only ask patiently the right questions, we'll get to the bottom of things. We don't think so. There is now a vast amount of evidence showing that such techniques do not uncover any truth, but largely create answers to questions that can later be relied upon by marketers.[18] And considering that the results of market research-based strategies tend to be ambiguous (because so many other factors affect actual sales), managers can almost always attribute success to their smart techniques or strategies and attribute failures to other causes.

On top of all that, relying on such "deep" research techniques is complicated by the influence of O, which makes predicting even more challenging. So it is reasonable to conclude that the use of market research techniques that rely on measures of individual consumers' preferences to predict future marketplace decisions will decline (or be reserved to situations where it has clear value, such as finding out consumers' reaction to yellow toothpaste). Increasingly, marketing will be about understanding what information sources consumers use, following trends, trying to offer the right products, and then following consumers' reactions. We said it before: Marketers in O–Dependent domains should stop thinking of themselves as drivers, and embrace their role as followers.

A funny thing has happened to market research. On the one hand, researchers can use increasingly sophisticated tools. Privacy aside, they can track consumers' every move and word on the Web and social media. There have also been developments in statistical and research techniques that a researcher might use to measure a consumer's preferences (at the time that the measurement takes place). One might think that such timely, detailed information would allow marketers to design just the right offers that consumers have been looking for, even before they realize what they want. However, the changes in the information sources consumers use (and as a result, in the way they make decisions) make such predictions less useful than marketers and the public might think. In fact, as we pointed out, predicting what individual consumers would end up doing is becoming harder than ever. The difficulty derives from the fact that when it's time to buy, the information that will influence the actual decision depends on what the consumer will happen to consider at that time. Stable dispositions are not as predictive as they used to be. Yet there are things that researchers will be able to do even in categories where time–of–purchase preferences are unpredictable. Recognizing the limits of such research, marketers should track, code, and quantify the content of reviews and other relevant evaluations created by O. We expect that future market research will focus more on tracking and responding to consumers' decisions as they occur, and less on long–term preference forecasting. Instead of measuring individual consumers' preferences, expectations, satisfaction, and loyalty, marketers should systematically track the readily available public information on review sites, user forums, and other social media.

12

SEGMENT EVOLUTION: FROM SUSCEPTIBLE TO SAVVY

IN SEPTEMBER 2010, a neurologist named Julius Bazan was invited to testify in front of the Subcommittee on Commerce, Trade, and Consumer Protection in the U.S. House of Representatives. Dr. Bazan wasn't there to speak about the inner workings of the brain or the susceptibility of the neocortex to judgment errors. He was there to tell the committee about his own experience as a consumer, and about what he called "legalized robbery."

A sixty-year-old man with a noticeable accent, Dr. Bazan was visibly upset as he told his story. He's originally from the former Czechoslovakia, he told members of the subcommittee, and he had been in the United States for thirty-one years. He said he had lost a big chunk of his savings in the stock market around the year 2001, and he was determined to stay away from Wall Street. A few years later, he was concerned about the dollar's decline and was hearing about gold on radio and TV, especially about a California-based company called Goldline International. What they were saying made sense to Dr. Bazan because gold was holding its value, and actually going up. Bazan contacted Goldline and opened an account.[1]

He wasn't alone. Goldline was advertising heavily on shows hosted by radio and TV personalities such as Glenn Beck and others, who were recommending buying gold. Our focus here is not on that advice, but about what happened when Bazan talked to Goldline's sales representative. To understand what happened we need to consider the difference between bullion coins and collectible coins. Bullion coins have a high "melt value" (the value of the actual gold in the coin) while collectible coins typically have a lower gold content. Their value comes from their scarcity and demand. Another relevant piece of information: Goldline's account executives are usually commissioned salespeople and their commissions are usually greatest on collectible coins and least on bullion.

"Initially I was thinking about the purchase of bullions, but I was told that bullion is not a good value to invest in," Bazan told the congressmen. He recalled that he was told that bullions were confiscated by the government in the 1930s and that coins with collector value were a better investment because they were excluded from confiscation back then.

Bazan continued: he bought collectible coins and started to watch gold prices. After six months, as gold prices were not moving up as fast as he expected them to, and since he found another investment opportunity, he decided to liquidate his holdings in gold. When he called Goldline to sell what he bought, he received a little surprise. Bazan's initial investment was around $140,000. Now the Goldline representative was telling him that the company was willing to buy it back for $83,000. Although the value of gold went up some during those six months, Bazan was about to lose around $57,000. He protested. The Goldline rep explained to him the concept of the spread—the difference between the buying price and the selling price.

"It felt like legalized robbery," Bazan told the subcommittee.

In 2011 the Santa Monica city attorney filed a criminal complaint against Goldline, accusing the company of running a "bait and switch" operation in which customers were sold gold coins although they contacted the company in order to invest in gold bullion.[2] In 2012, as part of a settlement agreement, the city attorney dismissed the criminal charges and Goldline, while denying all allegations, agreed to refund as much as $4.5 million to former customers, according to the *Los Angeles Times*.[3] Readers who are interested in the details of this story can look at the notes section of our book and will find links to press releases from both Goldline and the city attorney as well as some stories in the media. Our purpose with this example is to discuss a broader issue relating to the sources of information people use in making their decisions.

Imagine two people who contacted Goldline in 2011 with the intention of buying bullion. Whether or not they would end up buying collectible coins had a lot to do with their source of information. Would they rely solely on M? Or would they rely on O as well? Those who would rely on M were likely to hear the confiscation story (that was also promoted in the information kit sent to potential customers). Those who would rely on O were likely to encounter some red flags. For example, if they typed the words "Goldline International" in Google, they would find online articles from ABC News, *Consumer Reports*, *Mother Jones*, and other sources, alerting them to potential problems. These alerts may not have been there when Bazan made his purchase, but in 2011 they were all over the Web.[4]

And yet, despite the available information, some people repeated Bazan's course of action: They called with the intention of buying bullion but ended up with collectible coins. In writing this book, we came across similar cases again and again—people who were swayed to buy product X when they actually wanted product Y, people who ordered inferior gadgets, snake oil, or lemons, even though information about the true nature of these products was just a few clicks away.

The dramatic changes that are taking place in the mix of forces that influence purchase decisions are not happening overnight. As we saw earlier, they differ across product and service categories. In this chapter we'll see that they also evolve at different rates across different consumer segments. The reality is that many people do not use the available information that can help them make better decisions. People differ in their access to technology, their ability to use it, and in their inclination to take the time, short as it can be, to get the information they need for making better decisions. Exposure to absolute values is unevenly distributed, with some consumers already making decisions based on reliable sources, and those still relying on the traditional proxies for assessing quality. This means that as the trends we discuss here progress, some people will stay behind. In fact, it seems that at least for a while, those who take advantage of available information will often make better decisions, whereas those who get overwhelmed by the technology or the mountains of available information may become more susceptible to influence. This leads to an alarming phenomenon we call "Absolute Inequality." There are those who are more savvy and there are those who are still susceptible. Though we expect the share of the latter group to decline over time, this may take a while.

When we talk about access to technology, it's not simply about the ability to connect to the Internet. Slow access, old equipment, and poor Internet user skills can keep certain segments from taking full advantage of the information that is out there.[5] People also differ in terms of their motivation and inclination to take the time to get the information they need for making better decisions. Consumers with access to more options, more attributes, and more information about these attributes (and who can use such information efficiently) are less likely to make decision errors. Although this generalization has always been true, the growing access to information and sorting tools has expanded the spectrum of differences among consumers.

There's a catch, though. Some consumers can be heavy users of technology—active on newsgroups, chatting frequently with fellow consumers—but still not take full advantage of the most diagnostic information out there. How can that be? Think of a Linux enthusiast who interacts almost exclusively with other Linux fans, or a devoted member of the Harley-Davidson owner's club. Because of their narrow, like-minded reference groups, we can't expect them to take full advantage of the new information environment. A key prerequisite to finding absolute values is exposure to diverse sources and perspectives. So raving fans of a brand who only talk among themselves may be as susceptible to relative tactics as people who don't use O at all. We're talking about two distinguished concepts here. The first is the degree to which someone is exposed to other's views. The second is the degree to which that person uses heterogeneous sources.

This is a good place to briefly address a related issue. When we talk about our book, we're sometimes asked if the shift from relative to absolute will ever reach politics. In other words, when people can so easily access the most relevant information, will they quickly find out the merit of a proposition or any other political initiative? And consequently, is framing less likely to work in politics? Will persuasion techniques become less potent? Part of the answer has to do with the degree to which people use heterogeneous sources, an issue that in this domain is referred to as political or ideological segregation. Political segregation is driven by people's tendency to value and listen to others with similar points of view. The degree of political segregation in the United States (as well as how it's affected by the Internet) is a topic of heated debate that is tangential to our focus and we're not going to address or resolve it here.[6] The bottom line in our context is important, though—if significant political segregation exists, it can easily curb any possible shift from relative to absolute in politics. In other words, if the accusation "you live in a bubble," which is often exchanged between the political left and right, is true, then people are less likely to hear different perspectives. Even when the topic is factual, absolute values are less likely to be exposed when people only search for facts that support their prior beliefs. Fact-checking websites and apps such as FactCheck. org or PolitiFact try to serve as guides for voters (and to some extent they may), but if people use them mostly to see when political rivals are caught lying, these services are less likely to bring the trends we discuss to politics.

SEGMENTS AND LOCATION ON CONTINUUM

As we pointed out earlier, the location on the O–influence continuum may vary across customer segments. For example, a company
may identify two distinct segments: Segment A tends to purchase
the company's product through distribution channels that are less
conducive to O (for example, brick-and–mortar stores). This segment also tends to rely on information from M rather than O. In
contrast, Segment B heavily relies on review sites and other O content before purchase, and tends to buy the product through online
channels that are more conducive to O. Just so that we can illustrate
our point, we'll make some generalizations in the following example. Older consumers (such as baby boomers like us) may be that
Segment A, as they are relatively more inclined to watch TV, read
newspapers and magazines, are less active on social media, and are
still shopping offline. Segment B may include younger people who
tend to be more fluent in O-intensive media, can't imagine not
having the Web, cell phones, and social media, tend to watch less
TV, and pretty much live online. For them, O is the primary influence while, by and large, reaching and influencing them directly
is a big challenge for M. Identifying these O-influence segments
is essential for determining the marketing strategies to reach and
influence them. In communicating with Segment A, the company
can still use advertising to persuade, frame, or position its offering.
Using these same methods to appeal to Segment B is not likely to
work. Of course, more sophisticated analysis would be needed in
real life since such crude generalizations can be misleading due to
individual differences within broad segments. For example, while
both of us are in the baby boomer age group, we both rely heavily
on product review sites before shopping. However, we're quite different in our use of social media. (Emanuel is an active user whereas
Itamar's main social media activity consists of reviewing his Facebook News Feed.)

Let's consider how a marketing researcher (yes, those are still needed) might go about O-influence segmentation. Think about the familiar practice of psychographic segmentation—segmenting based on people's values and lifestyles. With this approach, the marketer may not know to which group each individual customer belongs, but the marketer knows that these segments exist out there. Similarly, although certain O-influence generalizations can be useful (such as the distinction between young and old consumers), segmentation along the O-influence continuum can be used by utilizing the same approach as psychographic segmentation, except that it's better grounded in facts and actual behavior, rather than selective ratings and subjective interpretations of often ambiguous data clusters.

Suppose we take a random sample of a thousand recent cell phone purchasers, and ask them about their pre-purchase behavior. The questionnaire will be designed to find out, for example, (a) the various information sources they consulted (this could be done using both unaided and aided measures), (b) the number of phones they considered, (c) when and where they gathered information about the phone they ended up getting, (d) where they bought the phone, and (e) whether they walked into the stores of the service provider knowing what they wanted or whether they followed the recommendation of the salesperson. In addition, the questionnaire will be designed to obtain more general information about each respondent, such as the time spent Web surfing, Web "research" practices, and demographic characteristics. With this additional information, the market researcher will be able to know more about the characteristics of each O-influence group. Of course, the details of the study will need to be tailored to each product and situation, and may vary to some degree based on the brand and country. But the guiding principle in each such study should be to focus as much as possible on typical (actual rather than predicted) behavior and facts rather than on subjective perceptions and hard-to-remember details. Having said that, adding some more subjective judgment questions at the end of the study (for example, regarding perceived usefulness of reviews versus information from marketers) might give some further insights.

Such a study should allow the researcher to identify (primarily) behavioral-based O-influence segments, their relative sizes, and the information sources and channels that will most effectively reach them. Grouping customers will still require some judgments by the researcher, but again, the behavioral and fact basis makes it much more reliable and robust than cluster analysis. It is important to repeat this O-influence segmentation study periodically, in order to track changes in information habits and sizes of the different segments. In particular, in the foreseeable future we can expect segment instability.

Brands may differ greatly in terms of the location of their buyers on the O-influence continuum. When ASUS entered the market using its own (and then still-unknown) name, buyers were likely to be those who listen to knowledgeable others and check specs and reviews. On the other hand, an emotional attachment to a brand (as has been the case for some Harley-Davidson and Corvette fans) often comes at the expense of doing one's due diligence and taking advantage of available diagnostic information. Market research may also uncover differences in the type of O sources that are used in a particular case. For example, decisions to get a new iPhone are probably weakly influenced by users' reviews. The phone is out, the press and experts give it their full attention, and users' reviews may be redundant (unless the phone's actual performance is much worse than expected).

FROM SUSCEPTIBLE TO SAVVY

Let's think about two imaginary countries: Oberya and Moberya. The citizens of the two countries are similar in many ways, except for in one major factor. The folks in Oberya get most of their information from O, while the folks in Moberya get most of it from M.

One day, a company in Oberya (the Oberya Gadget Corporation, or OGC) developed a new coffeemaker and introduced it to the citizens of Oberya with great fanfare. A few Oberyans bought the coffeemaker and it didn't take long before reviews and comments started to appear in review sites and other social media. The general verdict: thumbs down. The product wasn't malfunctioning or faulty; it just didn't work as well as expected. It was complicated to use and people said the buttons were confusing. The coffeemaker was a flop.

Left with a huge inventory of coffeemakers, OGC's management contacted a local distributor in Moberya, hired a brilliant ad agency, and got to work. They advertised the coffeemaker on Moberya's big TV networks, and the coffeemakers started flying off the shelves. While eventually Moberyans may reject the new product as well, one would expect it to take much longer. With a much less developed O ecosystem (review sites, social networking sites, etc.), the folks in Moberya will learn about the quality of the product either through personal experience or by word of mouth (which can be painfully slow).

It's not a coincidence that we use two fictitious countries in the above example. In reality, it's difficult to find cases where two similarly developed countries differ so dramatically in their reliance on O. Real-life cases like this usually happen between a *developed* and a *developing* country, in which case some alternative explanations come to mind: Having lower income in developing countries may mean that consumers in these countries tend to choose low-price products (that are considered inferior in developed countries) as long as their quality is just good enough. In some cases products from rich nations are prestigious in poor nations, a fact that can make the analysis even harder.

Yet even though it's hard to find clear-cut examples in real life, absolute inequality is out there and should be reduced. Having a well-developed O ecosystem has clear economic and social welfare implications. Policy makers should pay attention to this and make sure that consumers in their countries are not left behind with higher susceptibility to inferior products (either locally produced or imports). Taking a global perspective, our analysis means that the shift from relative to absolute will progress in certain markets slower than in others. While we expect markets to shift over time from "susceptible" to "savvy," in some cases this might take a long time, which means that there may be gaps in susceptibility to relative influence between different markets.

Switching back to the micro level, an individual company that tries to reach and influence potential customers should realize that the location on the O-influence continuum often varies across customer segments. One segment may rely primarily on O, while another may rely more on M, or use distribution channels that are less conducive to O. Similarly, a company may identify a segment with higher brand loyalty, which may be more open to hear directly from M. Identifying these O-influence segments should drive the marketing strategies to reach and influence each segment. In communicating with segments that rely on M, a company can still use advertising to build top-of-mind awareness or to persuade, frame, or position its offering. Using these methods when communicating with a segment that relies primarily on O is not likely to work very well. Instead, as we discussed in Chapter 10, the communication program should focus on generating interest (rather than top-of-mind awareness) and communicating quality *through* O rather than trying direct persuasion.

Keep in mind, however, that nothing stands still, which applies also to the location of segments on the O-influence continuum. A segment that has heavily relied on M up to a few months ago may be moving to the O-Dependent side. So segments' location on the continuum should be monitored on an ongoing basis. This is particularly true as new O tools (which are even easier to use) keep coming. We discuss this next.

13

THE FUTURE OF THE ABSOLUTE

IT HAPPENED TO Dara O'Rourke as he was applying sunscreen lotion to his three-year-old daughter's face. For Richard Barton and Lloyd Frink, it happened when they were shopping for homes. It happened to Oren Etzioni at thirty thousand feet in the air on his way to his brother's wedding.

That was when these men realized they were in the dark. Dara O'Rourke realized that he had no idea what the lotion he was applying so generously to his daughter's skin actually contained. (Did it have any toxic substances?) Frink and Barton were both in the market for new homes and they were struggling to figure out how much they should be paying for the houses they saw. Oren Etzioni was shocked to find out that people around him on the flight paid less for the same ticket, even though some of them bought their tickets later than he did. We're all in the dark about certain elements of our lives, but these men—separately and each in his own way— decided to take action. Dara O'Rourke went to his office at the University of California, Berkeley, and looked up the ingredients of the sunscreen lotion. Lloyd Frink and Richard Barton entered some comparable sales figures they got from the county's website into a spreadsheet and started analyzing how much the houses they were considering were actually worth.[1] Oren Etzioni, a computer scientist from the University of Washington, started working on a paper with some colleagues: Can they write an algorithm to guess when is the best time to buy a ticket?

This is how it often starts: Someone notices that they are in the dark, and they do something about it.

When Etzioni's paper was published, the university sent out a press release. Etzioni usually thinks about university press releases as "write-only." "You write them, but nobody reads them," he says. But things developed differently in this case. *NBC Nightly News*, *BusinessWeek*, *Wired* magazine, and other media outlets all ran stories about the paper. Suddenly everyone was asking Oren Etzioni when to book their flights. "Students were raising their hands in my class, asking when they should buy their ticket," he told us.[2]

This is another element that drives the trends we describe in this book: There's unquenchable demand among consumers for information that might help them make better decisions. As we argued earlier, people have a strong tendency to acquire seemingly relevant information, even when it's useless; and once acquired, they often feel they should use it.

The other driver can be found on the supply side. Etzioni was initially motivated by academic curiosity, but noticing that he struck a raw nerve, he started a company called Farecast.com. It was an airfare pricing comparison tool, with a predictive algorithm that suggested whether you should buy the ticket or wait until prices go down. In 2008 the company was acquired by Microsoft, and the algorithm is now incorporated into their Bing search engine.[3]

The other inquiries, too, led to the development of tools that let consumers make more informed decisions. Dara O'Rourke developed GoodGuide, a website and an app that helps consumers evaluate products on three dimensions. You enter a product (or scan its bar code) and the guide rates the product on its health, environmental, and social impact. This way you can answer questions such as: Which baby shampoo is healthiest for my baby? Which cell phone is most environmentally friendly? Which apparel company is the most socially responsible (for example, with its labor practices)? Richard Barton and Lloyd Frink developed Zillow.com, which estimates the price of a house or an apartment based on recent transactions in a neighborhood.

How do these tools reduce the power of relative influences? An airline can try to use all the promotional tricks in the book to convince you to buy your ticket *today*, but if your search engine suggests that prices are about to go down, you are likely to wait instead for the right time.[4] A real estate developer can try to use a variety of persuasion and positioning methods to boost a certain location, for example by comparing a new house to a selective and unrepresentative set of other houses in an area. But buyers get a good idea regarding the going prices in a neighborhood through Zillow or similar apps. Or consider GoodGuide: Companies do a lot to frame their products as green, natural, and healthy. Graphic designers and packaging experts know how to convey these concepts through various subtle (and not-so-subtle) hints on the package. Yet these proxies become less effective when a consumer knows the cold facts using the GoodGuide app or website. If a baby product gets 4 out of 10 on environmental friendliness, and 3 out of 10 on health, the messages on the package will have less impact, even if it features a mother hugging her baby, with lush green trees and waterfalls in the background. And of course, it can also go the other way as users look up products and choose those that are best rated: A brand that doesn't necessarily stand for "green" can benefit from very good ratings on GoodGuide.

We're not here to evaluate specific tools or predict which new technologies will take off. We want to make more general points about the future of the trends we've been discussing in this book: The first one is to explain why tools that provide access to absolute values will continue to emerge. We believe that the necessary ingredients will be around for a long time: (a) Inquisitive consumers or experts who notice that they are in the dark and do something about it, (b) unquenchable consumer demand for information that, over time, will benefit the broader consumer population, and (c) consumers' tendency to use easily accessible information they view as important. In fact, one can argue that we're caught in a loop that produces more and more information. Vendors, computer scientists, and entrepreneurs all over the world notice the demand for information, so they supply new tools and new information, which in turn are being used by consumers, and so on. . . . The cycle is in full swing.

Our second point is that this is just a snapshot. The discussion and the examples used in this book are based on technologies available around 2013, but things keep moving, and the nature of these tools may transform over time. Today, most of O consists of consumer and expert opinions. It's reasonable to believe that these opinions will remain an important part of O, but it doesn't have to stop there. Data can come from other sources as well and further reduce relative influences. The three examples above hint at the possibilities. None of them uses people's opinions as the main data source. GoodGuide is based on scientific data from government agencies and research institutes. Zillow pulls transaction data from county records. Farecast.com (or now Bing) predicts the price of a flight by making billions of price observations and searching for patterns.

New technologies may enable the absolute evaluations in ways that are still hard to imagine. We'll leave the wild scenarios to professional futurists, yet it's not hard to think of some hypothetical examples. Imagine, for example, that after every visit to your car mechanic, you click a button that forwards the invoice to a central database that collects all the car repair data in the country. The aggregate data from such a database gives consumers a very accurate picture on reliability and maintenance cost of different car models, which further erodes the value of brand as a quality proxy. This is hardly science fiction. It's possible, of course, that more disruptive innovations are on the horizon, and that they will affect our lives the way that mobile phones, GPS, or search engines have. It's likely that as you're reading this book, entrepreneurs are working on the next generation of tools that might get consumers closer to absolute values, perhaps in surprising ways.

The general direction has been set, but there are some conditions that can greatly affect the future of the trend toward the absolute. One is access to technology. As we explained in the last chapter, the trends we describe in this book are likely to emerge in certain markets slower than in others based largely on technology penetration. The other big factor to consider is the availability of data, which is driven by legislation and the priorities of policy makers, as we discuss next.

COOL TOOLS ARE NOT ENOUGH

If technology provides the flashlights that help people better navigate in the dark, the energy that is needed is data, and here, too, things are changing. In a recent article in the *Harvard Business Review*, Richard Thaler and Will Tucker predicted that government-owned data and private-company disclosures will become increasingly available in machine-readable formats, which will stimulate the development of new services they call "choice engines"—tools similar to the ones described above. While overall, the direction is more data and transparency, these things cannot be taken for granted. There are domains where data is obtained relatively easily (for example, airline flight prices) and there are domains where data is harder to get (especially in a machine-readable format). "It is not a lack of technology that has kept many choice engines from making the leap from beta testing to market disruption," Thaler and Tucker wrote.[5] "The missing ingredient is easy access to data." For example, if real estate transaction data is not available (as is the case in certain countries), a tool such as Zillow won't help. The future of the trends we discuss in this book depends not only on technology but also on disclosure laws, which are affected by the priorities of policy makers. As Thaler and Tucker point out, the current availability of data in the United States is driven in part by President Obama's push for transparency and open government.

As we were working on this book, we got a reminder of another obstacle that can emerge and curb the trend toward absolute evaluations. In late 2011 an ad campaign introduced a company called TrueCar.com to the public. Scott Painter, the serial entrepreneur behind the company, was going to take the automotive industry from "relative" to "absolute." Car dealers have traditionally tried to sell cars relative to arbitrary reference points. ("It's $5,000 below sticker price!" or "You're getting this beauty for just $300 above invoice!") TrueCar was going to change that. The company collects data from state vehicle-registration offices, insurance companies, car-loan providers, and other data aggregators. If you want to buy a car, you pick a specific model and you see what other buyers in your geographical area actually paid for it. Instead of thinking about your price relative to a sticker price or the invoice price, you see the actual prices people paid.[6] Next step: TrueCar finds you a price below the average price. You print a "TrueCar Price Protection Certificate," which you take to a participating dealer who will sell you the car for that price. No haggling. No "let me talk to my manager and see what we can do." You pay the price printed on the certificate and drive off happily into the sunset.

Immediately after TrueCar launched this ad campaign, its efforts were met with resistance from some in the industry. Concerned about their margins, dealers protested and dealer associations around the country issued complaints about TrueCar violating certain local laws. Regulators in some states looked into the company's business practices and TrueCar stopped its operation in several states. TrueCar's dealer network shrank and the company, which had been profitable before, started losing money.[7]

It's a reminder that the road to absolute can be bumpy. The tools that we're talking about are likely to threaten someone's territory, and companies on the defense are likely to exert political pressure to curb some of these tools. Yet the general trend has been set. In fact, after a period of restructuring, TrueCar seems to have regained its momentum, and even though it has changed some of its practices, it's clear that TrueCar and other tools that have emerged in the last decade make a car buyer much less susceptible to relative tactics than they were in the past.[8]

NEW TOOLS—NEW CHOICES

Remember trends like "couch tracking" or "faster verdict," which we discussed earlier in the book? These trends in decision making derive from the information that is available to us today. Or you may recall an experiment we described in Chapter 2: When people were asked to pick one of two toasters, they picked one option. When they were asked to *rate* two toasters, they preferred a different option.[9] The general point is that our choices are affected by the information and tools available to us. If these tools and information change, so may our choices. When the yellow pages served as the main source for information in certain domains, we tended to favor companies that appeared first in a category. As a result, being listed ahead of competitors used to be very important. So much so that businesses would name themselves accordingly, making names such as AAA Appliances very popular. Being first in any list is still very valuable, but when customers use tools like Yelp, the impact of being first is reduced. Now the average star rating becomes a key shortcut. Yet nothing stands still, and if consumers start to base their decisions on different sources, businesses may need to further adjust.

This is why it is important for businesses to watch for new technologies, track the information sources used by consumers, and adjust their strategies and tactics. Consider an app like Healthy-Out, which lets you find restaurants around your location. Actually, to be more exact, it lets you find *restaurant dishes* around your location. You stand on a street corner looking to grab a bite. You search this app based on things like your dietary desires (low carb? gluten-free? heart healthy?), the number of calories you're thinking of consuming, the type of dish you feel like having (salad? sandwich? wrap?). . . . Then the app shows you the dishes nearest you that match your preferences. Since you're searching the menus of restaurants, you may pay less attention to things like the atmosphere or restaurant names. Since the search engine offers you some pre-defined criteria, these may become more prominent in your decision. (For example, even if you never thought of gluten before, you may now attribute your digestive problems to gluten, and start paying attention to this.) If a significant number of people in a market start to base their decisions on HealthyOut or similar apps, restaurants in that market should make sure they provide the information these apps need.

It's impossible to predict what new tools will emerge. However, the likely candidates are tools that help us reach better decisions yet don't require too much effort on our part. Our tendency to be "cognitive misers" is here to stay. Because it's hard to process information systematically, we tend to base our decisions on whatever is easy and most accessible. We want the bottom line. Shortcuts. Summaries. Here are four examples for current tools that may hint to possibilities in the future:

Decide.com

Decide.com (Oren Etzioni's new startup) is a shopping search engine for consumer electronics, appliances, and other products. It gives you a brief answer to two questions: what to buy, and when to buy it. For example, if you're looking for a camcorder, you'll see a single score next to each model on the site. This number (from 0 to 100) summarizes all user and expert reviews. Simple icons tell you if new models are expected in the next six months and if any significant changes in price are likely in the next couple of weeks. You can, of course, dig much deeper (and some people do) but this is optional.

BrightScope

If you're like most people, you never read the long disclosure documents from your retirement plan administrators. But now a company called BrightScope rates your employer's 401(k) plan by giving it a grade between 0 and 100. Once you see the overall grade, you can see how your employer's program scores on specifics like cost, performance, and generosity (for example in terms of the plan's vesting schedule). BrightScope uses information that plan administrators have to file by law. By summarizing it in a user-friendly manner, and by rating plans across critical metrics, it can help you assess (or at least start to assess) the quality of your retirement plan.[10]

Digital wallets

Some solutions may lead to better outcomes by bypassing the decision process altogether. Here's an example: You stand at the store and it's time to pay. Today, your decision on which credit card to use may be affected by the latest promotion from your bank, or by how they frame their loyalty program, or by your perception of what card is most appropriate for a particular context, such as a fancy hotel. People often make bad choices in these situations (for example, increasing the balance on a high-interest credit card). If you let a digital wallet on your smartphone decide on the most cost effective payment method based on some pre-defined criteria (such as the card with the lowest interest rate, or the loyalty program with the best benefits) these irrelevant elements will play a reduced role in your decision. Google, PayPal, and other companies have been working on solutions in this arena.

Beyond any packaged, commercial tools, the web makes it much easier for consumers to conduct their own independent research, a trend that is likely to grow. Here's an example: As we mentioned earlier, one of us is a big consumer of dark chocolate (starting with a super-concentrated cocoa in the morning), a habit that began when the good news about the health benefits of dark chocolate started appearing in the media. So Itamar got a bit concerned when the news about a possible link between dark chocolate and Parkinson's disease arrived in April 2013.[11] Based on a study with rodents, the researchers encouraged people to limit their chocolate consumption. But Itamar was not going to give up his chocolate habit so quickly and looked for evidence against it (okay, you can call that biased information search). The Internet offered the tools for this "research project." Within a couple of minutes, he could find 1) the average chocolate consumption by country, and 2) the prevalence of Parkinson's disease by country. Itamar reasoned that, while there might be some confounding factors (such as genetic differences), if there is a strong link between chocolate and Parkinson's, countries with a higher chocolate consumption should have a higher incidence of Parkinson's. Fortunately, this two-minute exercise revealed no such correlation. Without further scientific evidence (preferably involving humans), Itamar has no intention of giving up his dark chocolate pleasure. More generally, as the available, easily accessible data continues to expand and the Web research tools further improve, we can expect more people to conduct more such independent studies. These amateur "studies" may sometimes lead to the wrong answers but can often produce answers that are closer to the absolute values.

To be clear, we don't see humans making decisions like robots in the future. People most likely will pick and choose where they want to use technology and how. Certain purchase decisions are based on things other than just sheer information (as high quality as it might be). For example, people have not stopped using real estate agents with the rise of Zillow and similar services. Despite the fact that brokers can be expensive[12] sellers still want the hand-holding, assistance, assurance, and expertise of brokers.[13] The same is true for buyers who usually want help negotiating such a big transaction. Having said that, the nature of real estate decision making has clearly changed in the past few years. Buyers are much more informed and less susceptible to certain influences than they used to be ten years ago. New tools may change things further.

We don't know what tools are coming next, but the trend is in full motion. It often starts with someone in the dark who decides to turn on the light. Now there's more for people to see and consider as they make decisions. People tend to use easily accessible information they view as important, and entrepreneurs keep supplying new flashlights. As long as we have data to power these light sources, the trends we described here will continue. No doubt there will be bumps along the way, but the big picture is clear: We can expect access to more data that will be better organized and interpreted through new tools. We can also expect the data to be more relevant to us. As we have more opportunities to observe our friends (on Facebook or alternative future platforms), we'll know much more about their experience as consumers—the good, the bad, and the ugly. This will further reduce marketers' ability to influence consumers through branding, positioning, or other "relative" strategies.

14

ABSOLUTE BUSINESS: A FINAL WORD

WHEN CONSUMERS CAN assess their likely experience, without having to rely on often-unreliable proxies such as brand names and prior experience or marketers' advertising messages everything changes. Marketing as we know it is not needed anymore. Yet most people think about marketing and business using the same old concepts. While textbooks have added references to the Internet, and many books have been written about social media, the presumed critical roles of branding, loyalty, positioning, and other principles of marketing have not changed.

As we conclude the book, we'd like to make a few final comments about the shape of things to come and illustrate how particular managerial practices might be revised to fit the new reality.

FOLLOW THE ABSOLUTE

How will the new environment affect a company's structure and organization? We can expect a shift in the importance of marketing within the organization, and there will be changes within the marketing arm itself. Let's start with the role of "Marketing" within a company. In the past the marketing function "protected" the organization in some cases. When things like positioning, branding, or persuasion worked effectively, a mediocre company with a good marketing arm (and deep pockets for advertising) could get by. Now, as consumers are becoming less influenced by quality proxies, and as more consumers base their decisions on their likely experience with a product, this is changing.

This means that the marketing function in the organization has less of an impact on the success or failure of a business. Another way to put it: The chances that the product failed or succeeded because of "marketing" have been greatly reduced. Since the impact of marketing is reduced, the impact of other functions in the organization increase, and specifically, those functions that affect absolute values. These may be different in different domains. R&D in consumer electronics and perhaps HR in the hospitality industry. Resources should be allocated to parts of the organization that have the biggest impact on absolute values as defined by prospective buyers. Follow the absolute.

There are also organizational changes we expect *within* marketing. While the organization as a whole will be less affected by this function, when organized correctly, marketing can still play an important role. As consumers can more easily assess the quality of products, and old marketing concepts have less impact, then the business as a whole and the marketing function in particular should emphasize those elements that make a difference—tracking what people want and generating interest. Marketing organizations (operating in O-Dependent markets) that will focus on these tasks should thrive. On the other hand, those who will keep their primary focus on persuasive advertising, building brand equity, and measuring customer satisfaction and loyalty are likely to stay behind. Correspondingly, one might expect marketing institutions outside the company to change. For example, advertising, media, market research, and marketing communication agencies will have to adapt or they may face increasing challenges in justifying their added value. Like internal marketing departments, they should specialize more in the things that matter—tracking and generating interest—and less in complex branding models, persuasion, or gimmicks.

CHANNELS

We can expect changes in distribution channels as well. Since absolute values are more easily assessed based on nonseller sources, in many situations there is less need for hand-holding during the buying process. This means that distribution channel decisions are likely to be less complex as well, with greater concentration and simplification. And yet, if you open existing distribution channel textbooks, you'll find chapters about rather complex distribution channel structures (such as various hybrid channel structures) to fit the information needs of different customer segments. When quality can be assessed accurately and most buyers check the Web to find out the absolute value of products, the differentiation among channels and their ability to sell to different segments becomes less important. Marketers can just focus on the most efficient sellers (while assuring enough competition among them); marketers' dependence on different areas of expertise of different channels has declined.

At the present time, channel strategy can also be used to try to influence the degree to which customers rely on the views of others, that is, their location along the influence continuum. For example, a company that chooses to rely primarily on the online channel (Amazon.com and the like) is inviting user reviews, which are likely to play a prominent role in the decisions of subsequent potential buyers. A reliance on brick-and-mortar channels, on the other hand, makes the sharing of opinions less likely, thereby making the product less O-Dependent. This is likely to become less relevant as shopping apps and other tools become ubiquitous among shoppers in brick-and-mortar stores as well.

PRICING

The closer your product (or any new market you consider entering) is to the O-Dependent end, the less control you have over pricing. That is, where experienced quality can be accurately predicted before purchase, price corresponds to quality relative to the competition and the going prices. If you are the first in a new market, there may be (at least initially) more flexibility to set standards, but even there, prices will eventually be based on fundamentals (for example, costs and, more important, competition).

Much has been made of the importance of value-based pricing, which focuses on how to assess true value advantage (often measured in dollars and cents) and charge accordingly. In the past, this concept had limited impact, in large part because the value analyses relied upon were many times perceived as theoretical and not relevant to the customer's situation. For example, generations of MBA students starting around 1976 and continuing to this day have practiced their value pricing skills using the entertaining Harvard Business School "Optical Distortion" case study.[1] The case describes a start-up with an unusual but apparently proven idea—contact lenses for chickens that are designed to tame chickens' behavior and decrease their tendency to attack their cell mates. A main use of the case in the MBA classroom is to illustrate value pricing— the figures in the case allow the student to derive the real value of the contact lenses to the chicken grower, which leads to the conclusion that the lenses are a great bargain. Unfortunately, despite its seemingly compelling value-based selling proposition chicken growers were not buying the value calculations, perhaps because they have been visited by too many other salespeople with superior value stories. Or perhaps because, as one person associated with the company put it: "the benefits are so great you get the reaction that it's too good to be true." Suppose, however, that economic value assessments, even if they are not as precise, were presented by actual users, such as chicken growers who have already tried the product and experienced savings. In that case, potential adopters might be more receptive to the message (assuming they believe that the product supporters do not have any ulterior motive). Thus O-based shared user data can make value pricing more effective and a better indicator of the product's absolute value.

The new information environment also means that consumers are more likely to obtain products at the best (or close to best) possible price. For example, product prices on websites such as Amazon often fluctuate over time within some unknown range. For consumers, tracking changing prices and knowing which price is relatively low is time consuming and hard to do. However, we would expect services to emerge (akin to what Decide.com already does) that will alert subscribing consumers to good prices and encourage timely prices. Similarly, many stores and websites offer lowest price guarantees, whereby the buyer can be reimbursed if the same retailer (or, in some cases, also competing retailers) later offers the same product at a lower price. The problem is that consumers rarely keep track of price changes, so they end up not getting potential refunds. We don't expect tools that address this problem to take off overnight (sellers have little incentive to cooperate, as automatic refunds can be very expensive) but suitable information services are emerging that alert consumers when prices decline and may even automatically arrange the refund (digital wallets may address this, too).

THE PACE OF THINGS TO COME

The new environment will also affect the pace of things to come. It's not that business is moving at a slow pace today, but there are reasons to believe that things will move even faster. First, as we said, consumers reach a faster verdict regarding the adoption or rejection of products. When people deliberately seek information, they are more likely to act on it. In addition, uncertainty about new innovations is resolved much faster than in the past.

Since businesses cannot count much on long-term assets like brand or loyalty, we can expect a further shift toward a short-term orientation. Forces that used to make things predictable, such as brand equity, loyalty, difficulty to assess quality, and slow-changing product perceptions, are declining. This will lead to less stability in the marketplace. Companies will have to get the right product to market without counting much on long-term assets because brand or loyalty won't help much if the product is wrong or fails to get attention.

Changes in market research practices and emphasis should reflect the importance of quickly detecting consumer sentiment and assessment and adapting products and services accordingly. Companies won't be able to rely much on research for predicting consumer choices and actions, particularly in O-Dependent categories. Thus fast trackers of market reactions are likely to have an advantage. It won't be only about rapid innovation. Fast imitators who supply high-quality products can gain from the new era as well. If they offer good products, consumers will be fast to recognize it. First-mover advantage is becoming less significant as well. When people can assess quality, first-mover advantage won't be such an asset for slowing down competition, and thus me-too strategies (as long as they are legal) may work better than before. Lower barrier to entry will mean that markets may be more crowded. And more intense competition, again, means faster pace.

We opened this book with five widely held beliefs, and we promised to explain why they are becoming less true today (and will be even less true in the future):

> " . . . *a company's brand is more important today than it has ever been.*"

" . . . *nurturing loyalty should be the marketer's primary, day-to-day concern.*"

"*All customers are irrational.*"

" . . . *an overload of options may actually paralyze people.*"

" . . . *positioning is the most important part of the marketing game.*"

We hope that we convinced you. While some of these things are still true for some domains, situations, or people, technology and entrepreneurial innovation have started to move things in a different direction. The dramatic increase in buyers' ability to assess quality before making most purchase decisions has fundamental implications for companies and other marketers. True, many consumers have not yet adopted the habit of taking advantage of the available information and some may get overloaded when they try. But the change process is undoubtedly penetrating the consumer decision making process slowly but surely, and it is just a matter of time till available information is even more widely exploited.

Some managers have started to adapt their practices and now place more emphasis on products that are likely to generate favorable reviews and less on marketing tools that have lost much of their effectiveness. Still, with the growing visibility of the idea of "irrationality," some managers think that they can easily sway purchase decisions using "irrationality-inducing tricks" such as asymmetric dominance or framing. We showed throughout the book why the opposite is true: People today can more easily figure out the quality of products and services they consider.

The consumer in O–Dependent domains is the big winner of the shift to absolute. On average, consumers will make better decisions and their ability to quickly assess their likely experience will push companies to provide better products and services. Although there always be segments that compromise on quality, overall the importance of high quality is going up. Yet consumers are not the only winners of this new age. Companies can win, too. Not companies that use smoke and mirrors, puffery and fluff. But those who learn to adjust quickly to the new era. Those that understand that it's not about brand, but about their next product. Those who will track effectively what customers say and want in current products and use that to innovate (or imitate) quickly will be most successful.

When marketing theories were developed, consumers made decisions differently. Yet in the socially intensive information environment around us, the manner in which consumers decide has transformed in numerous ways. If marketing were "invented" today, it would look very different from the way it is still taught in business schools, executive education programs, and textbooks. It would focus less on persuasion attempts or on trying to shape people's preferences. It would be less about what companies say or about how they say it, and more about what they do. Success in the new era is about tracking what people want, and then providing them with absolute value. Will relative forces still play some role in people's decisions? Of course. Will we see more and more decisions that are based on merit, on substance, and on the experienced quality of products and services? Absolutely.

ACKNOWLEDGMENTS

WE WOULD LIKE to thank Jim Levine of Levine Greenberg for his insights and guidance, especially in the initial stages of this project. Thanks to Hollis Heimbouch at HarperCollins for her absolute confidence in our concept, and for turning it into an actual book. We have discussed ideas in this book when presenting them in various universities and other forums and benefited from their points and counterpoints. We are grateful to Ran Kivetz (Columbia University) and Ravi Dhar (Yale University) for their suggestions and perspectives. We interviewed several people for this book and we'd like to thank each and every one of them. Here they are, in no particular order: Bing Liu (University of Illinois), Brett Hurt (Bazaarvoice), Dara O'Rourke (GoodGuide), Oren Etzioni (Decide .com), Ben Farkas (Synthesio), Peter Rojas (gdgt.com), Seth Greenberg (Intuit), Michael Luca (Harvard University), Suzette Jarding (Ristorante Machiavelli), Mark Rosenzweig (Euro-Pro), Myle Ott (Cornell University), Nancy Peterson (Homestars.com), Tom Thai (Bluefin Labs), Raj Rao (3M), Jonney Shih (ASUS), Jenny Sussin (Gartner). We are responsible for the accuracy, clarity, and opinions in this book but we are grateful for the help these people gave us.

Last but certainly not least, we would like to thank our families:

Itamar would like to thank Yael for her ideas, feedback, patience, and encouragement. Emanuel is grateful to Daria for her ongoing support and commitment. We'd like to thank our children, Asaf and Karen (Itamar) and Noam, Yonatan, Maya, and Mika (Emanuel) for their help and encouragement, and for making us even more familiar with the habits and views of a younger generation.

NOTES

Links mentioned in the notes can be accessed online from the book's website at www.AbsoluteValueBook.com

Introduction

1. There are numerous statements about these widely held beliefs. The ones we quoted happen to be from the following sources. About branding: Brian Solis, "The Importance of Brand in an Era of Digital Darwinism," *The Brian Solis Blog*, March 5, 2012, accessed May 15, 2013, http://www.briansolis.com/2012/03/the-importance-of-brand-in-an-era-of-digital-darwinism.

About loyalty: "Consumer Loyalty: Isn't that the Goal?" *Chief Marketer*, January 6, 2009, accessed May 15, 2013, http://www.chiefmarketer.com/database-marketing/loyalty-crm/consumer-loyalty-isnt-that-the-goal-06012009.

About irrationality: William J. Cusick, *All Customers Are Irrational: Understanding What They Think, What They Feel, and What Keeps Them Coming Back* (New York: AMACOM, 2009).

About choice: The quote is from an article by Alina Tugend who reports that "as psychologists and economists study the issue, they are concluding that an overload of options may actually paralyze people or push them into decisions that are against their own best interest." See Alina Tugend, "Too Many Choices: A Problem That Can Paralyze," *New York Times,* February 26, 2010, accessed May 15, 2013, http://www.nytimes .com/2010/02/27/your-money/27shortcuts.html.

About positioning: "Why Positioning Is the Most Important Part of the Marketing Game," *b2bmarketing Blog,* accessed May 15, 2013, http:// www.b2bmarketingblog.co.uk/strategies/why-positioning-is-the-most-important-part-of-the-marketing-game.

Chapter 1: From Relative to Absolute

1. Interview with Jonney Shih, Boston, January 29, 2013; Willy Shih et al., "ASUSTeK Computer Inc. Eee PC," Harvard Business School case study N9-608-156, 2008; Willy Shih and Howard H. Yu, "ASUS-TeK Computer Inc. Eee PC (B)," Harvard Business School case study N9-609-052, 2008; "Small but Destructive," *Economist,* June 11, 2009, accessed May 15, 2013, http://www.economist.com/node/13832588; Michael V. Copeland, "The Man Behind the Netbook Craze," *Fortune,* November 20, 2009, accessed May 15, 2013, http://tech.fortune.cnn .com/2009/11/20/the-man-behind-the-netbook-craze/; Suzanne Nam, "The Jonney Machine," *Forbes,* November 12, 2007, accessed May 15, 2013, http://www.forbes.com/global/2007/1112/024a.html.

2. "Worldwide Tablet Market Surges Ahead on Strong First Quarter Sales, Says IDC," *IDC,* May 1, 2013, accessed May 15, 2013, http://www .idc.com/getdoc.jsp?containerId=prUS24093213; Jon Fingas, "IDC and Gartner: PC Market Flattened Out in Q2 While Apple, ASUS, Lenovo Remain the Stars," *Engadget,* July 12, 2012, accessed May 15, 2013, http:// www.engadget.com/2012/07/12/idc-and-gartner-pc-market-flattened-out-in-q2-2012/.

3. "Asustek Computer," *Forbes,* May 2013, accessed May 14, 2013, http:// www.forbes.com/companies/asustek-computer/.

4. In September 2013, Decide.com was acquired by eBay.

5. Itamar Simonson and Amos Tversky, "Choice in Context: Tradeoff Contrast and Extremeness Aversion," *Journal of Marketing Research* 29 (August 1992): 281–95. This is also where the story about the bread-baking machine first appeared.

6. A note regarding the 2012 experiment: Consumer searches in real life are often even less structured. Participants were limited to Amazon and were asked to focus on Canon PowerShot cameras.

7. People differ in their tendency to compromise, and the new information environment may affect a tendency to prefer as well as a tendency to avoid compromise options. A study involving identical and fraternal twins conducted by Aner Sela and Itamar has shown that a tendency to select or avoid middle options is to a significant degree a heritable tendency. See Itamar Simonson and Aner Sela, "On the Heritability of Consumer Decision Making: An Exploratory Approach for Studying Genetic Effects on Judgment and Choice," *Journal of Consumer Research* 37 (2011): 951–66. A recent study by Briley, Frederick, Sela, and Simonson replicated this finding using a large sample of identical and fraternal twins in Australia.

8. See Susan Fiske and Shelley Taylor, *Social Cognition* (Reading, MA: Addison-Wesley, 1984).

9. Facebook's Graph Search launched a few months before this book went to print. Emanuel used it occasionally and we can see the potential of such a search tool. Somini Sengupta, "Facebook Unveils a New Search Tool," *New York Times*, January 15, 2013, accessed May 15, 2013, http://bits.blogs.nytimes.com/2013/01/15/facebook-unveils-a-new-search-tool/.

10. Kathryn Zickuhr and Aaron Smith, "Internet Adoption over Time," *Pew Internet*, April 13, 2012, accessed May 15, 2013, http://pewinternet.org/Reports/2012/Digital-differences/Main-Report/Internet-adoption-over-time.aspx.

11. Benjamin Scheibehenne, Rainer Greifeneder, and Peter M. Todd, "Can There Ever Be Too Many Options? A Meta-Analytic Review of Choice Overload," *Journal of Consumer Research* 37 (October 2010): 409–25.

12. "Consumer Trust in Online, Social and Mobile Advertising Grows," *Nielsen Blog*, April 10, 2012, accessed May 9, 2013, http://www.nielsen.com/us/en/newswire/2012/consumer-trust-in-online-social-and-mobile-advertising-grows.html. And there are signs that trust in strangers may be stronger among younger people. For example, see "Bazaarvoice and the Center for Generational Kinetics Release New Study on how Millennials Shop," *Bazaarvoice,* January 31, 2012, accessed May 9, 2013,

http://www.bazaarvoice.co.uk/about/press-room/bazaarvoice-and-center-generational-kinetics-release-new-study-how-millennials-shop.

13. On Amazon's influence, see T. J. McCue, "Amazon Influences Consumers More Than Google (and Perhaps Facebook and Apple)," *Forbes*, July 31, 2012, accessed May 9, 2013, http://www.forbes.com/sites/tjmccue/2012/07/31/amazon-influences-consumers-more-than-google-and-possibly-facebook-and-apple/.

14. Jim Lecinski, *Winning the Zero Moment of Truth* ([Mountain View,CA]: Google, 2011), accessed May 15, 2013, http://www.zeromomentoftruth.com/,17.

15. Roger Yu "Rising Tech Firm ASUS Seeks to Improve U.S. Brand," *USA Today,* January 8, 2013, accessed May 15, 2013, http://www.usatoday.com/story/tech/2013/01/08/asus-global-tech-player/1809487/.

Chapter 2: The Decline of "Irrationality"

1. See, for example, Itamar Simonson, "Get Closer to Your Customers by Understanding How They Make Choices," *California Management Review* 35, no. 4 (1993): 68–84; Itamar Simonson, "Shoppers' Easily Influenced Choices," *New York Times*, November 6, 1994.

2. Daniel Kahneman, *Thinking, Fast and Slow* (New York: Farrar, Straus & Giroux, 2011), 411.

3. Peter Eavis and J. B. Silver-Greenberg, "15 of 19 Big Banks Pass Fed's Latest Stress Test," *New York Times*, March 13, 2012, accessed May 9, 2013, http://www.nytimes.com/2012/03/14/business/jpmorgan-passes-stress-test-raises-dividend.html; "Federal Reserve Annual Stress Test Fails 4 of 19 Big Banks," *USA Today*, March 14, 2012, accessed May 9, 2013, http://usatoday30.usatoday.com/money/industries/banking/story/2012-03-12/fed-stress-test/53514988/1.

4. Irwin Levin and Gary Gaeth, "How Consumers Are Affected by the Framing of Attribute Information Before and After Consuming the Product," *Journal of Consumer Research* 15 (December 1988): 374–78.

5. Michael Moss, "Safety of Beef Processing Method Questioned," *New York Times,* December 30, 2009, accessed May 15, 2013, http://www.nytimes.com/2009/12/31/us/31meat.html. See also E. J. Schultz, "Beef Industry Bruised by 'Pink Slime' Battle," *Advertising Age*, April 2, 2012,

accessed May 9, 2013, http://adage.com/article/news/beef-industry-bruised-pink-slime-battle/233855/.

6. See also http://www.beefisbeef.com. Bettina Siegel's blog "The Lunch Tray" can be found at http://www.thelunchtray.com/; the petition against "pink slime" in school food can be found on Change.org: "Tell USDA to STOP Using Pink Slime in School Food!," March 2012, accessed May 9, 2013, http://www.change.org/petitions/tell-usda-to-stop-using-pink-slime-in-school-food.

7. Shlomit Tzur and Shani Shiloh, "[Why Are Real Estate Prices Soaring? Distortions of Internet Boards]," July 31, 2010, accessed May 9, 2013, http://www.themarker.com/realestate/1.587730 (in Hebrew).

8. The situation in Israel, at least at that time, was different. Some progress seems to be happening in regards to consumers' access to real estate transactions data. For more, see this article (in English): Arik Mirovsky, "Tax Authority Pledges Public Access to Property Database," *Haaretz*, February 3, 2010, accessed May 9, 2013, http://www.haaretz.com/print-edition/business/tax-authority-pledges-public-access-to-property-database-1.262673.

9. Stephen Nowlis and Itamar Simonson, "Attribute–Task Compatibility as a Determinant of Consumer Preference Reversals," *Journal of Marketing Research* 34 (May 1997): 205–18.

10. James N. Druckman, "Political Preference Formation: Competition, Deliberation, and the (Ir)relevance of Framing Effects," *American Political Science Review* 98 (2004): 671–86. Similar results were obtained by Yaniv. See Ilan Yaniv, "Group Diversity and Decision Quality: Amplification and Attenuation of the Framing Effect," *International Journal of Forecasting* 27, no.1 (2011): 41–49.

11. Eric Johnson and Daniel Goldstein, "Do Defaults Save Lives?," *Science* 302, no. 5649 (2003): 1338–39.

12. Richard Thaler and Cass Sunstein, *Nudge: Improving Decisions About Health, Wealth, and Happiness* (New York: Penguin Books, 2008).

13. Amos Tversky and Daniel Kahneman, "Judgment Under Uncertainty: Heuristics and Biases," *Science* 185, no. 4157 (1974): 1124–31.

14. Itamar Simonson and Aimee Drolet, "Anchoring Effects on Consum-

ers' Willingness-to-Pay and Willingness-to-Accept," *Journal of Consumer Research* 31 (December 2004): 681–90.

15. David Brooks, *The Social Animal: The Hidden Sources of Love, Character, and Achievement* (New York: Random House, 2011), 181.

Chapter 3: New Patterns in Consumer Decision Making

1. Ann Blair, "Reading Strategies for Coping with Information Overload ca. 1550–1700," *Journal of the History of Ideas* 64, no. 1 (2003): 11–28.

2. Scheibehenne et al., "Can There Ever Be Too Many Options? A Meta-Analytic Review of Choice Overload," 409–25.

3. For example: Amos Tversky and Eldar Shafir, "The Disjunction Effect in Choice Under Uncertainty," *Psychological Science* 3, no. 5 (1992): 305–309.

4. George Stigler, for example, wrote back in 1961 that the amount of search is inversely related to the cost of search.

5. Matt Ridley, "Internet On, Inhibitions Off: Why We Tell All," *Wall Street Journal*, February 18, 2012, accessed May 9, 2013, http://online.wsj.com/article/SB10001424052970204795304577221164189123608.html.

6. Interview with Peter Rojas, August 7, 2012. Article about gdgt.com on TechCrunch: Darrell Etherington, "Gdgt Refocuses As the Remedy for Overwhelmed Gadget Shoppers," *TechCrunch,* September 4, 2012, accessed May 9, 2013, http://techcrunch.com/2012/09/04/gdgt-refocuses-as-the-remedy-for-overwhelmed-gadget-shoppers/.

Chapter 4: Why We're Bullish About Absolute Values

1. Robin Henry, "Publisher Fakes Reviews of Books," *Sunday Times*, September 9, 2012, accessed May 9, 2013, http://www.thesundaytimes.co.uk/sto/news/uk_news/Arts/article1121933.ece.

2. David Streitfeld, "The Best Book Reviews Money Can Buy," *New York Times*, August 26, 2012, accessed May 9, 2013, http://www.nytimes.com/2012/08/26/business/book-reviewers-for-hire-meet-a-demand-for-online-raves.html. Rutherford's website can be found on the Internet Archive, "GettingBookReviews.com," October 1, 2010, accessed May 9,

2013, http://web.archive.org/web/20101001080542/http:/www.getting-bookreviews.com/Home_Page.html.

3. Sharon Bernstein, "Better Business Bureau Says It Will Change Its Rating System," November 19, 2010, accessed May 9, 2013, http://articles.latimes.com/2010/nov/19/business/la-fi-bbb-ratings-20101119.

4. Charles Walford, " 'There Were Hairs in My Quiche': TripAdvisor troll admits smearing reputation of award-winning vegetarian restaurant she hadn't even visited," *MailOnline*, February 16, 2012, accessed May 9, 2013, http://www.dailymail.co.uk/news/article-2101957/TripAdvisor-troll-takes-advert-national-newspaper-apologise-smearing-reputation-award-winning-vegetarian-restaurant.html; "TripAdviser [*sic*] User Apologises for False Reviews," February 16, 2012, accessed May 9, 2013, http://www.telegraph.co.uk/foodanddrink/9085715/TripAdviser-user-apologises-for-false-reviews.html.

5. For example, with Facebook's Graph Search you can instantly find all "Restaurants in Austin, Texas, visited by my friends."

6. Press release: Federal Trade Commission, "Firm to Pay FTC $250,000 to Settle Charges That It Used Misleading Online 'Consumer' and 'Independent' Reviews," March 15, 2011, accessed July 13, 2013, http://ftc.gov/opa/2011/03/legacy.shtm.

7. The book on Amazon UK's site can be seen here: http://www.amazon.co.uk/The-Mistress-Martine-McCutcheon/dp/0330504487, accessed May 9, 2013. Incidentally, *The Mistress* sold pretty well, which is a reminder of the importance of generating interest, which we discuss later in the book. McCutcheon is a household name in the United Kingdom (readers in the United States may remember her as Hugh Grant's secretary/lover in the movie *Love Actually*). Like most Amazon reviewers, professional critics did not give it high marks, but the book got extensive publicity.

8. Interview with Bing Liu, November 8, 2012.

9. Streitfeld, "The Best Book Reviews Money Can Buy."

10. Christopher Elliott, "Some Hotels Stuffing Online Ballot Boxes," *New York Times*, February 7, 2006, accessed May 9, 2013, http://www.nytimes.com/2006/02/07/technology/07iht-hotels.html.

11. David Streitfeld, "Giving Mom's Book Five Stars? Amazon May Cull Your Review," *New York Times,* December 23, 2012, accessed May 9, 2013, http://www.nytimes.com/2012/12/23/technology/amazon-book-reviews-deleted-in-a-purge-aimed-at-manipulation.html.

12. Queena Kim, "Yelp Starts Branding Companies for Buying Fake Reviews," October 18, 2012, accessed May 9, 2013, http://www.market place.org/topics/business/yelp-starts-branding-companies-buying-fake-reviews.

13. Myle Ott, Claire Cardie, and Jeff Hancock, "Estimating the Prevalence of Deception in Online Review Communities," in *WWW '12: Proceedings of the 21st International Conference on the World Wide Web* (New York: ACM, 2012), 201–210.

14. Angie Hicks, interview by Emanuel Rosen, July 23, 2007.

15. Interview with Bing Liu, November 8, 2012. The estimate was mentioned in Streitfeld, "The Best Book Reviews Money Can Buy."

16. Interview with Myle Ott, November 12, 2012.

17. "Gartner Says By 2014, 10–15 Percent of Social Media Reviews to Be Fake, Paid for By Companies," September 17, 2012, accessed May 15, 2013, http://www.gartner.com/newsroom/id/2161315.

18. Regarding Hamas and BBB: Joseph Rhee and Brian Ross, "Terror Group Gets 'A' Rating from Better Business Bureau?," ABC News.com, November 12, 2010, accessed May 9, 2013, http://abcnews.go.com/Blotter/business-bureau-best-ratings-money-buy/story?id=12123843; Brian Ross interviews the blogger who did this: Brian Ross, "Hamas Got A Rating from BBB," ABCNews.com, http://abcnews.go.com/Blotter/video/hamas-rating-bbb-12188207, accessed May 15, 2013. Lynn Mucken, "Can You Trust the Better Business Bureau?," *MSN Money,* March 14, 2011, accessed May 15, 2013, http://money.msn.com/saving-money-tips/post.aspx?post=83b8d5a6-3cdf-46c2-bf59-691223b9e00a. Survey shows that consumers still trust BBB: "Which Contractor Listing Services Do Consumers Trust the Most?," May 22, 2012, accessed May 15, 2013, http://www.buildzoom.com/talk/which-contractor-listing-services-do-consumers-trust-the-most/. Press release: Better Business Bureau, "Better Business Bureau Expels Los Angeles Organization for Failure to Meet Standards," March 12, 2013, accessed July 13, 2013, http://

www.la.bbb.org/article/Better-Business-Bureau-Expels-Los-Angeles-Organization-for-Failure-to-Meet-Standards-40711.

19. Johanna Somers, "Yelp's Ad Pitch Gets Bad Reviews from Some Seattle-Area Business Owners," *Seattle Times,* August 2, 2012, accessed May 9, 2013, http://seattletimes.com/html/businesstechnology/2018837016_yelp03.html. For Yelp's position see http://www.yelp.com/faq#removing_reviews, accessed July 13, 2013.

20. Todd Wasserman, "Yelp by the Numbers: 61 Million Visitors a Month, $58 Million Revenue," November 17, 2011, accessed May 15, 2013, http://mashable.com/2011/11/17/yelp-ipo-numbers-stats/.

21. "Consumer Trust in Online, Social and Mobile Advertising Grows," *Nielsen Online,* April 10, 2012, accessed May 15, 2013, http://www.nielsen.com/us/en/newswire/2012/consumer-trust-in-online-social-and-mobile-advertising-grows.html.

22. "FTC Publishes Final Guides Governing Endorsements, Testimonials," October 5, 2009, accessed May 15, 2013, http://www.ftc.gov/opa/2009/10/endortest.shtm.

23. Interview with Peter Rojas, August 7, 2012.

24. Interview with Michael Luca, November 26, 2012.

25. See Loretti Dobrescu, Michael Luca, and Alberto Motta, "What Makes a Critic Tick? Connected Authors and the Determinants of Book Reviews," Harvard Business School Working Paper No. 12–080, 2012.

26. Interview with Nina and Tim Zagat, October 29, 2007.

27. Alexi Mostrous, "Woman Forced to Apologise for Fake TripAdvisor Review," *Times,* February 16, 2012, accessed May 15, 2013, http://www.thetimes.co.uk/tto/life/food/article3321640.ece.

Chapter 5: When Brands Mean Less

1. Interview with Michael Luca, November 26, 2012.

2. Michael Luca, "Reviews, Reputation, and Revenue: The Case of Yelp.com," Harvard Business School Working Paper No. 12-016, September 2011.

3. Kendall J. Wills, "Disks and More Disks," *New York Times*, June 19, 1983, accessed May 9, 2013, http://www.nytimes.com/1983/06/19/busi ness/discs-and-more-disks-by-kendall-j-wills.html; see also Wikipedia, "Disc film," *Wikipedia*, accessed May 9, 2013, http://en.wikipedia.org/ wiki/Disc_film.

4. "Disc Set Photo Sales Spinning," *Chain Store Age—General Merchandise Edition* 60 (April 1984): 100.

5. According to one study, 89 percent of new products are line or brand extensions. David A. Aaker, *Managing Brand Equity: Capitalizing on the Value of a Brand Name* (New York: Free Press, 1991), 208. See also Kevin Lane Keller, *Strategic Brand Management: Building, Measuring, and Managing Brand Equity*, 2nd ed. (Upper Saddle River, NJ: Prentice-Hall, 2003), 581. Keller says it's 80–90 percent.

6. "Toshiba Slips Further Down in Notebook Sales," *Notebook Review*, December 9, 2003, accessed May 9, 2013, http://www.notebookreview. com/default.asp?newsID=1665.

7. Regarding Nokia, see Hayley Tsukayama, "Nokia Broadens Its Smartphone Lineup," *Washington Post*, February 25, 2013, accessed May 9, 2013, http://www.washingtonpost.com/business/technology/nokia-broadens-smartphone-lineup/2013/02/25/f49aba30-7f5e-11e2-b99e-6baf4ebe42df_story.html.

8. "Espresso Machine Manufacturers—CoffeeRatings.com," accessed May 15, 2013, http://coffeeratings.com/machine-listings.php.

9. Amazon.com, "Customer Reviews DeLonghi BCO120T Combination Coffee/Espresso Machine," accessed May 11, 2013, http://www .amazon.com/DeLonghi-BCO120T-Combination-Espresso-Machine/ product-reviews/B000F2HGVE.

10. Barbara L. Kilfoyle "BG," customer review on Amazon.com, "Find Something Else," September 23, 2009, accessed May 15, 2013, http:// www.amazon.com/review/R2IAX37B6BY9GJ.

11. Jen, customer review on Amazon.com, "Great if You Want to Wash Your Counters and Floor!," July 15, 2011, accessed May 15, 2013, http:// www.amazon.com/review/R1WTYA85SPX0L8.

12. "What's Noka Worth? (Part 10)," December 18, 2006, accessed May 15, 2013, http://dallasfood.org/2006/12/noka-chocolate-part-10/.

13. These, for example, were the two first results of a Google search done February 27, 2013: "NOKA Chocolate Exposed!" on SlashFood, and "Noka Chocolate Is a Scam" on Consumerist (links available in the next note).

14. Regarding NōKA: "What's Noka Worth? (Part 1)," December 9, 2013, accessed May 15, 2013, http://dallasfood.org/2006/12/noka-chocolate-part-1/; NōKA's response to accusations: NOKA_Chocolate, December 31, 2006 (10:54 a.m.), "Statement from NOKA Chocolate," comment on DallasFood.org, accessed May 15, 2013, http://dallasfood.org/forums/index.php?/topic/119-statement-from-noka-chocolate/; Damon Darlin, "Figuring Out Gift Giving in the Age of $2,000-a-Pound Chocolate," *New York Times*, February 10, 2007, accessed May 15, 2013, http://www.nytimes.com/2007/02/10/business/10money.html; Nicole Weston, "NOKA Chocolate Exposed!," December 19, 2006, accessed May 15, 2013, http://www.slashfood.com/2006/12/19/noka-chocolate-exposed/#ixzz1utINklfL; "Noka Chocolate Is a Scam," December 22, 2006, accessed May 15, 2013, http://consumerist.com/2006/12/22/noka-chocolate-is-a-scam/.

15. "Consumer Reports Blender Ratings," Consumer Reports.org (subscription required), accessed May 9, 2013, http://www.consumerreports.org/cro/appliances/kitchen-appliances/blenders/blender-ratings/ratings-overview.htm.

16. Interview with Mark Rosenzweig, February 4, 2013.

17. "How Sony Fell Behind in the Tech Parade," *New York Times,* April 15, 2012, accessed May 12, 2013, http://www.nytimes.com/2012/04/15/technology/how-sony-fell-behind-in-the-tech-parade.html. Regarding Sony's return to profitability see Hiroko Tabuchi, "Sony Doubles Annual Profit Estimate," *New York Times*, April 25, 2013, accessed May 12, 2013, http://www.nytimes.com/2013/04/26/business/global/26iht-sony26.html.

18. "A Pocket Camera Even Pro Photographers Can Love," *New York Times*, June 28, 2012, accessed May 12, 2013, http://www.nytimes

.com/2012/06/28/technology/personaltech/a-pocket-camera-even-pro-photographers-can-love-state-of-the-art.html.

19. Kevin Lane Keller, *Strategic Brand Management: Building, Measuring, and Managing Brand Equity*, 3rd ed. (Upper Saddle River, NJ: Pearson/Prentice-Hall, 2008).

20. Brad Stone, "Can Amazon Be the Wal-Mart of the Web?," *New York Times*, September 19, 2009, accessed May 9, 2013, http://www.nytimes.com/2009/09/20/business/20amazon.html.

21. David Aaker, "Why I Bought a No-Name Computer from a Components Firm," accessed May 12, 2013, December 15, 2011, http://blogs.hbr.org/cs/2011/12/why_i_bought_a_no-name_compute.html.

Chapter 6: Satisfaction, Loyalty, and the Future of Past Experience

1. Video of Rasmussen's presentation can be seen here: "Google Wave Developer Preview at Google I/O 2009," YouTube video, May 28, 2009, accessed May 9, 2013, http://www.youtube.com/watch?v=v_UyVmI-TiYQ. The video was viewed more than 9 million times, indicative of the attention this project has gotten.

2. More on the Deloitte study here: "New Deloitte Survey Uncovers the Erosion of Travel Loyalty," January 22, 2013, accessed May 12, 2013, http://www.deloitte.com/view/en_US/us/Industries/travel-hospitality-leisure/b8f3794f6d36c310VgnVCM1000003256f70aRCRD.htm; "A Restoration in Hotel Loyalty: Developing a Blueprint for Reinventing Loyalty Programs," Deloitte, October 2012, accessed May 12, 2013, http://www.deloitte.com/view/en_US/us/Industries/travel-hospitality-leisure/72ce4f52478ab310VgnVCM1000003256f70aRCRD.htm.

3. Jane Black, "Pushing into BlackBerry's Sweet Spot," *BloombergBusinessweek*, April 3, 2002, accessed May 9, 2013, http://www.businessweek.com/stories/2002-04-03/pushing-into-blackberrys-sweet-spot.

4. Robert Baillieul, "BlackBerry's Decline in 7 Charts," *The Motley Fool*, July 1, 2013, accessed July 13, 2013, http://beta.fool.com/robertbaillieul/2013/07/01/blackberrys-decline-in-6-charts/38850/.

Study regarding BlackBerry: J. D. Speedy, "Blackberry users are ready to move on: Study," *Computing Canada*, January 20, 2012, accessed May 9, 2013, http://www.itworldcanada.com/news/blackberry-users-are-ready-to-move-on-study/144717. Also see Engadget article suggesting that as early as 2010, 50 percent already were looking elsewhere: Paul Miller, "BlackBerry Users Running Out of Loyalty: 50 Percent Plan to Defect to iPhone or Android," August 2, 2010, accessed May 9, 2013, http://www.engadget.com/2010/08/02/blackberry-users-running-out-of-loyalty-50-percent-plan-to-defe/.

5. "Mobile Phone Users Lack Loyalty but Rely Heavily on Services," CMO Council, August 30, 2012, accessed May 9, 2013, http://www.cmocouncil.org/press-detail.php?id=3709.

6. David Aaker, *Building Strong Brands* (New York: Free Press, 1996), 21.

7. "Measuring your Net Promoter Score," accessed May 11, 2013, http://www.netpromotersystem.com/about/measuring-your-net-promoter-score.aspx.

8. Regarding Hyundai: Warren Brown, "Hyundai's Mission Possible: Beat the Luxury Brands," *Washington Post*, April 1, 2007, accessed May 9, 2013, http://www.washingtonpost.com/wp-dyn/content/article/2007/03/29/AR2007032901431.html. ABC News about Hyundai: "The Hyundai Cinderella Story," ABC News, April 13, 2009, accessed May 9, 2013, http://abcnews.go.com/Nightline/video?id=7312406. See also Nick Bunkley, "Hyundai, Using a Safety Net, Wins Market Share," *New York Times*, February 4, 2009, accessed May 9, 2013, http://www.nytimes.com/2009/02/05/business/media/05auto.html.

9. Danny Hakim, "Hyundai Near Top of a Quality Ranking," *New York Times,* April 29, 2004, accessed May 9, 2013, http://www.nytimes.com/2004/04/29/automobiles/29auto.html. See also Joseph B. White, "Hyundai's U.S. Sales Gains to Lag Market," *Wall Street Journal*, July 12, 2013, accessed July 15, 2013, http://online.wsj.com/article/SB10001424127887324425204578601640134140784.html?mod=WSJ_qtoverview_wsjlatest.

10. For example: the general rise in income has not affected happiness ratings, as documented for example by Richard Easterlin. See Richard Easterlin, "Will Raising the Incomes of All Increase the Happiness of All?," *Journal of Economic Behavior & Organization* 27 (1995): 35–47.

11. Incidentally, Lars Rasmussen also headed the development of Facebook Graph Search. See Alyson Shontell, "The Guy Who Led the Charge on Facebook 'Graph Search' Also Created Google's Biggest Flop," *Business Insider*, January 15, 2013, accessed May 9, 2013, http://www.businessinsider.com/lars-rasmussen-facebook-graph-search-google-wave-2013-1.

Chapter 7: Absolute Diffusion: From Pinehurst to Pinterest

1. Everett M. Rogers, *The Fourteenth Paw: Growing Up on an Iowa Farm in the 1930s: A Memoir* (Singapore: AMIC, 2008), 92.

2. Emanuel Rosen, *The Anatomy of Buzz: How to Create Word-of-Mouth Marketing* (New York: Doubleday, 2000).

3. Everett M. Rogers, *Diffusion of Innovations*, 5th ed. (New York: Free Press, 2003).

4. Bryce Ryan and Neal C. Gross, "The Diffusion of Hybrid Seed Corn in Two Iowa Communities," *Rural Sociology* 8, no. 1 (1943): 15–24.

5. Mark S. Granovetter, "The Strength of Weak Ties," *American Journal of Sociology* 78, no. 6 (1973): 1360–80.

6. For example, a recent study by researchers from Facebook and the University of Michigan confirms the fundamental role of weak ties in such an environment. See Eytan Bakshy, "Rethinking Information Diversity in Networks," January 17, 2012, accessed May 9, 2013, https://www.facebook.com/notes/facebook-data-team/rethinking-information-diversity-in-networks/10150503499618859.

7. Geoffrey Moore, *Crossing the Chasm: Marketing and Selling Technology Products to Mainstream Customers* (New York: HarperBusiness, 1991). The Bowling Alley strategy is covered in Geoffrey Moore, *Inside the Tornado: Strategies for Developing, Leveraging, and Surviving Hypergrowth Markets* (New York: HarperBusiness, 1995).

8. For background about the tablet PC see Youngme Moon, "Microsoft: Positioning the Tablet PC," Harvard Business School Case study 9-502-051, 2002.

9. "Why Tablet Computing Hasn't Been Big Business," *PCWorld*, No-

vember 18, 2010, accessed May 9, 2013, http://www.pcworld.com/arti
cle/211066/why_tablet_computing_isnt_big_business.html.

10. About Pinterest: Jenna Wortham, "A Site That Aims to Unleash the
Scrapbook Maker in All of Us," *New York Times*, March 11, 2012, accessed May 9, 2013, http://www.nytimes.com/2012/03/12/technology/
start-ups/pinterest-aims-at-the-scrapbook-maker-in-all-of-us.html.

11. Josh Constine, "Pinterest Hits 10 Million U.S. Monthly Uniques
Faster than Any Standalone Site Ever—ComScore," *TechCrunch*, February 7, 2012, accessed May 9, 2013, http://techcrunch.com/2012/02/07/
pinterest-monthly-uniques/.

12. Silbermann's quote is from an interview at Startup Grind in San Francisco: "Pinterest CEO, Ben Silbermann, Speaking at Startup Grind,"
YouTube video, March 2, 2012, accessed May 9, 2013, http://www.you
tube.com/watch?v=1JLc2PYyCao.
  Silbermann's talks at SXSW in 2012 here: Ben Silbermann, interview
with Christopher Dixon, "Pinterest Explained: Q&A with Co-Founder
Ben Silbermann," March 13, 2012, accessed May 9, 2013, http://schedule
.sxsw.com/2012/events/event_IAP992413.

13. For February 2013 data, see "Start-up Pinterest Wins New Funding,
$2.5 Billion Valuation," Reuters, February 20, 2013, accessed May 9, 2013,
http://www.reuters.com/article/2013/02/21/net-us-funding-pinterest-
idUSBRE91K01R20130221. For April 2012 data, see Alex Knapp, "New
Study Pegs Pinterest as the Number 3 Social Website," *Forbes*, April 9, 2012,
accessed May 9, 2013 http://www.forbes.com/sites/alexknapp/2012/04/09/
new-study-pegs-pinterest-as-the-number-3-social-website/.

Chapter 8: Pointless Positioning and Persuasion

1. HTC Status commercial with Blink-182 can be seen here: "blink-
182—HTC Status Commercial," YouTube video, uploaded by user
ft182tk, August 1, 2011, accessed May 9, 2013 http://www.youtube.com/
watch?v=3K3LTdlIyhA.

2. Greg Kumparak, "Failbook Phone: AT&T Already Looking to Ditch
the HTC Status, Says Source," TechCrunch, August 23, 2011, accessed
July 14, 2013, http://techcrunch.com/2011/08/32/att-discontinuing-htc-
status/.

3. The quote is from Gdgt.com, which gave the phone 71 points: "HTC First," gdgt.com, accessed May 15, 2013, http://gdgt.com/htc/first/. See also Charles Arthur, "AT&T dumps Facebook phone as Home limps past 1m downloads," *Guardian*, May 14, 2013, accessed July 14, 2013, http://www.guardian.co.uk/technology/2013/may/14/facebook-home-app-htc-problems.

4. Greg Sandoval, "HTC to Acquire Majority Stake in Dr. Dre's Beats," *CNET*, August 10, 2013, accessed May 15, 2013, http://news.cnet.com/8301-31001_3-20090967-261/htc-to-acquire-majority-stake-in-dr-dres-beats/.

5. HTC Rezound commercial can be seen here: "HTC Rezound, the First Phone with Beats Audio Built In," YouTube video, uploaded by user HTC, November 11, 2011, accessed May 9, 2013, http://www.youtube.com/watch?v=QoWBACFnmXo.

6. See, for example, Jack Dorsey's interview with Kara Swisher at the Commonwealth Club of California: "Jack Dorsey (5/21/11)," YouTube video uploaded by user commonwealthclub, June 10, 2011, accessed May 9, 2013, http://www.youtube.com/watch?v=4oi21TBCo20.

7. Eric Taub, "Nintendo at AARP Event to Court the Grayer Gamer," *New York Times*, October 30, 2006, accessed May 15, 2013 http://www.nytimes.com/2006/10/30/technology/30aarp.html; Marcus Yam, "Wii Invades Retirement Home," *DailyTech*, February 22, 2007, accessed May 9, 2013, http://www.dailytech.com/Wii+Invades+Retirement+Home/article6191.htm.

8. Andrew Gershoff, Ran Kivetz, and Anat Keinan, "Consumer Response to Versioning: How Brands' Production Methods Affect Perceptions of Unfairness," *Journal of Consumer Research* 39, no. 2 (August 2012): 382–98. See consumers' perception of versioning under "Damaged Good," *Wikipedia*, http://en.wikipedia.org/wiki/Damaged_good (accessed May 9, 2013).

9. John McDermott, "Why AT&T Can Afford to Sell the Facebook Phone for Less than a Dollar," *AdAge Digital*, May 9, 2013, accessed May 11, 2013, http://adage.com/article/digital/t-sell-facebook-phone-a-dollar/241373/.

10. Robert B. Cialdini, *Influence: The Psychology of Persuasion* (New York: William Morrow, 1993), 227.

11. Noah J. Goldstein, Steve J. Martin, and Robert B. Cialdini, *Yes! 50 Scientifically Proven Ways to be Persuasive* (New York: Free Press, 2008), 6.

Chapter 9: The Influence Mix

1. "Does 'Liking' a Brand Drive User Loyalty?," *eMarketer*, February 8, 2012, accessed May 9, 2013, http://www.emarketer.com/Article/Liking-Brand-Drive-User-Loyalty/1008822. Also see Matthew Creamer, "Even Sexy Brands Struggle with Low Engagement on Facebook," *AdAge Digital*, February 28, 2012, accessed My 9, 2013, http://adage.com/article/digital/sexy-brands-struggle-low-engagement-facebook/232993/.

2. See, for example, George J. Stigler, "The Economics of Information," *Journal of Political Economy* 69, no. 3 (June 1961): 213–25.

3. We came across the connection with *Duck Soup* in John Tierney's article, "Facts Prove No Match for Gossip, It Seems," *New York Times*, October 16, 2007, accessed May 15, 2013, http://www.nytimes.com/2007/10/16/science/16tier.html.

4. See "Asch Conformity Experiments," *Wikipedia*, http://en.wikipedia.org/wiki/Asch_conformity_experiments, accessed May 19, 2013. See also Ralf D. Sommerfeld, "Gossip as an Alternative for Direct Observation in Games of Indirect Reciprocity," *PNAS* 104, no. 44 (2007):17435–40.

5. Philip Nelson, "Information and Consumer Behavior," *Journal of Political Economy* 78 (March–April 1970): 311–29.

6. There is a third category, "credence goods/attributes," such as many vitamin supplements, for which quality cannot be assessed even after experience.

7. Neil Buckley "Atkins Puts Hole in Krispy Kreme Profits," *Financial Times*, May 8, 2004, 1; Burton D. Cohen, "Krispy Kreme: The Franchisor That Went Stale," Kellogg School of Management case study, KEL454.

8. Some research that suggests Black Friday deals are not necessarily the best: Stephanie Clifford, "Friday's Deals May Not Be the Best," *New York*

Times, November 24, 2011, accessed May 9, 2009, http://www.nytimes .com/2011/11/25/business/fridays-deals-may-not-be-the-best.html.

9. Amazon.com, "Customer Reviews LitterMaid LME9000 Elite Mega Advanced Automatic Self-Cleaning Litter Box," accessed May 9, 2013, http://www.amazon.com/LitterMaid-LME9000-Advanced-Automatic-Self-Cleaning/product-reviews/B000H6AK7A.

10. Douglas Rushkoff, *Coercion: Why We Listen to What "They" Say* (New York: Riverhead, 1999), 93.

Chapter 10: Communication: Match Your Customers' Influence Mix

1. Regis McKenna, *Relationship Marketing: Successful Strategies for the Age of the Customer* (Reading, MA: Addison-Wesley, 1991), 12.

2. Al Ries and Laura Ries, *The Fall of Advertising and the Rise of PR* (New York: HarperBusiness, 2002), xii. As we point out later, we agree with Al and Laura Ries that PR is increasingly important, but this doesn't mean that advertising is dead, or that it can only be used to maintain brands that have been created by publicity.

3. We are starting to see evidence for the decline in the importance of top-of-mind recall. A study by McKinsey found that consumers increasingly evaluated brands that were not part of their initial consideration set. For example, consumers added, on average, 2.2 brands to their consideration set of 3.8 cars, 1.4 brands to an initial set of 3.2 auto insurance companies, and 1 brand to an initial set of 1.7 personal computers. David Court, Dave Elzinga, Susan Mulder, and Ole Jørgen Vetvik, "The Consumer Decision Journey," *McKinsey Quarterly* (June 2009): 4, accessed May 14, 2013, http://www.mckinsey.com/insights/marketing_sales/ the_consumer_decision_journey.

4. "LeBron's Day with the Samsung Galaxy Note II," YouTube video uploaded by user samsungmobileusa, October 30, 2012, accessed May 9, 2013, http://www.youtube.com/watch?v=IeomAnjz1Oc. Article in *Slate* about this commercial: John Swashburg, "Rebranding LeBron," *Slate*, December 5, 2012, accessed May 9, 2013, http://www.slate.com/blogs/ browbeat/2012/12/05/lebron_james_samsung_ad_galaxy_note_ii_ad_ wins_over_old_lebron_hater_video.html.

5. About Samsung's ads, see John McDermott, "Samsung's Ads Are Most Effective of the Year, but Fail to Take Bite Out of iPhone," *AdAge Digital*, January 4, 2013, accessed May 12, 2013, http://adage.com/article/digital/samsung-s-ads-effective-bite-iphone/238997/.

6. About Amazon Vine: "What is Amazon Vine?," accessed May 9, 2013, http://www.amazon.com/gp/vine/help.

7. Interview with Raj Rao, October 22, 2012.

8. PowerReviews was recently acquired by Bazaarvoice.

9. Interview with Brett Hurt, September 21, 2012.

10. Itamar Simonson, Stephen Nowlis, and Yael Simonson, "The Effect of Irrelevant Preference Arguments on Consumer Choice," *Journal of Consumer Psychology* 2, no. 3 (1993): 287–306.

11. Ries and Ries. *The Fall of Advertising and the Rise of PR*, xx.

12. Laura Petrecca, "Small Business Challengers Work on Marketing," *USA Today*, April 1, 2011, accessed May 14, 2013, http://usatoday30.usatoday.com/money/smallbusiness/startup/2010-06-04-marketing_N.htm.

13. "Poppa D's Nuts Debuts in 7-Eleven," *Orlando Business Journal*, April 27, 2011, accessed May 14, 2013, http://www.bizjournals.com/orlando/news/2011/04/27/poppa-ds-nuts-debuts-in-7-eleven.html.

14. The Lysol Community can be found here: http://www.lysol.com/lysol-community, accessed May 14, 2013.

Chapter 11: Market Research: From Predicting to Tracking

1. Jemima Kiss, "'iPhone Set to Struggle,'" *Guardian*, June 29, 2007, accessed May 14, 2013, http://www.guardian.co.uk/media/2007/jun/29/digitalmedia.news.

2. "Anytime, Anyplace: Understanding the Connected Generation," Universal McCann, 2007, accessed July 12, 2013, http://universalmccann.bitecp.com/um_report_pttp_lr3.pdf.

3. Some background about the difference between markets in this case: Sixty percent of mobile phone users in the United States already had

three or more devices like an MP3 player, a portable media device, and a digital camera. So when asked for their opinion about a converged device, only 31 percent of respondents in the United States showed interest in multiple capabilities. The picture was different in countries like Mexico or India, where people liked the concept.

4. For example see, David Pogue, "The iPhone Matches Most of Its Hype," *New York Times*, June 27, 2007, accessed May 15, 2013, http://www.nytimes.com/2007/06/27/technology/circuits/27pogue.html.

5. For a review, see for example Paul E. Green and V. Srinivasan, "Conjoint Analysis in Marketing: New Developments with Implications for Research and Practice," *Journal of Marketing* 54, no. 4 (October 1990): 3–19.

6. Interview with Tom Thai, August 2, 2012.

7. Background articles about Bluefin: David Talbot, "A Social-Media Decoder," *MIT Technology Review*, October 18, 2011, accessed May 14, 2013, http://www.technologyreview.com/featuredstory/425787/a-social-media-decoder/; Rachel Z. Arndt, "Bluefin Mine Social Media to Improve TV Analytics," *Fast Company*, December 2011/January 2012, accessed May 14, 2013, http://www.fastcompany.com/1793473/bluefin-mines-social-media-improve-tv-analytics.

8. John Jannarone, "When Twitter Fans Steer TV," September 17, 2012, accessed May 14, 2013, http://online.wsj.com/article/SB10000872396390444772804577623444273016770.html.

9. In 2013, Bluefin Labs was acquired by Twitter.

10. Chris Ziegler, "Nokia CEO Stephen Elop Rallies Troops in Brutally Honest 'Burning Platform' Memo? (Update: It's Real!)," Engadget, February 8, 2011, accessed May 14, 2013, http://www.engadget.com/2011/02/08/nokia-ceo-stephen-elop-rallies-troops-in-brutally-honest-burnin/.

11. Willy Shih and Howard H. Yu, "ASUSTeK Computer Inc. Eee PC (B)," Harvard Business School case study N9-609-052, 2008. See also HBR blog: Scott Anthony, "Netbooks: Disruption Interrupted?," *HBR Blog Network*, March 17, 2009, accessed May 15, 2013, http://blogs.hbr.org/anthony/2009/03/netbooks_disruption_interrupte.html. Clive Thomp-

son, "The Netbook Effect: How Cheap Little Laptops Hit the Big Time," *Wired*, February 23, 2009, accessed May 15, 2013, http://www.wired.com/gadgets/wireless/magazine/17-03/mf_netbooks.

12. Interview with Brett Hurt, September 21, 2012. Regarding the Samsung example, see Tara DeMarco, "Revisiting the Cliché, 'The Customer Is Always Right,'" *bazzarvoice:blog*, May 16, 2011, accessed May 14, 2013, http://blog.bazaarvoice.com/2011/05/16/revisiting-the-cliche-the-customer-is-always-right/.

13. Interview with Brett Hurt, September 21, 2012.

14. Accor case: Ben, "My Forrester Groundswell Awards (Submission)," *Synthesio*, August 4, 2011, accessed May 14, 2013, http://synthesio.com/corporate/2011/awards/forrester2011/.

15. Interview with Brett Hurt, September 21, 2012; Steve Fuller, Senior Vice President & CMO, L.L.Bean, Presentation at Bazaarvoice Social Commerce Summit 2011, accessed January 17, 2013, http://www.bazaarvoice.com/video-playback/how-customer-conversations-transform-operations.html.

16. This discussion is consistent with prior work on the effect of diagnosticity and accessibility on judgment. J. M. Feldman and J. G. Lynch Jr., "Self-Generated Validity and Other Effects of Measurement on Belief, Attitude, Intention and Behavior," *Journal of Applied Psychology* 73 (1988): 421–35

17. Only 6 percent of women surveyed in North America said it's very important to find information about fashion, jewelry, or accessories, while 12 percent (twice as many) said that they are very likely to share information about this category. Similarly, 19 percent said it's very important to find information about entertainment, while 38 percent (again, twice as many) said they are very likely to share information about this category. See "How Women Get and Spread Word on Products and Services Tied to Lifestage and Product Category," Harbinger, October 6, 2010, accessed May 14, 2013, http://www.harbingerideas.com/consumer_insight_research.asp.

18. Richard Nisbett and Timothy Wilson, "Telling More than We Can Know: Verbal Reports on Mental Processes," *Psychological Review* 84 (1977): 231–59.

Chapter 12: Segment Evolution:
From Susceptible to Savvy

12. A video of the session is available here: "Sep. 23, 2010—A Hearing on H.R. 6149, the 'Precious Coins and Bullion Disclosure Act,'" YouTube video uploaded by user EnergyCommerce, July 20, 2011, accessed May, 15 2013, http://www.youtube.com/watch?v=pAQCkrsbUjA#t=0h30m5s. Dr. Bazan's testimony starts at thirty minutes into the session.

2. Press release: Santa Monica City Attorney's Office, "Goldline International and Executives Charged with Fraud, False Advertising and Conspiracy," November 1, 2011, accessed May 14, 2013,_http://www .smgov.net/departments/cao/Content.aspx?id=27883.

3. *Los Angeles Times* coverage of the settlement: Stuart Pfeifer, "Goldline Agrees to Refund up to $4.5 Million to Former Customers," *Los Angeles Times*, February 23, 2012, accessed May 14, 2013, http://articles.latimes. com/2012/feb/23/business/la-fi-0223-goldline-settlement-20120223. For Goldline's press release, see "All Charges Dismissed, Goldline Announces; Precious Metals Company Will Continue to Set Standard for Customer Disclosures," Goldline International, accessed May 14, 2013, http://www.goldline.com/santa-monica-dismisses-misdemeanor-criminal-charges; "Goldline Responds to City Attorney's Misleading Press Release," Goldline International, accessed May 14, 2013, http:// www.goldline.com/goldline-international-charges-response. Press release: Santa Monica City Attorney's Office, "Goldline International Placed Under Injunction, Ordered to Change Sales Practices," February 22, 2012, accessed May 14, 2013 http://www.smgov.net/departments/ cao/Content.aspx?id=29440.

4. For example: Matthew Mosk, Brian Ross, and Avni Patel, "Goldline: We'll Fight Fraud Charges," November 2, 2011, accessed May 15, 2013, ABC News, http://abcnews.go.com/Blotter/goldline-fight-fraud-charges/ story?id=14864468#.UZR6-LVwpas; Jeff Neumann, "Glenn Beck's Goldline International Under Investigation for Ripping People Off," *Gawker*, July 20, 2010, accessed May 15, 2013, http://gawker.com/5591413/glenn-becks-goldline-international-under-investigation; Stephanie Mencimer, "Glenn Beck's Gold Gurus Charged with Fraud," *Mother Jones*, May 19, 2010, accessed May 15, 2013, http://www.motherjones.com/poli tics/2010/05/glenn-beck-goldline-weiner. *Consumer Reports* warned that

Goldline's prices for collectible coins were inflated: Consumer Reports Money Adviser, "Can You Trust Goldline's Advice?," ConsumerReports .org, August 2010, accessed May 15, 2013, http://www.consumerreports .org/cro/2010/08/can-you-trust-goldline-s-advice/index.htm.

5. Data provided to us by Nielsen suggests some link to education and income level, at least as of 2011. Mobile users in the United States with higher income or more years of formal education were more likely to use their mobile device to read product reviews prior to purchase or to compare prices of products. For example, while 68 percent of those with a graduate degree read a product review on their mobile device, only 52 percent of those with a high school diploma did the same. Proprietary data provided by Nielsen, Q2 2012 Mobile Connected Device Report, pp. 25–26, 37–38.

6. Some observers like Cass Sunstein (in his book *Republic.com*) argue that the Internet contributes to polarization as people choose not to expose themselves to different points of view. On the other hand, scholars like Matthew Gentzkow and Jesse Shapiro argue that most Internet users, even those we would call "extremists," do not stay within their communities. See Matthew Gentzkow and Jesse Shapiro, "Ideological Segregation Online and Offline," *Quarterly Journal of Economics* 126, no. 4 (2011): 1799–1839.

Chapter 13: The Future of the Absolute

1. A video on how Zillow was born can be seen here: "How Zillow started," YouTube video uploaded by user 3oceans, October 29, 2006, accessed May 15, 2013, http://www.youtube.com/watch?v=kfVoM6jEiHo.

2. Interview with Oren Etzioni, January 27, 2012.

3. Mark Hendrickson, "Microsoft Acquires Farecast for $115M," *TechCrunch*, April 17, 2008, accessed May 15, 2013, http://techcrunch .com/2008/04/17/microsoft-acquires-farecast-for-115m/.

4. Etzioni pointed out to us that the click-through was very much affected by the program's advice.

5. Richard H. Thaler and Will Tucker, "Smarter Information, Smarter Consumers," *Harvard Business Review*, January–February, 2013.

6. The difference can be significant. Fast Company calculated that on a $20,000 car, there can be a $5,000 gap between what the most susceptible consumers and the savviest buyers pay.

7. Tara Siegel Bernard, "Car Dealers Wince at a Site to End Sales Haggling," *New York Times*, February 10, 2012, accessed May 14, 2013, http://www.nytimes.com/2012/02/11/your-money/car-dealers-wince-at-a-site-to-end-sales-haggling.html; "The TrueCar Challenge," *Economist*, January 7, 2012, accessed May 14, 2013, http://www.economist.com/node/21542456; Gregory Ferenstein, "Yahoo Autos Partners with Truecar, Brings Transparency to Car Buying," *Fast Company*, January 3, 2012, accessed May 14, 2013, http://www.fastcompany.com/1804517/yahoo-autos-partners-truecar-brings-transparency-car-buying.

8. Dinah Wisenberg Brin, "TrueCar Aims to Foster Hassle-Free Auto Deals," CNBC, March 22, 2013, accessed May 14, 2013, http://www.cnbc.com/id/100582285.

9. Stephen Nowlis and Itamar Simonson, "Attribute–Task Compatibility as a Determinant of Consumer Preference Reversals," *Journal of Marketing Research* 34 (May 1997): 205–218.

10. Thaler and Tucker, "Smarter Information, Smarter Consumers."

11. Oliver Nieburg ,"Chocolate Over-Consumption May be Linked to Parkinson's Disease—Review," *Confectionary News*, April 11, 2013, http://www.confectionerynews.com/Sectors/Chocolate/Chocolate-over-consumption-may-be-linked-to-Parkinson-s-Disease-review.

12. Douglas Bernheim and Jonathan Meer, "Do Real Estate Brokers Add Value When Listing Services Are Unbundled?," February 2008, accessed May 15, 2013, Working Paper No. 13796, http://www.nber.org/papers/w13796.pdf. In addition, Steven D. Levitt and Chad Syverson found that homes owned by real estate agents sell for about 3.7 percent more than other houses. Steven D. Levitt and Chad Syverson, "Market Distortions When Agents Are Better Informed: The Value of Information in Real Estate Transactions," January 2005, accessed May 15, 2013, NBER Working Paper No. 11053, http://www.nber.org/papers/w11053.

13. Brad Stone, "Why Redfin, Zillow, and Trulia Haven't Killed Off Real Estate Brokers," *BloombergBusinessweek*, March 7, 2013, accessed

May 15, 2013, http://www.businessweek.com/articles/2013-03-07/why-redfin-zillow-and-trulia-havent-killed-off-real-estate-brokers.

Chapter 14: Absolute Business: A Final Word

1. Darrel G. Clarke and Randall E. Wise, "Optical Distortion, Inc.," Harvard Business School case study 9-575-072, 1975; Patrick J. Kaufmann, "Optical Distortion, Inc. (C): The 1988 Reintroduction," Harvard Business School case study 9-589-011, 1990.

INDEX

Aaker, David, 62, 75-76

ABC News, 21, 165

ABC TV, 44-45, 52, 53

absolute advantage, 97

absolute evaluations
  future of, 175-183
  perfect information and, 9-10
  shift from relative evaluations to, 3-9, 167
  what drives the shift from relative to, 10-16

absolute inequality, 166, 171-172

Accor, 157

Acer, 16, 153

adoption model/adopter categories, 91-100

advertising
  in generating consumer interest, 135-138
  persuasive, 108-111
  testing of TV commercials, 151

top-of-mind, 136, 143, 172

  see also marketing

Allen, Woody, 108

Amazon.com, 12, 23
  couch tracking on, 34, 36
  as distribution channel, 186
  diversification of, 75
  fake reviews on, 44, 48, 49-50
  pricing on, 188
  product reviews on, 7, 8, 11, 15, 26, 69, 129, 138, 149, 159
  review of, 55
  Vine program, 138

Anatomy of Buzz, The (Rosen), 91, 93

anchoring, 31

Angie's List, 51

Angry Birds, 90, 91

Annie Hall (movie), 108

Apple, 5, 16, 66, 80, 95-96, 130-131

ASUS, 71, 170
  brand consideration, 75–76
  launch of Eee PC, 5–6, 15, 16, 153
  shift away from relative evalua-
    tions, 3–5
asymmetric dominance, 22–23,
  190
AT&T Wireless, 107
Attensity, 152
authority, persuasion and symbols
  of, 108
automotive industry, 39–40, 102,
  104–105, 127, 159–160, 178–179
Avis, 102, 104

B2B companies, 110
baby boomers, 168
bait and switch, 164
Bakodo, 11
banner ads, 136
Barton, Richard, 173–174, 175
Bastardi, Anthony, 37
Bazaarvoice, 52, 141, 142, 156
Bazan, Julius, 163–165
Beats Electronics, 104
Beck, Glenn, 163–164
behavioral-based O-influence
  segments, 170
behavioral decision theory, 29–30,
  121
BestBuy.com, 11, 52, 141, 149
Better Business Bureau, Santa
  Monica, CA, 44–45, 52–53
Bezos, Jeff, 75
Bing search engine, 174, 176
Black Friday purchases, 128–129,
  130

BlackBerry, 79–80
Blair, Ann, 33
Blink-182, 101, 102
Block, Ryan, 41
blogs/bloggers, 21, 41, 45, 53, 54,
  70
Bluefin Labs, 151–152
Bowling Alley strategy, 95, 99,
  100
brand awareness, 3
brand equity, 16
  in consumer decision making,
    68, 189
  four components of, 62
  as a proxy for quality, 72
brand loyalty, 28, 140, 170
  decline in, 16, 62, 66, 79–82,
    189
  satisfaction and, 84–87
brand names
  declining impact of, 61–62,
    86
  diversification, 73–76
  early role as proxy for quality,
    63–65
  liking on Facebook, 118
  reduced role as a proxy for qual-
    ity, 69–71, 73, 126
  strong, 130–131
  in top-of-mind ads, 136
  volatility of, 65–68
  Yelp reviews and, 59–61
brick-and-mortar stores, point of
  purchase at, 129–130
BrightScope, 180–181
bullion coins, 164–165
BusinessWeek, 174

Cameras, 6–8, 22, 26–27, 63–64, 73, 133–134, 142
Canon PowerShot cameras, 7–8, 26–27
Car and Driver, 39
Cardie, Claire, 51
CarsDirect.com, 154
cell phones
  commercials on, 127
  Facebook phone, 101–102, 103, 107
  HTC Rezound (sound phone), 103–104
  iPhone, 16, 98, 147, 148, 149, 153, 170
  pre-purchase behavior, 169–170
  Samsung Galaxy Note II, 137–138
channels, distribution, 186–187
choice context effects, 22–24
choice engines, 177
choice overload, 13, 34–35, 41–42, 66
choice set, 22
choices. see consumer decision making
CMO Council, 80
CNET, 4, 11, 36, 118, 149
cognitive misers, 8–9, 180
collectible coins, 164–165
communication
  communicability, 97
  in matching customers' Influence Mix, 133–146
compatibility, consumer preferences and, 97–98
compromise effect, 7, 8

computer industry. see PC industry
comScore, 99
confirmation bias, 62, 85–86
conjoint analysis, 149–150
consumer decision making
  access to technology and, 165–167
  behavioral decision making, 29–30, 121
  brand-based choices in, 66–68
  brand equity in, 68
  consumer choices and task effects, 24–25
  couch tracking, 35–37
  emotions in, 38–40
  faster verdicts in, 37–38, 179, 189
  importance of, 124
  independent research, 181–182
  influences in, 19–25
  information for better, 173–175
  language in, 39
  new patterns in, 33–35
  new tools for, 179–182
  noise in, 25–28
  risk and uncertainty in, 124–125
  tools used in, 14–15
  usefulness of evaluations in, 13–14
Consumer Reports, 39, 47, 118, 120, 165
consumers
  advertising and consumer interest, 135–138
  compatibility and preferences, 97–98
  and decline in brand loyalty, 79–82

consumers (*cont.*)
and decline of past experience, 82–84
and inferior products, 170–172
influence in market research, 15
Influence Mix, 115–132
lack of trust of marketers, 118
and marketing communication, 97, 133–146
measurement of customer satisfaction, 155–158
persuasion techniques on, 108–111
product quality and differentiation, 124
satisfaction and customer loyalty, 84–87, 140
segmentation strategies on, 106–107
trust in review sites, 46–47
couch tracking, 35–37, 41, 42, 179
country of origin, in determining quality, 69
crippleware, 107
customers. *see* consumers

Decide.com, 5, 11, 149, 180, 188
decision making. *see* consumer decision making
default choice, 30
Dell, 4, 153
DeLonghi, 69
diagnosticity, 158
differentiation
product, 102–103
quality and, 124

diffusion theory, 90–100
digital wallets, 181
distribution channels, 186–187
Dobrescu, Loretti, 55
Drolet, Aimee, 31
Druckman, James, 28
Dyson vacuum cleaners, 71, 72, 73

e-books, 48
emotions
in consumer decision making, 38–40
persuasive techniques and, 108
social media and emotional ties, 140
end-of-aisle display (end cap), 24
Engadget (blog), 35, 36, 41, 54
Etzioni, Oren, 173, 174, 180
Euro-Pro, 71, 72–73
expectations and experience, 85–86, 155
Expedia, 51, 52
experts
access to, 11–12, 13, 46–47
influence not reflected in market research, 15
and product success or failure, 154
usefulness of evaluations by, 14

Facebook
couch tracking on, 36
and sale of Likes, 45
liking on, 118
marketing on, 136, 139, 144–145, 183

product recommendations through, 11, 47

weak ties connection, 93

Facebook phone, 101-102, 103, 107

FactCheck.org, 167

fake reviews, 12-13, 45, 46, 47-52

Fall of Advertising and the Rise of PR, The (Ries and Ries), 135

Farecast.com, 174, 176

Fast Company, 122

Fast Food Calorie Lookup, 128

fast trackers and imitators, 189

faster verdicts, 37-38, 179, 189

Federal Trade Commission, 48, 54

first-mover advantage, 189

Fisman, Raymond, 25

focus groups, 149

food

   beef, 20-22

   chocolate, 69-70, 120, 121, 181-182

   doughnuts, 122

   nuts, 144-145

   restaurant industry, 55-56, 59-61, 128, 179-180

   school lunches, 21

framing, 20-22, 28, 190

Frink, Lloyd, 173-174, 175

future trends, 175-177

gadget websites, 36, 41

gadgetwise, 36

Gaeth, Gary, 20

Gartner, 52

gdgt.com., 4, 41-42, 54, 149

Gershoff, Andrew, 107

GettingBookReviews.com, 44, 48

Gizmodo (blog), 36, 41, 54

Goldline International, 163-165

Goldstein, Daniel, 30

GoodGuide, 25, 174-175, 176

Google, 15, 16, 26, 50, 66, 77, 98, 153, 181

Google Maps, 77

Google Wave, 87

Granovetter, Mark, 92, 93-94

Guardian, 147

Hamas, 44-45, 52-53

Hancock, Jeff, 51

Harley-Davidson, 140, 166, 170

Hartman, Terri, 52-53

Harvard Business Review, 177

Harvard Business School, "Optical Distortion" case study, 187-188

HealthyOut, 128, 179-180

hotel industry, 79, 106-107, 117, 157

Hotels.com, 51

Houzz, 90

HP, 4, 153

HTC, 16, 103, 153

HTC First, 107

HTC Rezound, 103-104

Huber, Joel, 22

Hurt, Brett, 52, 142

Hyundai, 16, 83-84

IDC, 3

ideological segregation, 167

IMDb, 78

impulse purchases, 129-130

independent research, 181–182
inferior products, 170–172
Influence Mix framework, 115–132
  matching customers' Influence
    Mix, 133–146
  what is your customers' Influ-
    ence Mix?, 123–126
information
  access to data, 177–178
  for better decision-making, 173–
    175
dissemination, weak ties and new,
    92–93
information overload, 13
innovation, adoption model and,
    91–98
Internet
  expert reviews on, 11–12
  independent research, 182
  new decision-making tools,
    179–181
  top-of-mind advertising on the
    Web, 136
iPad, 95
iPhone, 16, 98, 147, 148, 149, 153,
    170
irrationality concept, 18–20, 190
choice context effects, 22–24
framing effects, 20–22, 28, 190
task effects, 24–25
Iyengar, Sheena, 25

James, LeBron, 137
J.D. Power, 83, 120
Jobs, Steve, 5
Johnson, Eric, 30
Johnson, Magic, 137

Kahneman, Daniel, 19, 31
Kamenica, Emir, 25
Keinan, Anat, 107
Kidman, Nicole, 122
Kivetz, Ran, 107
Kodak, 63–64
Kohl's, 156
Krispy Kreme, 122

laddering technique, 161
laminator, 138
Langfield, Joanna, 55
Lego, 141
Lenovo, 153
Letterman, David, 83
Levin, Irwin, 20
LG, 16, 74, 141
liking, 108, 118
LinkedIn, 93
Linux, 5
Liu, Bing, 51–52
L.L. Bean, 157–158
Locke, John, 48
Los Angeles Times, 165
loyalty. see brand loyalty
loyalty programs, 87
Luca, Michael, 55, 60–61
"The Lunch Tray" (blog), 21

McCutcheon, Martine, 44
Machiavelli (restaurant), 59–60,
    61
McKenna, Regis, 135
McLuhan, Marshall, 108
MacUser, 90
Maberry, Porter, 137
Madhok, Michelle, 49

manufacturing defects, 156–157

market research, 147–162

  changes in, 189

  in determining location on the influence continuum, 158–162

  in groups, 149

  measuring satisfaction, 155–158

  in O-influence segmentation, 169–170

  product development and, 15–16

  shift in focus, 151–155

Marketers (M) (in Influence Mix), 117, 118, 119, 120, 121, 123, 126, 131

  and communicating through O, 139, 141

  O-influence segments and, 172

marketing

  adoption model in, 94–95

  communication, 133–146

  couch tracking, 36–37

  and customers' influence mix, 123–126

  and decline of past experience, 82–84

  distribution channels, 186–187

  emotional appeal in, 39–40

  end cap displays, 24–25

  fake reviews, 48, 54

  framing in, 21–22

  Influence Mix framework and, 115–146

  invention of marketing today, 191

  loyalty and, 79–82

  online reviews manipulation in, 45

  organizational aspects, 184–186

  persuasion techniques, 108–111

  positioning strategies, 101–111

  price anchors in, 31

  pricing, 187–188

  product differentiation, 102–103

  relative evaluations in, 6–9

  segmentation strategies, 105–107

  on social media, 115, 124, 136, 139–140

  target, 95–96

  versioning strategies, 107

Marx Brothers, 119

Miami Heat, 137

Microsoft, 5, 95–96, 141, 153, 174

Minolta cameras, 6–7

Mistress, The (McCutcheon), 44, 48

mobile apps, 11, 25

Moore, Geoffrey, 94, 95

Mother Jones, 165

Motta, Alberto, 55

NBC Nightly News, 174

Net Promoter Score, 81–82

netbooks, 5, 153

New York Times, 20, 21, 44, 48, 49, 50, 51, 73, 99

Nielsen, 14–15, 53

Nike, 105

Ninja Blender, 16, 72

Nintendo, 106

noise, 25–28

NôKA Chocolate, 69–70

Nokia, 66, 153

Nowlis, Stephen, 24
Nudge (Thaler and Sunstein), 30

O-Dependent domains, 123–126,
   129, 134–135, 136, 139, 190
O-Dependent marketers, 148, 185,
   186, 187
O-Dependent products, 148
O ecosystem, 171
O-Independent domains, 123–126,
   134–135, 144–145
O-influence continuum
   customers' location on, 126
   market research and location on,
      158–162
   segments and location on, 168–
      170, 172
O-Influencers/O-Dependent
   communicating through O, 139–
      141, 143
   Influence Mix, 116, 117–132
   market research and, 149, 150
   market research and determining
      location on the continuum,
      158–162
   matching customers' Influence
      Mix, 133–146
   what is your customers' Influ-
      ence Mix?, 123–126
observability, consumer, 97
Oliver, Jamie, 21
Oltman, Stacy, 53
Orbitz, 51
O'Reilly, Gary, 44
organic segmentation, 105–107
O'Rourke, Dara, 173, 174–175
Other people and information

services (O) (in Influence Mix),
   116, 117–118, 119, 120, 121, 122,
   126–132, 139–141
Ott, Myle, 51, 52

Painter, Scott, 178
Pan Macmillan, 44, 48
Parker, Robert, 70
past experience, decline of, 82–84
PayPal, 181
PC industry
   brand consideration, 75–76,
      170
   brand name volatility, 66
   launch of Eee PC, 5–6, 15, 16,
      153
   review sites, 11, 12–13
   shift away from relative evalua-
      tions in, 3–6
   software developers, 77, 87
   tablet computing, 3, 95–96
PC Magazine, 11, 90
perceptions
   framing effects and, 20–22
   questioning consumer, 161
perfect information, 9–10
persuasion techniques, 108–111
PhoneDog.com, 36, 86, 104
Pinehurst Farm, Iowa, 89–90, 98,
   99
Pinterest, 16, 36, 98–99
point of purchase, 129–130
political segregation, 167
PolitiFact, 167
Poppa D's Nuts, 144–145
portable devices study, 2007, 147,
   148, 149

positioning and persuasion, 101–111

positioning statements, 110–111

PowerReviews, 141

pre-purchase search/behavior, 34–35, 37, 169–170

preference formation, 141, 143

preference reversal, 29

preferences
  prior (P), 116–117, 118, 120, 121, 122, 123, 126, 131
  limitation of market research, 161
  stable, 120–121

price anchors, 31

price comparison sites, 61

price versioning, 107

Priceline, 51

pricing, 187–188
  as a proxy for quality, 69–71

product placements, movie and TV, 136

promoters, 81–82

psychographic segmentation, 169

public consumption, 125–126

public relations, 135, 143

Puck, Wolfgang, 52

quality, product
  assessment of, 10, 78, 166, 189
  brand names and, 62, 63–65, 86
  and differentiation, 124
  pricing and, 187

quality proxies
  country of origin, 69
  price, 69–71
  reduced role of, 69–71, 73

Rao, Raj, 138

Rasmussen, Lars, 77, 87

rating systems, review site, 45, 46, 47, 49, 50, 51

rational information, 39

rational utility-maximizers, 18–19

real estate (Zillow), 24, 175, 176, 177, 182

reciprocation, persuasion and, 108–109

Red Herring, 41

Reevoo, 141, 142

reference prices, 31

Reich, Taly, 7, 22, 23

relative advantage, 97

relative evaluations
  experimental evidence for decline, 6–9
  shift from relative to absolute evaluations, 3–9, 167
  what drives the shift from relative to absolute evaluations, 10–16

Research in Motion, 79–80

research, independent, 181–182

retirement planning, 180–181

review sites, 11
  conjoint analysis and, 149–150
  curbing manipulations on, 49–52
  on Facebook phone, 102
  hotel, 117
  on HTC Rezound phone, 104
  manipulating, 12–13, 45, 46, 47–49, 141
  and marketers' role, 141–144
  rating systems, 45, 46, 47, 49, 50, 51

review sites (*cont.*)
  reviewers under review, 52–56
  Yelp reviews and brand names,
    59–61
  see also Amazon.com
reviews, product
  emotional appeal and, 39, 40
  moderating, 141–143
  negative, 142, 157–158
  and O-influence continuum,
    159–160
Ries, Al, 102, 135, 143
Ries, Laura, 135, 143
RIM, 153
risk, and uncertainty in decision
  making, 124–125
Rogers, Everett M., 90, 91, 93, 94,
  97, 99–100
Rojas, Peter, 40–41, 54
Rosenzweig, Mark, 71, 72–73
Rotten Tomatoes, 55, 78
Roy, Deb, 152
Rutherford, Todd Jason, 44, 48–
  49, 50

Salesforce.com, 152
Samsung, 16, 66, 141, 153, 156,
  157
Samsung Galaxy Note II, 137–
  138
satisfaction
customer loyalty and, 84–87
measuring, 155–158
Sciarra, Paul, 98
Scotch Thermal Laminator, 138
Scott, Willard, 122
Seattle Times, 53

segmentation strategies
  O-influence segmentation, 168–
    170, 172
  positioning and, 105–107
  from susceptible to savvy, 170–
    172
Sela, Aner, 121
self-publishing, 48–49
Sephora.com, 34
Shafir, Eldar, 37
Shark Navigator vacuum cleaner,
  16, 71–72, 73
Sharp, Evan, 98
Shih, Jonney, 3–5, 15, 16, 71, 76,
  153
ShopSavvy, 11, 25, 130
shredder experiments, 22–23
Siegel, Bettina, 21
Silbermann, Ben, 98–99
Silicon Valley, 98, 99
social media
  fake social media reviews, 52
  market research and, 151, 152
  marketers on, 115, 124, 136, 139–
    140
  in shift from relative to absolute
    evaluations, 11
  weak ties network on, 93
  website rankings, 99
Sony, 73, 78, 136
source credibility theory, 108
special offers, 140
speed dating experiment, 25–26
spread concept, 164
stable preferences, 120–121
Streitfeld, David, 44
Strength of Weak ties theory, 92

Subcommittee on Commerce, Trade, and Consumer Protection, U.S. House of Representatives, 163–164
Sunday Times, 44
Sunstein, Cass, 30
surveys, satisfaction, 157
Sussin, Jenny, 52
Synthesio, 152, 157

target marketing, 95–96
task effects, 24–25
TechCrunch, 99
technology
  the absolute and new, 176–177
  decision-making and access to, 165–167
  gadgets and, 41
  market research and, 154
  portable devices study (2007), 147, 148, 149
  in shift from relative to absolute evaluations, 10–11, 12, 32
technology adoption model, 91–92, 94
television, 127, 151, 152
Thaler, Richard, 30, 177–178
Thinking, Fast and Slow (Kahneman), 19
Thomas, Keir, 95
3M, 138, 141, 157
top-of-mind advertising, 136, 143, 172
Toshiba, 66
transparency, data, 177–178
Trevathan, Jeremy, 44, 48
TripAdvisor, 45, 49, 51, 55, 106

Trout, Jack, 102
TrueCar.com, 178–179
Tucker, Will, 177–178
Tversky, Amos, 6, 19, 31, 37
20/20 (ABC TV), 44–45, 52, 53
Twitter, 99
  couch tracking on, 36
  and selling followers, 45
  marketing on, 139, 144–145, 151
  positioning and segmentation of, 105
  product recommendations through, 11, 12, 47
  weak ties connection, 93

uncertainty, and risk in decision making, 124–125
uncertainty resolution, 90, 91, 189
Universal McCann, 147, 148, 149
U.S. Department of Agriculture, 21
USA Today, 20, 145

vacuum cleaner industry, 71–73
value-based pricing, 187–188
value maximization, 19
values and lifestyles, segmentation based on, 169
Verizon, 103
versioning strategies, 107
video games, 106, 121–122
Vilsack, Tom, 21
Visible Technologies, 152

Walmart.com., 52, 71, 141
weak ties theory, 92–94

Where 2 Technologies, 77
Wii video games, 106
Williams-Sonoma, 6
wine, 70-71
Wired, 41, 174
wishlists, 36

yellow pages, 179
Yelp
  brand names and Yelp reviews,
    59-61

competitor listings, 179
fake reviews on, 49, 50, 51, 53,
    55
product reviews, 11, 122
YouTube, 45, 74, 97, 104, 128, 137,
    139

Zagat, 11, 60, 83
Zagat, Tim and Nina, 55
Zillow.com, 24, 175, 176, 177, 182
Zirnstein, Gerald, 21

ABOUT THE AUTHORS

ITAMAR SIMONSON is the Sebastian S. Kresge Professor of Marketing at the Graduate School of Business, Stanford University. His award-winning work has been featured in the *New York Times*, the *Washington Post*, and many other outlets worldwide, and he serves on eight editorial boards of leading journals.

EMANUEL ROSEN is the author of the national bestseller *The Anatomy of Buzz*. He was previously vice president, marketing, at Niles Software, where he launched the company's flagship product, End-Note. His work has been featured in *Time* and *Advertising Age*, and on CNN. He received a Bronze Lion from the Cannes International Advertising Festival as well as several other national awards, including two gold medals.